W9-CGQ-380

New Regulation of the Financial Industry

Also by Dimitris N. Chorafas

FINANCIAL MODELS AND SIMULATION: Concepts, Processes and Technology

HANDBOOK OF COMMERCIAL BANKING: Strategic Planning for Growth and Survival in the New Decade

New Regulation of the Financial Industry

Dimitris N. Chorafas

First published in Great Britain 2000 by
MACMILLAN PRESS LTD
Houndmills, Basingstoke, Hampshire RG21 6XS and London
Companies and representatives throughout the world

A catalogue record for this book is available from the British Library.

ISBN 0–333–77548–1

First published in the United States of America 2000 by
ST. MARTIN'S PRESS, INC.,
Scholarly and Reference Division,
175 Fifth Avenue, New York, N.Y. 10010

ISBN 0–312–22899–6

Library of Congress Cataloging-in-Publication Data
Chorafas, Dimitris N.
New regulation of the financial industry / Dimitris N. Chorafas.
p. cm.
Includes bibliographical references and index.
ISBN 0–312–22899–6 (cloth)
1. Banks and banking, International—Law and legislation. 2. Financial services industry—Law and legislation. I. Title.

K1066 .C49 1999
332.1—dc21

99–050145

This book is printed on paper suitable for recycling and made from fully managed and sustained forest sources.

10 9 8 7 6 5 4 3 2 1
09 08 07 06 05 04 03 02 01 00

Printed and bound in Great Britain by
Antony Rowe Ltd, Chippenham, Wiltshire

Contents

List of Figures

List of Tables

Foreword

Lowering our bank's risks while improving the rewards is a main goal of every self-respecting senior management. But making that happen is not easy. Changing interest rates, volatile exchange rates, complex financial products, unknown factors leading to disasters and other risks have led to new rules and regulations, increasing supervisory awareness and prompting analytical scrutiny of how financial institutions operate.

'Competition brings out the best in products and the worst in men', David Sarnoff once suggested. Because organisations are made up of people, the regulation of financial markets, the criteria which it uses, the checkpoints it puts in place and the reporting practices, cannot leave human nature out of the equation.

Regulators now want to see that a bank's board of directors is confronted with increased fiduciary responsibility, takes a leadership position in risk management, and is accountable for maintaining sound banking practices. Sound practices require a firm understanding of today's most pressing issues and challenges, which are addressed in this book.

While in the early 1980s a focal point of interest was deregulation, to which were added globalisation and technology, today the central point has become re-regulation, but in a global setting. The new rules of supervision look at the management of exposure and ensure that it includes an analysis of how trading strategies and lending patterns affect the value of assets and liabilities.

Written for managers of institutions which want to know how the new regulatory environment developed, and which are the forces that help to give it muscle and teeth, this book divides into three parts. Part One addresses the regulation of financial institutions as:

- globalisation expands the frontiers of banking;
- technology changes the pace of our work.

Chapter 1 discusses the evolving role of regulators in the banking industry, emphasising the rules of the Committee of Sponsoring Organisations (COSO), which constitute the basis of 'A New Capital Adequacy Framework' by the Basle Committee (nicknamed 2000+); the challenges presented by Internet banking and commerce (IBC); and the need for regulatory action because of the huge losses suffered by banks in the aftermath of their loans to hedge funds.

Chapter 2 focuses on one of today's most popular regulatory issues: the search for a new global financial architecture. The text brings into perspective the moral hazard from the current fire-brigade approaches, explains the synergy between monetary policy and bank supervision, and examines FDIC as a model for deposit insurance.

By focusing on systemic risk and the follow-the-sun overdraft, Chapter 3 directs the reader's attention to the dangers from delaying action on the financial architecture for the new millennium. Systemic risk is a key issue because of overleveraging in financial markets and bank-to-bank derivatives trades, which continue to increase.

It would not be easy to structure the global regulatory environment, but as Chapter 4 explains there are precedents which provide food for thought. The Federal Reserve System in the USA is an example. Chapter 5 discusses the changes taking place in bank legislation, presenting practical examples from the German Federal Republic.

Cognisant people in the financial industry suggest that the way to shape bank regulation is through well documented responses to such queries as: how can we arrive at a credit institution's true value? How can we best utilise market value concepts, including discounted cash flows? What changes in our strategies are likely to impact on debt and equity in the future? Keeping these queries in mind, Part Two addresses itself to the many aspects of bank supervision.

Among the examples offered in Chapter 6 are differences in regulation and supervision among the Group of Ten (G-10) countries, and their effect on systemic risk. Because the trend today is towards an integration of regulatory duties, Chapter 7 looks at the new powers of the British Financial Services Authority (FSA), and the role of regulators in controlling exposure.

Chapter 8 addresses the difficult issue of cross-border supervision of banks, non-banks and Internet commerce. This is largely uncharted territory, with the merger of technology and of the marketplace providing both challenges and opportunities. To exploit these opportunities supervisors must manage the evolving financial risk factors. This is the theme of Chapter 9.

The Basle Committee on Banking Supervision and the G-10 central bankers are well on their way to capitalising on the possibilities presented by technology, particularly the use of models. But there is also model risk, as Chapter 10 demonstrates. Supervisors are aware of this and therefore they control the eigenmodel's output. As it has been found with Long-Term Capital Management (LTCM), however, the data and the procedures have also to be controlled in a steady manner, otherwise it is garbage in/garbage out.

The theme of Part Three is the cornerstone of the regulatory environment: the capital base of financial institutions. Chapter 11 explains why it is important to rethink and revamp the 1998 Capital Accord by the Basle Committee. It also looks into the EU's Capital Adequacy Directive (CAD), and the possible conflicts between CAD and Basle Committee regulatory guidelines.

Chapter 12 addresses itself to repurchase agreements (repos) and what they mean in terms of systemic risk. It also examines whether there is a dividing line between custodian duties and repos. Chapter 13 brings to the reader's attention similarities and differences between British, American, Swiss and German approaches to the management of exposure, as well as the role played by technology. It does so by presenting to the reader the predefined financial reporting requirements and the new frontiers these open.

Mergers in banking are the focal point of Chapter 14. The text brings to the reader's attention the consequences of these mergers for competition, the concentration of risk, and the health of the banking industry as a whole. The book concludes with debt management strategies by sovereigns and associated restructuring policies in Chapter 15, which addresses the question of whether or not investments in equities by governments is a good solution. It does so in the context of the larger subject of debt management strategies and the restructure of assets and liabilities by sovereigns.

* * *

The practical examples from Britain, Germany, Switzerland, Austria and the USA present to the reader solutions which are already on hand in at least some of these countries. By contrast, concepts such as the financial architecture for the new millennium are still in a state of flux. Good sense should see to it that the decisions to be reached are rigorous, and are taken in a timely manner.

'I wasted time and now doth time waste me', wrote Shakespeare in Richard II. There is no time to be wasted with improving the regulatory standards, setting a proactive framework for systemic stability, using the Internet in the best possible way and getting ahead of the commercial and investment banks themselves in advanced applications of technology. In the longer run, a comprehensive and proactive regulation works in the interest of everybody.

* * *

I am indebted to a long list of knowledgeable people, and organisations, for their contribution to the research which made this book feasible, and also to several senior executives and experts for constructive criticism during the preparation of the manuscript. The complete list of the 124 senior executives and 70 organisations who participated in this research is shown in the Acknowledgements.

Let me take this opportunity to thank Samantha Whittaker for suggesting this project and seeing it all the way to publication, and Keith Povey and Gail Sheffield for the editing work. To Eva-Maria Binder goes the credit for compiling the research results, typing the text, and preparing the camera-ready artwork and index.

Valmer and Vitznau DIMITRIS N. CHORAFAS

Acknowledgements

(Countries are listed in alphabetical order.)

The following organizations, through their senior executives and system specialists participated in the recent research projects that led to the contents of this book and its documentation.

AUSTRIA

National Bank of Austria

Dr. Martin OHMS
Finance Market Analysis Department

3, Otto Wagner Platz
Postfach 61
A-1011 Vienna

Association of Austrian Banks and Bankers

Dr. Fritz DIWOK
Secretary General

11, Boersengasse
1013 Vienna

Bank Austria

Dr. Peter FISCHER
Senior General Manager, Treasury Division

Peter GABRIEL
Deputy General Manager, Trading

2, Am Hof
1010 Vienna

Creditanstalt

Dr. Wolfgang LICHTL
Market Risk Management

Julius Tandler Platz 3
A-1090 Vienna

Wiener Betriebs- and Baugesellschaft mbH

Dr. Josef FRITZ
General Manager

1, Anschützstrasse
1153 Vienna

GERMANY

Deutsche Bundesbank

Hans-Dietrich PETERS
Director

Hans Werner VOTH
Director

Wilhelm-Epstein Strasse 14
60431 Frankfurt am Main

Federal Banking Supervision Bureau

Hans-Joachim DOHR
Director Dept. I

Jochen KAYSER
Risk Model Examination

Ludger HANENBERG
Internal Controls

71-101 Gardeschützenweg
12203 Berlin

European Central Bank

Mauro GRANDE
Director

29 Kaiserstrasse
29th Floor
60216 Frankfurt am Main

Deutsches Aktieninstitut

Dr. Rüdiger Von ROSEN
President

Biebergasse 6 bis 10
60313 Frankfurt-am-Main

Commerzbank

Peter BÜRGER
Senior Vice President, Strategy and Controlling

Markus RUMPEL
Senior Vice President, Credit Risk Management

Kaiserplatz
60261 Frankfurt am Main

Deutsche Bank

Professor Manfred TIMMERMANN
Head of Controlling

Hans VOIT
Head of Process Management, Controlling Department

12, Taunusanlage
60325 Frankfurt

Dresdner Bank

Dr. Marita BALKS
Investment Bank, Risk Control

Dr. Hermann HAAF
Mathematical Models for Risk Control

Claas Carsten KOHL
Financial Engineer

1, Jürgen Ponto Platz
60301 Frankfurt

GMD First-Research Institute for Computer Architecture, Software Technology and Graphics

Prof. Dr. Ing. Wolfgang K. GILOI
General Manager

5, Rudower Chaussee
D-1199 Berlin

FRANCE

Banque de France

Pierre JAILLET
Director, Monetary Studies and Statistics

Yvan ORONNAL
Manager, Monetary Analyses and Statistics

G. TOURNEMIRE, Analyst, Monetary Studies

39, rue Croix des Petits Champs
75001 Paris

Secretariat Général de la Commission Bancaire – Banque de France

Didier PENY
Head of Big Banks and International Banks Department

Michel MARTINO
International Affairs

Benjamin SAHEL
Market Risk Control

73, rue de Richelieu
75002 Paris

Ministry of Finance and the Economy, Conseil National de la Comptabilité

Alain LE BARS
Director International Relations and Cooperation

6, rue Louise WEISS
75703 Paris Cedex 13

HUNGARY

Hungarian Banking and Capital Market Supervision

Dr. Janos KUN
Head, Department of Regulation and Analyses

Dr. Erika VÖRÖS
Senior Economist, Department of Regulation and Analyses

Dr. Géza NYIRY
Head, Section of Information Audit

Csalogany u. 9-11
H-1027 Budapest

Hungarian Academy of Sciences

Prof. Dr. Tibor VAMOS
Chairman, Computer and Automation Research Institute

Nador U. 7
1051 Budapest

ITALY

Banca d'Italia

Eugene GAIOTTI
Research Department, Monetary and Financial Division

Ing. Dario FOCARELLI
Research Department

91, via Nazionale
00184 Rome

Istituto Bancario San Paolo di Torino

Dr. Paolo CHIULENTI
Director of Budgeting

Roberto COSTA
Director of Private Banking

Pino RAVELLI
Director Bergamo Region

27, via G. Camozzi
24121 Bergamo

LUXEMBOURG

Banque Générale de Luxembourg

Prof. Dr. Yves WAGNER
Director of Asset and Risk Management

Hans Jörg PARIS, International Risk Manager

27, avenue Monterey
L-2951 Luxembourg

POLAND

Securities and Exchange Commission

Beata STELMACH
Secretary of the Commission

1, Pl Powstancow Warszawy
00-950 Warsaw

SWEDEN

Skandinaviska Enskilda Banken

Bernt GYLLENSWÄRD
Head of Group Audit

Box 16067
10322 Stockholm

Irdem AB

Gian MEDRI
Former Director of Research at Nordbanken

19, Flintlasvagen
S-19154 Sollentuna

SWITZERLAND

Swiss National Bank

Dr. Werner HERMANN
Head of International Monetary Relations

Dr. Christian WALTER
Representative to the Basle Committee

Robert FLURI
Assistant Director, Statistics Section

15 Börsenstrasse
Zurich

Federal Banking Commission

Dr. Susanne BRANDENBERGER
Risk Management

Renate LISCHER
Representative to Risk Management Subgroup, Basle Committee

Marktgasse 37
3001 Bern

Bank for International Settlements

Mr. Claude SIVY
Head of Internal Audit

Herbie POENISCH
Senior Economist, Monetary and Economic Department

2, Centralplatz
4002 Basle

Bank Leu AG

Dr. Urs MORGENTHALER
Member of Management
Director of Risk Control

32, Bahnhofstrasse
Zurich

Bank J. Vontobel and Vontobel Holding

Heinz FRAUCHIGER
Chief, Internal Audit Department

Tödistrasse 23
CH-8022 Zurich

Union Bank of Switzerland

Dr. Heinrich STEINMANN
Member of the Executive Board (Retired)

Claridenstrasse
8021 Zurich

UNITED KINGDOM

Bank of England, and Financial Services Authority

Richard BRITTON
Director, Complex Groups Division, CGD Policy Department

Threadneedle Street
London EC2R 8AH

British Bankers Association

Paul CHISNALL
Assistant Director

Pinners Hall
105-108 Old Broad Street
London EC2N 1EX

Accounting Standards Board

A.V.C. COOK
Technical Director

Sandra THOMPSON
Project Director

Holborn Hall
100 Gray's Inn Road
London WC1X 8AL

Barclays Bank Plc

Brandon DAVIES
Treasurer, Global Corporate Banking

Alan BROWN
Director, Group Risk

54 Lombard Street
London EC3P 3AH

ABN-AMRO Investment Bank N.V.

David WOODS
Chief Operations Officer, Global Equity Directorate

199 Bishopsgate
London EC2M 3TY

Bankgesellschaft Berlin

Stephen F. MYERS
Head of Market Risk

1 Crown Court
Cheapside, London

Standard & Poor's

David T. BEERS
Managing Director, Sovereign Ratings

Garden House
18, Finsbury Circus
London EC2M 7BP

Moody's Investor Services

Samuel S. THEODORE
Managing Director, European Banks

David FROHRIEP
Communications Manager, Europe

2, Minster Court
Mincing Lange
London EC3R 7XB

Fitch IBCA

Charles PRESCOTT
Group Managing Director, Banks

David ANDREWS
Managing Director, Financial Institutions

Travor PITMAN
Managing Director, Corporations

Richard FOX
Director, International Public Finance

Eldon House
2, Eldon Street
London EC2M 7UA

Merrill Lynch International

Erik BANKS
Managing Director of Risk Management

Ropemaker Place
London EC2Y 9LY

The Auditing Practices Board

Jonathan E.C. GRANT
Technical Director

Steve LEONARD
Internal Controls Project Manager

P.O.Box 433
Moorgate Place
London EC2P 2BJ

International Accounting Standards Committee

Ms. Liesel KNORR
Technical Director

166 Fleet Street
London EC4A 2DY

City University Business School

Professor Elias DINENIS
Head, Department of Investment
Risk Management & Insurance

Frobisher Crescent
Barbican Centre
London EC2Y 8BH

Dr. Giovanni BARONE-ADESI
Professor of Finance
Faculty of Business

University of Alberta
3-20H Faculty of Business
Edmonton, Alberta
Canada T6G 2R6

UNITED STATES

Federal Reserve System, Board of Governors

David L. ROBINSON
Deputy Director, Chief Federal
Reserve Examiner

Alan H. OSTERHOLM, CIA, CISA
Manager, Financial
Examinations Section

Paul W. BETTGE
Assistant Director, Division of
Reserve Bank Operations

Gregory E. ELLER
Supervisory Financial Analyst,
Banking

Gregory L. EVANS
Manager, Financial Accounting

Martha STALLARD
Financial Accounting, Reserve
Bank Operations

20th and Constitution, NW
Washington, DC 20551

Federal Reserve Bank of Boston

William McDONOUGH
Executive Vice President

James T. NOLAN
Assistant Vice President

P.O.Box 2076
600 Atlantic Avenue
Boston, MA

Federal Reserve Bank of San Francisco

Nigel R. OGILVIE, CFA
Supervising Financial Analyst
Emerging Issues

101 Market Street
San Francisco, CA

Seattle Branch, Federal Reserve Bank of San Francisco

Jimmy F. KAMADA
Assistant Vice President

Gale P. ANSELL
Assistant Vice President,
Business Development

1015, 2nd Avenue
Seattle, WA 98122-3567

Office of the Comptroller of the Currency (OCC)

Bill MORRIS
National Bank Examiner/Policy Analyst,
Core Policy Development Division

Gene GREEN
Deputy Chief Accountant
Office of the Chief Accountant

250 E Street, SW
7th Floor
Washington, D.C.

Federal Deposit Insurance Corporation (FDIC)

Curtis WONG
Capital Markets, Examination Support

Tanya SMITH
Examination Specialist,
International Branch

Doris L. MARSH
Examination Specialist,
Policy Branch

550 17th Street, N.W.
Washington, D.C.

Office of Thrift Supervision (OTS)

Timothy J. STIER
Chief Accountant

1700 G Street Northwest
Washington, DC, 20552

Securities and Exchange Commission, Washington DC

Robert UHL
Professional Accounting Fellow

Pascal DESROCHES
Professional Accounting Fellow

John W. ALBERT
Associate Chief Accountant

Scott BAYLESS
Associate Chief Accountant

Office of the Chief Accountant
Securities and Exchange Commission
450 Fifth Street, NW
Washington, DC, 20549

Securities and Exchange Commission, New York

Robert A. SOLLAZZO
Associate Regional Director

7 World Trade Center
12th Floor
New York, NY 10048

Securities and Exchange Commission, Boston

Edward A. RYAN, Jr.
Assistant District Administrator (Regulations)

Boston District Office
73 Tremont Street, 6th Floor
Boston, MA 02108-3912

International Monetary Fund

Alain COUNE
Assistant Director, Office of Internal Audit and Inspection

700 19th Street NW
Washington DC, 20431

Financial Accounting Standards Board

Halsey G. BULLEN
Project Manager

Jeannot BLANCHET
Project Manager

Teri L. LIST
Practice Fellow

401 Merritt
Norwalk, CN 06856

Citibank

Dr. Daniel SCHUTZER
Vice President, Director of Advanced Technology

909 Third Avenue
New York, NY 10022

Prudential-Bache Securities

Bella LOYKHTER
Senior Vice President, Information Technology

Kenneth MUSCO
First Vice President and Director, Management Internal Control

Neil S. LERNER
Vice President, Management Internal Control

1 New York Plaza
New York, NY

Merrill Lynch

John J. FOSINA
Director, Planning and Analysis

Corporate and Institutional Client Group
World Financial Center, North Tower
New York, NY 10281-1316

International Swaps and Derivatives Association (ISDA)

Susan HINKO
Director of Policy

600 Fifth Avenue, 27th Floor
Rockefeller Center
New York, NY 10020-2302

Standard & Poor's

Clifford GRIEP
Managing Director

25 Broadway
New York, NY 10004-1064

Moody's Investor Services

Lea CARTY
Director, Corporates

99 Church Street
New York, NY 10022

State Street Bank and Trust

James J. BARR
Executive Vice President, U.S. Financial Assets Services

225 Franklin Street
Boston, MA 02105-1992

MBIA Insurance Corporation

John B. CAOUETTE
Vice Chairman and President, Structured Finance Division

885 3rd Avenue No 14
New York, NY 10022

Global Association of Risk Professionals (GARP)

Lev BORODOVSKI
Executive Director, GARP, and Director of Risk Management, Credit Suisse First Boston (CSFB), New York

Yong LI
Director of Education, GARP, and Vice President, Lehman Brothers, New York

Dr. Frank LEIBER
Research Director, and
Assistant Director of Computational Finance, Cornell
University, Theory Center, New York

Roy NAWAL
Director of Risk Forums, GARP

980 Broadway, Suite 242
Thornwood, NY

Group of Thirty

John WALSH
Director

1990 M Street, NW
Suite 450
Washington, DC, 20036

Edward Jones

Ann FICKEN (Mrs)
Director, Internal Audit

201 Progress Parkway
Maryland Heights, MO 63043-3042

Teachers Insurance and Annuity Association/College Retirement Equities Fund (TIAA/CREF)

Charles S. DVORKIN
Vice President and Chief Technology Officer

Harry D. PERRIN
Assistant Vice President, Information Technology

730 Third Avenue
New York, NY 10017-3206

Massachusetts Institute of Technology

Ms. Peggy CARNEY
Administrator, Graduate Office

Michael COEN, PhD Candidate, ARPA Intelligent Environment Project

Department of Electrical Engineering
and Computer Science
Building 38, Room 444
50 Vassar Street
Cambridge, MA, 02139

School of Engineering and Applied Science, University of California, Los Angeles

Dean A.R. Frank WAZZAN
School of Engineering and Applied Science

Prof. Richard MUNTZ
Chair, Computer Science Department

Prof. Dr. Leonard KLEINROCK
Telecommunications and Networks

Westwood Village
Los Angeles, CA 90024

University of Maryland

Prof. Howard FRANK
Dean, The Robert H. Smith School of Business

Prof. Lemma W. SENBERT
Chair, Finance Department

Prof. Haluk UNAL
Associate Professor of Finance

Van Munching Hall
College Park, Maryland 20742-1815

Part One

The Regulation of Financial Institutions

1
The Evolving Role of Regulators in the Banking Industry

1 Introduction

Bank regulators have a unique responsibility for maintaining public confidence in the financial system. The assurance of stability in the financial services industry has become increasingly important with the internationalisation of banking and the rapid advancement of technology. High technology and a shrinking world present enormous opportunities but also amplify the effects of volatility and of exposure.

Prior to globalisation, national regulators, whether the central bank or another agency such as the Financial Services Authority (FSA) in the UK, the Federal Banking Supervision Bureau in Germany, or the Office of the Comptroller of the Currency (OCC) and the Federal Deposit Insurance Corporation (FDIC) in the USA, stood ready to take hold of failing financial institutions in the event that these experienced temporary disruptions or if their failure posed a systemic risk.

Today, systemic risk can be instantly communicated to the four corners of the globe as huge transborder cash flows, of up to $2 trillion per day, have changed the formerly nation-centred perspective. Cross-border investment and speculation, made possible by globalisation and technology, have brought the markets to decisive new highs. But as the Asian meltdown in 1997 and Russian bankruptcy in 1998 demonstrated, past performance is no guarantee of future stability. The central banks' efforts in connection with globalisation are co-ordinated by:

- the Group of Ten (G-10) central bankers: USA, UK, Japan, Germany, France, Italy, Canada, Holland, Belgium, Sweden, Switzerland (and Luxembourg as observer); and
- the Basle Committee on Banking Supervision, of the Bank for International Settlements (BIS), and its working groups.

However, many financial institutions (as for instance the hedge funds and other non-bank banks) escape prudent supervision. Similarly, the responsibility for handling distressed countries, and by extension their failing banks, is most diffused. It is the International Monetary Fund (IMF), not a member of the G-10, which acts as lender of last resort for 'emerging' countries going bankrupt and, indirectly, for the banks and non-banks of the G-10 that lend them money without any collateral or without a rigorous examination of their creditworthiness.

While a system of global bank regulation is slowly coming into place following the 1988 Capital Accord, the 1996 Market Risk Amendment and the 1999 New Capital Adequacy Framework by the Basle Committee on Banking Supervision (see D.N. Chorafas, *The 1996 Market Risk Amendment. Understanding the Marking-to-Model and Value-at-Risk*, McGraw-Hill, Burr Ridge, IL, 1998), there is nothing in place which can handle in an efficient manner overexposed countries whose economy is falling apart. Neither is there a global net for financial institutions in distress because they unwisely lend huge sums of money to the non-creditworthy.

Yet there is a model, albeit on national scale, which has worked perfectly for two-thirds of a century. Following the Great Depression of 1929–32, the US government instituted the FDIC, whose role is explained in Chapter 2. In 1999, there are nearly 11 000 FDIC-insured depository institutions which:

- range from less than $10 million to mega-banks with more than $500 hundred billion in assets; and
- are characterised by a variety of structures and different chartering authorities, with common ground FDIC insurance.

A question posed by many cognisant bankers in my seminars and during the research meetings I conduct is: 'Do we *really* need global regulation?' The evident answer is: 'Yes, because it sets the framework for how credit institutions conduct their business on a global scale.' Regulation also induces the financial entities to establish high internal standards in terms of ethics, performance, internal audit and risk control.

2 A closer look at the regulators' role and their contribution

The rapid transborder movements of financial assets and liabilities by banks, hedge funds and institutional investors are too frequent and too large for the flimsy regulatory structures that encase them country-by-country. During the last two decades, George Soros and his ilk have outgrown whatever supervisory system has been in place. On one hand, they owe the public nothing. On the other, the way they act brings the existing system of checks and balances to its limits – and beyond.

What are the regulatory system's limits? A factual and documented answer to this query requires taking a closer look at the role of supervisors, down to its fundamentals. The role of financial services regulators is to promote the protection of investors, depositors and other counterparties, as well as to look after the survival of financial markets. An integral part of this role is to ensure that business and the public have confidence in the ability of the financial industry:

- to guarantee adequate business continuity; and
- to avoid disruptions or even the downgrading of services.

By the mid-1980s a shift in the policy of prudential regulation became evident, away from rules pre-set within a strictly national framework, and towards a broader international collaboration at least between the G-10 central bankers. Apart from the timid start towards the globalisation of supervision, the 1990s have seen an emphasis on:

- a more flexible regulatory framework which starts working transborder;
- greater weight on case-by-case evaluation of institutions;
- mathematical models using volatilities, simulation, non-linearities and other tools; and
- a major weight given to the reliability of financial reports by banks and other institutions.

Central bankers and regulators now look at reliable financial reporting as a prerequisite to the proper execution of the assurance of the functions of the intermediary. Fraudulent reporting represents serious risks to the financial system and those doing business with it: the business community and the general public.

Although the stronger institutions welcome the stance by supervisors outlined above, not everybody likes regulation because it imposes constraints. In my research, many senior bankers made the point that regulators tend to be reactive rather than proactive. They learn from the different banks they supervise and from their failures, but most often they trail behind the facts. This, commercial and investment bankers said, is true not only of new standards, rules and directives but also of technology: in mathematical models, for example, tier-1 investment and commercial banks are way ahead of regulators.

Yet it is difficult to imagine a financial system which functions like a clock without supervisory and control action. Regulation sees to it that when a company wishes to have access to public capital, and therefore the credit markets, it must accept and fulfil certain obligations necessary to protect the public interest. One of the basic ones is the full and fair public disclosure of corporate information, including financial results.

An excellent example of proactive measures taken by regulators is the work of the Committee of Sponsoring Organisations (COSO) of the Treadway Commission. This Commission was a private initiative, in the late 1980s, by James C. Treadway, Jr, formerly a Commissioner of the Securities and Exchange Commission (SEC). The Commission has been jointly sponsored and funded by the American Institute of Certified Public Accountants (AICPA) the American Accounting Association (AAA), the Financial Executives Institute (FEI), the Institute of Internal Auditors (IIA) and the National Association of Accountants (NAA).

COSO is not just a matter of regulatory guidelines: it is a complete system of management controls and financial reporting rules which in 1998 was successfully implemented by the Federal Reserve Banks of New York, Boston and Chicago. (For more information on COSO see Chapter 6.) In 1999, all other banks of the Federal Reserve System are implementing COSO. Thereafter, its application becomes mandatory for all credit institutions in the USA with assets of $500 million or more. To my way of thinking, COSO is the perfect example of the new regulatory environment in terms of reliable financial reporting and internal control. The wise policy is that the Basle Committee adopts COSO for the G-10 countries, and its implementation expands to all markets with a role to play in the global economy (see also the discussion on financial reporting in Chapter 4).

The control environment defined by COSO can exist both within and outside the financial industry. It includes integrity, ethical values, management philosophy, competence, organisational structure, operating style, assignment of authority and responsibility, and human resource policies. Risk assessment incorporates:

- risk analysis of external and internal factors faced by the institution; and
- the handling of exposure associated with change, as well as the ability to manage change.

Control activities defined by COSO are the policies and procedures established by senior management to meet objectives. Information and communication prerequisites concern the capture and dissemination of relevant information in order to ensure that an organisation's own people carry out their job responsibilities, and also that people external to the bank – including the regulators – trust the way the entity conducts its business.

COSO makes the point that the company's own management is not the only party responsible for the accuracy of financial statements. For instance, as the US Supreme Court has ruled, when independent public accountants express an opinion on a public company's financial statements they assume a public responsibility that transcends the contractual relationship with their client. The independent public accountant's responsibility extends to the corporation's stockholders, creditors, customers, and the rest of the investing public. The regulations and their standards for auditing public companies are there to safeguard that public trust. Auditors must adhere to those standards and ethical values at all times.

The reference to the accountability of certified public accountants is most important because in many countries they perform an examiner's function on behalf of regulators. The Bank of England (and now the FSA), for example, does not carry out on-site examinations on a regular basis. The supervision of banks under its authority has been based on reports by external auditors which detail the supervised institution's business and the correctness of its accounts. The Banking Act of 1987 formally empowered the regulators to require an institution to commission financial reports by a *reporting accountant*.

Regulators, however, can neither regulate nor legislate human nature out of financial reporting. As they have moved to reduce or mitigate risk, those engaged in fraudulent reporting have come up with new inventions, such as 'creative accounting'. Therefore it is necessary both to reinforce and modernise the controls. Part and parcel of this responsibility is to use high technology and analytical studies in order to exercise steady vigilance.

Reliable financial reporting is not the only issue with which regulation is concerned. Bank supervisors must be leaders in many fields. Nelson Mandela once said that to be a good leader one must act like the shepherd: the shepherd walks behind the sheep, but takes action to keep them in safe valleys. As shown in Figure 1.1, a regulatory environment rests on four pillars.

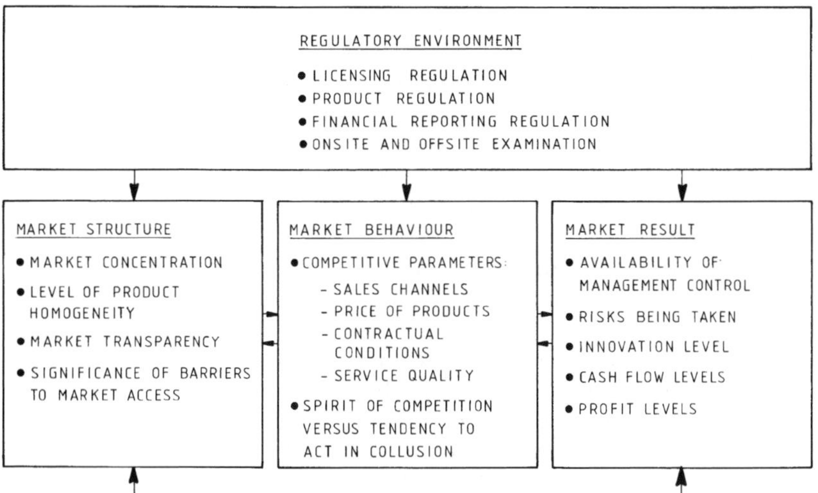

Figure 1.1 The three pillars on which a regulatory environment rests

Through its action, it influences market structure, market behaviour, and obtained results. The concept behind this figure is a modification of the Harvard paradigm of industrial economics. Notice that both the forward processes and the feedback are important for an effective bank regulation.

Each one of the component parts of Figure 1.1 is a domain where regulators should be proactive and show leadership; in other terms, where they should make their contribution. Mandela did not mention it, but an integral part of a complete paradigm of the shepherd are the watchdogs who keep the flock within the safe valley. This is the role played by analysts, and by model-literate auditors, examiners and inspectors.

3 The expanding notion of regulating the markets in an Internet setting

Whether one wants to admit it or not, markets, including financial markets, play a central role in any economy, whether they are liberal or centrally directed. The role of markets is that of facilitating the exchange of goods, services, information and payments. To function properly, markets require not only rules but also an institutional infrastructure. Through the exchange of wealth this infrastructure makes possible, markets create opportunity and therefore economic value for sellers and buyers. This exchange benefits society at large (a statement true of traditional markets and of the emerging Internet banking and commerce, or IBC).

Because the Internet puts unparalleled amounts of information at its users' fingertips, it brings consumers almost to a par with professionals on market news and insights. Consequently, it exerts an enormous price pressure on intermediaries everywhere, particularly the most inefficient. It also threatens brokers' margins and all sorts of fees which they currently receive.

To better appreciate IBC's contribution to the global economy during the first decade of the twenty-first century, one should take the proverbial long, hard look at how new industries are born and old ones fade away. Since the Industrial Revolution gained steam, new industries have been born out of ideas which were turned into everyday necessities. Examples are:

- the railroad boom of the 1890s; and
- the automobile's rapid market expansion in the 1920s.

Like those events the Internet's market appeal stems from the addition of a whole new industry to the economy. The rush to adapt IBC technology to all sorts of purposes to create supports able to take the Web everywhere is encouraging a tremendous surge in investments. It also creates new business opportunities leading to the industrial base of the future. No doubt, somewhere along the way, there will be a brutal sorting out of winners and losers; the survivors will consolidate, expand and thrive.

Another (barely appreciated) contribution of the Internet is that it has knocked down obstacles of *place* and *time*. The IBC space is vast and anyone operating in that space is more or less on a level playing field with anybody else. This has a very important impact on costs as well as on choices. It has also prompted many experts to:

- predict an unprecedented growth in Internet-led business, including new ways of trading; and
- suggest that what has taken place so far is nothing more than a preview of some of the things to come.

The consensus which is now developing is that investments in Internet-led business would suffer only if venture capitalists lost faith in Internet commerce, as opposed to particular firms going bust. While the pessimists are of the opinion that a surge of trading among people unskilled in analysis and valuation and unburned by past losses is dangerous, the optimists say that individual failures are not important. They are the paving stones of the future highway.

As once promising innovations turn out to be dead ends, many companies that led the Internet boom may disappear. While the stock market value of these companies created in the boom evaporates and investors realise that the risks can be deadly, this sorting-out process triggers relatively minor disruptions in the economy, while at the same time pushing other Internet firms to the forefront of public attention.

In terms of market valuation of Internet stocks few investors are aware of one of the key advantages of Internet companies: they have little debt. And because of the nature of IBC they will probably need, in the future, a rather limited amount of external financing, which sets them apart from the railroads, automobiles and other industries created by the Industrial Revolution.

Let me explain in a couple of paragraphs some of the basic concepts behind IBC, because in the new millennium these will be the cornerstone of any effective regulatory action concerning the financial markets. Like everybody else, until now I have applied the more commonly used terms: electronic banking and electronic commerce (see D.N. Chorafas, *Internet Financial Services. Secure Electronic Banking and Electronic Commerce?*, Lafferty Publications, London and Dublin, 1998). But these no longer correspond to the new business realities. 'Electronic banking' has been traditionally associated with home banking which is yesterday's issue and, anyway, it never really took off.

Shortly after the year 2000, the broadband Internet and its filials, the bank's own intranet (private internal networks, based on Web software), and the private extranets connecting business partners (also based on Web software) will alter the way financial institutions look at their business and the sort of transactions they carry out. Therefore, regulators should be ahead of the curve in comprehending the *broadband Intranet's* impact on the banking industry and in establishing the IBC rules. Quite similarly, my extensive research in the USA and Europe in 1998 and 1999 convinced me that, for the future, 'Internet commerce' is a better term than electronic commerce because it identifies the channel of the global process.

At the core of IBC is the understanding that the developing institutional infrastructure should be both transborder and polyvalent in every aspect: regulatory, legal and technological. Only when there are world-wide regulatory rules it is possible to monitor market behaviour and enforce a fair code of action. The legal infrastructure includes global commercial register, commercial code, contract law, intellectual property protection and dispute resolution through the courts (see also Chapter 8 on IBC opportunities and scams).

For its part, Internet's technological infrastructure provides the moving gear for the wheels of commerce and financial services. Broadened connectivity will see to it that the pace of transactions steadily increases, and so does their volume, because advances in technology make feasible solutions which were not even imaginable some years ago. That is the good news.

The other side of this reference is that well-focused rules and regulations should be in place to facilitate transactions and provide assurances. In a high-tech society such as ours, they do so only when they keep pace with technological evolution. Logistics systems looking after payments and settlements are central to functioning markets. No deal would be consumed without transfer of payment from buyer to seller. This requires trust, a credit system and a payments solution built on reputation because both sellers and buyers are able to deliver. It also calls for dematerialisation (delivery versus payment, or DVP) because moving reliable information is more efficient than moving paper.

Given the right infrastructure, whether through registered exchanges or over-the-counter (OTC), the mechanics provided by markets are instrumental in matching buyers and sellers. That is what IBC is doing. Trust, however, will not come by itself. Regulation should be in place to help all the way, from the correct determination of product offerings and assurance for buyers, to the establishment of prices assisted through price discovery and effective negotiations between counterparties. While practically everybody understands that markets work by matching demand and supply, few people appreciate that this process cannot work if there is no confidence. Regulation fills the confidence gaps by levelling the playing field and ensuring that no persistent advantages occur to some of the players, and also by:

- seeing to it that there are no market manipulations; and
- putting in place the checks and balances necessary to avoid systemic risk.

Supervisors consider it particularly important that banks adopt a co-ordinated approach to risk management and pay special attention to the possible correlation of different types of risk, both within the individual bank and the banking system as a whole. To do so in an able manner, the financial institution's board and senior management must appreciate:

- the risks being taken through new transactions;
- the exposure already embedded in the trading book and the banking book; and
- the synergy between different types of risk, which today works faster than ever.

Both for the more traditional ways of doing business and for IBC, nothing applies better to risk management than Winston Churchill's aphorism about the events which led to the Second World War: 'When the situation was manageable it was neglected, now that it is thoroughly out of hand we apply too late the remedies which then might have effected a cure.' The cure is the control of exposure by addressing in a rigorous manner both credit risk and market risk.

4 The synergy of credit risk and market risk

All transactions involve both credit and market exposure, though for some credit risk is higher and for others the greater danger is in the market risk side. Figure 1.2 outlines the four main channels of banking which lead to gains and losses, and whose measurement helps in appreciating and controlling the institution's performance. Regulators are greatly interested in

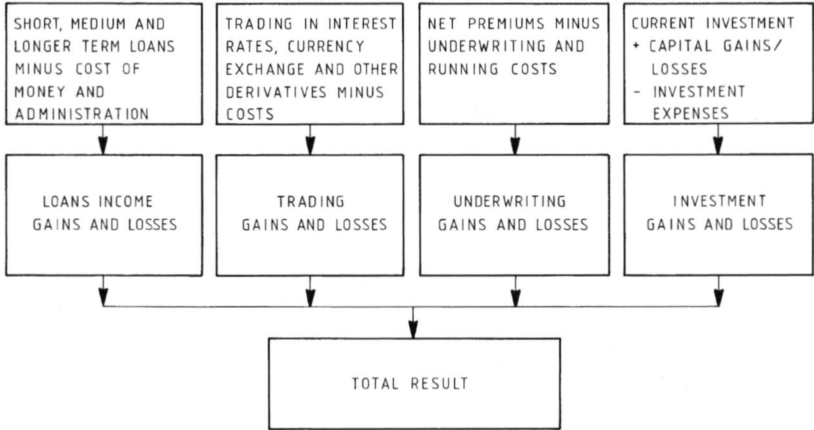

Figure 1.2 Four main channels for gains and losses in the banking industry

how an entity under their supervision performs in these four channels, but they often do not pay enough attention to the synergy of credit risk and market risk, until events such as the near bankruptcy of Long-Term Capital Management (LTCM) bring home that message.

The four channels in Figure 1.2 and their content are in full evolution, because over the years there have been major changes in banking. Both the institutions themselves and their customers have changed. In the late 1950s, for example, about 90 per cent of all loans by major credit institutions went to the large manufacturing and merchandising companies. By the late 1990s that figure is 4 per cent, a process often called the *disintermediation* of the banking industry.

The action has gone to the capital markets, but these do not have the same commitment to a credit relationship that a commercial bank used to have, and their time horizon is much shorter. The strategy of borrowers, too, has changed. They manage financing sources as a portfolio of choices, which is a demanding task. Because they obtain better terms than those of a traditional loan, rather than asking a commercial bank for money, big companies hire an investment bank as counsel, and address the capital market by issuing commercial paper. Partly to compensate for the loss of income in loans, commercial banks have rushed into derivative financial instruments (see D.N. Chorafas, *Managing Derivatives Risk*, Irwin Professional Publishing, Burr Ridge, IL, 1996), sometimes without properly mastering this steadily evolving field of financial trades.

Derivatives embody the synergy of credit risk and market risk better than any other instrument. There is no greater proof of this than financial reporting on 'other assets' and 'other liabilities' as it is now practised in Switzerland.

From 1996, the Swiss regulatory authorities have required that recognised but not yet realised gains with derivatives are shown in the Annual Report as 'other assets'; while recognised but not yet realised losses are written as 'other liabilities'. Depending on its market value on 31 December, the same instrument will show either in the 'other assets' or the 'other liabilities' chapter:

- if it is an 'other asset', then the holder has made a paper profit and carries credit risk;
- if it is an 'other liability', the holder has paper losses and the name of the game is market risk.

While regulation and supervision of off-balance-sheet activities differs significantly from one country to another – and in some countries it does not exist at all – this and similar examples suggest that since the mid-1990s regulators have appreciated both the amount of exposure banks take with derivatives and the synergy existing between the two types of risk.

Many supervisors consider that the information about derivatives exposure presently supplied in the published accounts of financial institutions is generally insufficient to give counterparties, shareholders and depositors a reasonable picture of the bank's health. The value-at-risk (VAR) model was expected to provide factual evidence in regard to the bank's exposure, but it has not fulfilled the expectations (see Chapter 15). Transparency is another issue. The more transparent a financial reporting structure is, the easier it is to understand the nature of transactions, and the better the net worth of the banking book and trading book can be appreciated.

The same is true of gains and losses. At root, that is what COSO is about. Reliable financial reporting and transparency make it possible to access the right information for factual and documented decisions, and to develop a navigation map which is well-founded rather than depending on rumours, personal connections and data which cannot be verified. For this reason, practically no one should disagree on the benefits of highly dependable disclosures. Everybody must appreciate that the more timely and reliable is the information, the better the markets work, and the more efficient is risk management.

South Korea, Indonesia, Malaysia, Brazil, Mexico and other countries might have avoided sudden exchange-rate crises and panics if investors had had a more accurate idea of their foreign reserve levels and of the risks taken by their banks and other companies. These countries might have steered clear of the abyss if their firms had been forced to disclose the size of their foreign liabilities in connection with the huge debts they had contracted, as well as their financial staying power.

Lack of transparency encourages governments, companies and people to indulge in reckless behaviour or use second-rate criteria compared to outstanding credit risk and market risk. Indeed, even some regulators' rules distort investment decisions. An example from the 1990s has been lending short-term to Asian and Russian borrowers because such loans carried a lower risk-weighting in the Basle Committee's rules for capital adequacy.

At the end of 1997, 60 per cent of the $380 billion in international bank lending outstanding to Asia had a maturity of less than one year. One of the Basle capital adequacy shortcomings is that short-term lending requires less provisioning than long-term loans. Short-term lending was one of the basic background reasons of the mid- to late 1997 meltdown in East Asia and the August 1998 débâcle in Russia. In Russia, investors had bought lots of lucrative but very risky short-term government debt. When the day of reckoning came, 33 separate short-term Treasury debt issues (GKO), with a total face value of $33 billion, traded at about 9 cents to the dollar, while another 12 separate long-term debt issues (OFZ), with a face value of $9.7 billion, also hit foolish investors like a thunder bolt. The loan moratorium decreed by a bankrupt Russian government included five multilateral loans originated under the London Club restructuring agreement totalling

$22 billion, plus a $150 million facility provided by ING Bank for the Russian Republic of Tartaristan.

In conclusion, banks are not as careful as one might think with their loans, particularly when they sense an opportunity for big profits. Also, while many items which affect gains and losses are recorded on the balance sheet, the notes to the accounts are not always explicit, and there is some degree of 'creative accounting' in financial reporting to supervisors, with the result that the real exposure is not transparent. Therefore, supervisory authorities are now revising the reporting rules, particularly those having implications for management accounts and, most importantly, for published financial statements (see section 2 on COSO).

5 The information economy and the role of global networks in finance

As a consequence of any-to-any real-time networks, international finance is no longer restricted to a relatively small number of large institutions. With global networks providing for rapid communications, commercial and investment banks, mutual funds, hedge funds and insurance companies, as well as multinational corporations, can enter and exit markets much faster, more effectively and at a lower cost that has ever been the case.

While the Internet, the intranets and the extranets provide the medium, rocket scientists are creating swarms of new types of security, many of them being derivatives financial instruments (see D.N. Chorafas, *Rocket Scientists in Banking*, Lafferty Publications, London and Dublin, 1995; 'rocket scientists' are physicists, engineers and mathematicians who carry into banking their analytical experience gained from the aerospace and nuclear industry). They customise financial products, often overnight; restructure assets; repackage and sell debt. Through credit derivatives, they transfer all or part of the credit risk borne by the originator of a loan to investors willing and able to assume it. But, with novel products, market risk and credit risk are hard to assess a priori, and to price correctly. However, the proper pricing of risk is an issue of great importance to regulators because new instruments change the time-honoured rules of supervisory functions.

The synergy of marketing strategy and technology sees to it that in international consumer banking, particularly in catering to high net-worth individuals, institutions try to cross borders and make themselves the bank of choice for wealthy customers around the world. One of the prerequisites for success is that senior management must be not only customer-friendly but also computer literate, and they must lead in technology. Such prerequisites are necessary to offer private banking services in many currencies, as well as to provide investment advice around the globe.

For instance, capitalising on its ability to lead in the globalisation of retail banking which it built over the years, Citibank talks of becoming to retail banking what Coca-Cola is to soft drinks. This broadening of scope of internationalisation towards other layers of the retail market is attempted without driving away the high net-worth customers who favour Citi's services. Because of being leader in real-time technology, Citibank has gained some significant advantages in the global battle for the consumer, and the knowledge engineering artefacts which Citibank technologists have developed over the years to enrich the bank's information technology (IT) have been instrumental in its market thrust.

The number of expert systems and agents now active in its network show that Citibank has invested heavily in consumer-friendly technology (D.N. Chorafas, *Agent Technology Handbook*, McGraw-Hill, New York, 1998; agents are knowledge artifacts residing on the network and serving their master). This blends well with the bank's global strategy: it is already present in 99 countries, while many of its would-be rivals are limited to investment banking markets, provide less broad coverage, and are way behind in IT. In short, this means that Citibank is well-positioned in the IBC economy described in section 3.

The issue which should retain the regulators' attention is that the Internet economy sees to it that entire industries are reinventing themselves and are refocusing their activities. They are moving quickly into lucrative integrated markets and bypassing current rules and obsolete procedures. The drive is to partner and acquire an IBC position, making it feasible to emerge as a leader in the market which is shaped by the *Internet economy*.

Regulators must be very sensitive in this transition because the Internet economy also brings to the foreground new risks such as the high leveraging of financial assets and a rapid growth in liabilities, as in the case of the nearly bankrupt LTCM documents. This is clearly shown in Figures 1.3 and 1.4 which, for evident reasons, should retain the regulators' attention.

Figure 1.3 shows a fairly rapid growth in financial assets from 1975 to the year 2000. The growth of financial assets as a percentage of GDP particularly accelerated in 1985–8 and during the last five years of this century. Compared to this, the liabilities of the financial industry show an erratic trajectory, even more so during the last 15 years. While they accelerated in 1985–7, subsequently, for a few years, they deflated.

In 1990 the financial liabilities accelerated again and only after 1997 did they reach for the stars, leaving the growth of assets way behind, as illustrated in Figure 1.4. It is not just the hedge funds who have inordinate gearing; the liabilities of the whole banking industry are expanding most rapidly.

The leveraging of financial assets because of deregulation, globalisation and technology is not a priori unwanted; in fact, some financial experts say that 'leverage suggests that we are clever enough and skilful enough to employ a tool that can multiply our power ... Using leverage is something to boast about, not something to conceal.' I do not subscribe to such statements, and LTCM as well as East Asia and Russia have shown how dangerous

Figure 1.3 The rapid growth of assets in the financial industry: financial assets as a percentage of GDP

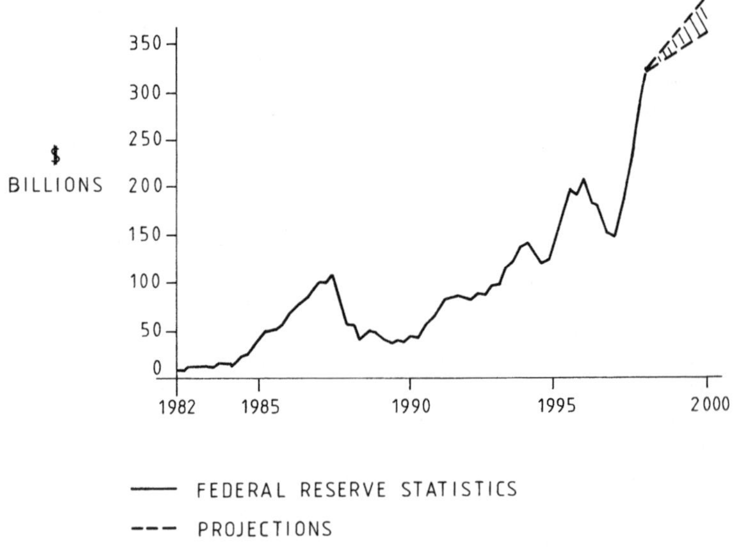

Figure 1.4 The rapid growth of liabilities in the financial industry: 4-quarter moving sum of net bond issues in $ billions

gearing can be. But the number of people being proselytised to leverage is on the increase, and therefore the regulators are getting nervous about the control of exposure taken by financial institutions and are searching for new ways to avoid a major bubble.

The positive aspect of the new landscape in international banking is that, during the 1990s, in the G-7 countries economic growth is being driven by high technology. Part of the expansionary equation is that prices are falling, not rising. Computers, communications, software and other information-related industries now account for 40 per cent of economic growth. In the Western economy, the high-tech sector grows at a 15 per cent annual rate, while the economy of old smoke stack-type industries only grows at 1.5 per cent.

This combination of rapid but non-inflationary growth in the technology-driven sector of the economy, and moderate expansion everywhere else, is exploited very effectively in the USA and Britain, but it has thus far eluded Japan and Continental Europe, because their economy is still characterised by old smoke-stack arteriosclerosis. Nothing has been learned from the fact that in the USA and the UK high-tech is a recipe for sustainable economic growth of 3 per cent to 4 per cent per year.

Economists now predict that the potential growth rate of technology-driven economies and their financial systems is likely to rise further as the high-tech sector continues to expand. This has an evident effect on the banking industry, bringing to the foreground another issue concerning regulators: among financial institutions, information technology has definitely become a core business in banking, and prudential supervision is expanding into the IT sector, particularly the companies serving the banking industry.

The proactive position taken by American regulators in connection with the Year 2000 (Y2K) problem provides a good example of what I am saying. The guidelines established by FDIC (see Chapter 2) on choosing a software house or service bureau outsourcer by American banks will eventually be generalised throughout the G-10 countries.

First and foremost, because information technology is core business in banking, the Federal Reserve, FDIC, OCC and Office of Thrift Supervision (OTS) have examined 350 software companies and service bureaux in the USA in connection with Y2K compliance. Second, the regulators have explained to senior bank management that failure in outsourcing can be as fatal to a financial institution as failure of its own IT resources. Precisely for this reason the regulators rounded up and phased out of banking a weak service bureau which, in their judgement, would have created problems that would have filtered into the banks which it served.

Third, the action of regulators extended beyond banking, not only in connection with Y2K compliance but also to provide assurance for correct functioning of all mission critical systems. As these real-life references document today, and even more in the new millennium, banking and IT are indivisible. Technology provides an institution's infrastructure. No bank can function with defective IT, but those institutions and those regulators who master technology are ahead of the curve.

6 The phase shift in the market calls for new regulatory policies and procedures

Despite the return of confidence and liquidity to most markets after the débâcle of LTCM in September 1998, both Dr Alan Greenspan, the chairman of the Federal Reserve Board, and William McDonough, president of the New York Federal Reserve Bank, have suggested in recent speeches that an emergency such as the one at LTCM could occur again. Neither is this wounded hedge fund totally out of the woods.

Part and parcel of the *phase shift* which is currently taking place is the fact that Wall Street and the City are no longer mainly funding a more or less real economic activity, but spend a great deal of their time and money on derivatives and on speculation. Today, the real economy is viewed mainly as a vehicle for leveraging in the financial markets: that is to say, the virtual economy.

Apart from the high gearing, a big chunk of the risk embedded in the current phase shift comes from abandoning sound fundamentals. In LTCM's case, many otherwise sound investors ignored basic rules because they were seduced by the reputation of John Meriwether, formerly of Salomon Brothers, and his Nobel Prize-winning team of advisers as fast-buck makers. With a leverage ratio which ultimately soared to 50 : 1, LTCM could be sitting on some undisclosed positions that continue to deteriorate. This risk is all the more pronounced as LTCM executives refused to comment, for the record, on how well the fund is doing, or to divulge precisely what is in its portfolio.

Bankers and other investors threw money at LTCM based on the track record of the managers and their consultants rather than paying attention to basic, time-honoured investment principles. This marvelling at the jewels masked the fact that in 1991 John Meriwether was forced to resign from Salomon in the wake of a government bond scandal in which the investment bank's traders tried to corner the market in Treasury bonds at several auctions by falsifying bids.

Although never personally implicated as head of the government bond department at Salomon Brothers, Meriwether took responsibility for the incident. This came back in the headlines after the LTCM fiasco. As we will see in Chapter 8, there is more than one reason why hedge funds are a kind of anomaly in the financial system. While they greatly contribute to its leverage, for any practical purpose they are not regulated or even inspected. As a result, they act *as if* they have been given a blank cheque. This suggests that:

- any assessment of where LTCM and its like really stand necessarily involves some guesswork; and

- because of the huge positions which are at risk, it is possible that the world's financial markets will once again sink into crisis.

Because solutions to these problems are so complex, Bill Clinton has instituted the President's Working Group on Financial Markets which includes, among other members, the Secretary of the Treasury, the chairman of the Federal Reserve and the SEC chairman. The members of this group do not comment on their deliberations, but from what is learned there is no unanimity on the best course to follow.

In the answers he gave to the House Banking Committee on 16 September 1998, Dr Alan Greenspan stated that hedge funds 'are very strongly regulated by those who lend them money'. Robert Rubin, however, countered this argument by stating, 'It assumes that the creditors are careful.' Rubin, a former Wall Street trader, believes that when times are good even smart people can do very stupid things.

The bottom line is that we all formulate hypotheses and make assumptions. The Federal Reserve Bank of New York, which brokered LTCM's rescue, the commercial and investment banks which poured money in to refloat the hedge fund, and the fund's own managers have been betting, in essence, on an improvement in the health of the financial markets and a lower, more predictable volatility. The bet is that:

- price fluctuations will shrink over time, or at least will not accelerate;
- confident investors will increase their appetite for securities; and
- during the coming years the capital market will remain liquid.

Liquid capital markets means that there would be plenty of bidders around whenever anyone wants to sell. But none of these three elements are sure bets and, besides, the regulators know that the problem is much more fundamental. It has become evident for some time that when events become too complex, and the markets move rapidly in their way, regulators, investment bankers and commercial bankers (in short the experts) are demonstrably less able to cope with them. Because LTCM was hardly unique in its approach to investing, the risks of the global market place look far sharper after its near bankruptcy than they did before that long week in late September 1998, when so much seemed to depend on the fate of a single institution.

Most worrisome to regulators is the relatively new phenomenon of the use of borrowed money for speculation which has been provided by banks and institutional investors. This has become a mainstay of many players in today's markets, culminating in the fact that speculation is done by proxy by the banking industry, which is regulated, while the speculators themselves are not. With LTCM this occurred on a scale very much larger than many investors had thought possible or which other hedge funds had manipulated to their advantage in the past.

One of the most flagrant gearing exercises in the LTCM case is that banks lent money to the hedge fund and then entered into bilateral derivatives trades with their overexposed debtor. This not only magnified the leverage of the lenders and of the hedge fund, but also linked them tightly together. A default by LTCM would have had catastrophic consequences for both the lender and gambler counterparty. Such deals involved credit arrangements so complex that none of the players (lenders, investors, trading partners, regulators) could respond to the fund's troubles in the old, time-honoured way. The bottom line is that today the globalised financial markets feature a whole series of structural changes so profound that when we come to the edge of risk-taking we find the old formulas no longer work. 'That is what this [LTCM] crisis was about', said Dr Henry Kaufman.

Many regulators now fear that what happened with LTCM is a result of developments in the financial market that have permanently altered the way the system works. Investors can ignore the lessons of this crisis at their own peril, and the same is true of supervisors and legislators.

7 Regulating the partnership between credit institutions and hedge funds

In terms of prudential supervision, the regulators had other worries besides LTCM. Following the huge losses announced by the global banks and hedge funds in mid-August to early October 1998, because of Asia, Russia and other light-hearted investments, their stocks suffered the sharpest decline in the decade of the 1990s as investor confidence was shaken.

In the aftermath of the Russian meltdown, Quantum Fund lost $2 billion. Ironically it was George Soros who triggered this Russian crisis by calling for the devaluation of the rouble and gambling on it. Among British credit institutions Barclays Bank lost £250 million ($420 million) and NatWest Bank, £100 million ($165 million). NatWest stated that it 'felt comfortable' with that amount of red ink.

Other banks were worse hit. Bankers Trust lost $480 billion, of which $350 million is represented by the 85 per cent of its investments in Russia. The take-over by Deutsche Bank came in the wake of this torrent of red ink. Credit Suisse lost $250 million, mainly in Russia. BankAmerica originally revealed Russian losses of $200 million out of $350 million lost in trading. This number, however, ballooned when BankAmerica provided for $1.4 billion against losses in the third quarter of 1998, including $400 million against a loan to D.E. Shaw, a rocket-scientist outfit turned derivatives trader.

Salomon Smith Barney originally said that it lost $150 million. Later it was stated that the quarterly loss in the wholesale business of Citigroup stood at $336 million due to the bigger than expected $1.3 billion of red ink which went down the drain in trading at Salomon. Chase Manhattan announced a $3.25 billion exposure, mainly due to its lending to hedge funds.

This runs contrary to the principle that the distinguishing charateristic of a bank is its deposit-taking function, and depositors' money has to be protected at all times. Chase was not alone in its exposure to hedge funds. As noted in section 6, banks are heavily regulated institutions, while hedge funds have so far escaped anybody's control. When lending money or securities to speculators, credit analysis is at its lowest; yet, for any well-run bank, the borrower's willingness and ability to repay a loan is the cornerstone of its business.

Lending to hedge funds is a far cry from the way credit institutions used to work. Traditionally, banks took the view that because their deposit base was short term, they should only make short-term loans. Regulators see to it that this still prevails in some countries (for instance, Italy). Longer-term loans were introduced in the 1930s and became general practice in the post-Second World War years. Then, in the 1980s, there were loans to junk bond outfits and, in the 1990s, to hedge funds.

Junk bond and hedge fund loans violate the first principle of commercial banking: determine the purpose of the credit and the quality of the risk. They also make a joke out of sound banking practices which call for concentrating on the underlying economics of the deal and evaluating risk and reward.

Most importantly, junk bonds and hedge fund loans by commercial banks exploit a gaping hole in regulation and prudential supervision, under the nose of the regulators themselves. It makes no sense to be meticulous in examining the soundness of small loans when billion-dollar loans go undetected in terms of their purpose, the quality of their recipients and the use to which the funds are put.

Sometimes, even the government complots to push banks the wrong way. In an early announcement after the Russian default, Deutsche Bank said that it lost DM 280 million ($140 million) in that crisis, but that 80 per cent was covered by Hermes, the German government's guarantee for risky loans abroad. This initial amount grew to $750 million not covered by guarantees. In the aftermath, Deutsche Bank lost its AAA credit rating from Standard & Poor's. Rabobank of the Netherlands is now the world's only private bank with AAA.

Silly loans to risky business may also be made at home. Japan Leasing Corporation, a daughter of Long-Term Credit Bank, defaulted. This was the largest default yet in Japan. The good news is that it led to the nationalisation, and therefore the salvage of Long-Term Credit Bank with public money. Nomura Securities, too, fell victim to the turbulence in the financial markets. It lost Yen 207 billion ($1.73 billion) net in the first six months of fiscal 1998–99.

Even when it is so large, as shown in the foregoing examples, the mere size of the losses does not convey the full drama which is unsettling to regulators. A comparison may do a better job. Financial analysts estimate that, at the end of 1997, European banks had $426 billion worth of debt exposure to emerging markets; this is equivalent to approximately 7 per cent of Euroland's GDP.

By contrast, the American banks' exposure came to $117 billion, or about 1.5 per cent of US GDP. The irony is that even in Latin America the exposure of European banks was double that of US banks: $133.6 billion as against $64.3 billion. This speaks volumes as to who will be hurt the most because of the January 1999 troubles in Brazil. With economic growth in Europe running at 2.0 to 2.5 per cent on a year-over-year basis, compared with 3.5 to 4.0 per cent in the USA, Europe has a far smaller growth cushion should credit scarcity foster a slowdown or, even worse, a downturn.

2
The Search for a New Global Financial Architecture

1 Introduction

Chapter 1 has documented that not only has the financial market changed but it is still undergoing change. The profit margins in the banks' classical product lines have been squeezed. There is a trend towards disintermediation in loans compensated for by trading activities, which involve a high quotient of credit risk and market risk.

Increasingly, banks come to appreciate that new products are necessary for survival. But innovation cannot be enacted, let alone sustained, without a technological leap forward. Networks, and most particularly Internet-type any-to-any connectivity have created a new level of competitiveness. Among other things, this has meant that not only banking but also other dynamic branches of industry have become global.

Globality presents new business opportunities but also poses complex regulatory problems. It is therefore to be expected that legislators and regulators will push for revamping existing laws and rules conditioning the banking industry, albeit at a slower pace than new events evolve. This leaves some gaping holes in the prudential supervision of the banking industry.

The capital market's role in the world economy has expanded sharply in the 1990s. Traditionally, the capital market functioned mostly as a vehicle for raising capital for investment, but today it performs a multiple duty by financing:

- capital investments;
- domestic consumption;
- trade deficits; and
- new, leveraged financial instruments.

What is global regulation all about? Webster's defines *regulation* as: 'The act of reducing to order; disposing in accordance with rule or established custom.' A new regulatory environment implies changes in existing relations regarding future and forward interest rates; OTC trades on currency exchange rates; lines of business such as the securitisation of all types of loans; the development and marketing of new banking products; and trading in derivatives.

Other regulatory changes, for instance in America, concern the Glass–Steagall Act and interstate banking, but more and more the focal point of interest is transborder banking, including the internationalisation of exchanges, huge money flows to emerging countries, loans which no longer abide by established rules, and high stakes in exposure which a few years ago would have been incompatible with sound banking practice. Is this state of affairs really of interest to the long-term health of the banking industry?

The answer cannot be black or white. Asia's financial crisis in 1997, Russia's default in 1998 and LTCM's near bankruptcy have been so large and unexpected that they shook the complacency surrounding the global financial markets. Increasingly regulators, and some politicians, recommend that we should move towards establishing the following on a global scale:

- better macroeconomic policies;
- tighter financial supervision; and
- greater transparency in financial reporting

Yet, more than two years after the Asian crisis hit, and in spite of the fact that Thailand, Indonesia and South Korea have been followed into the abyss by Russia and Brazil while other countries in Latin America are also on the brink, this new financial architecture is still at a philosophical level. At this point, the global financial crisis is big enough to force a most rigorous questioning of the current order. The reader will find the evidence in this chapter.

2 The doubts arising from disfunctioning rules and markets

In the academic world, many economists are now challenging the wisdom of capital account liberalisation which characterises the way the global market currently works. They feel uncomfortable with the supposed efficiency of international capital markets and with the role of the IMF as lender of last resort.

One of the facts brought to the forefront by the East Asian financial crisis is that financial meltdown can also happen to relatively good economies. South Korea had developed an appreciable industrial base and, at least theoretically, it has the talent and means to rank among the world's sound economies. But when, in late 1997, its central bank nearly ran out of reserves, investors panicked and the currency collapsed.

To avert such panics, the IMF wants to see that countries could be *prequalified* for emergency aid, in the hope that the mere existence of a big, secured credit line would reassure investors. But as Brazil demonstrated, this argument does not stand. In 1998, the IMF, as well as the US and other G-10 nations, offered Brazil a $41 billion bailout. That package, however, failed to prevent a run on the real, and Brazil's currency lost more than 40 per cent of its foreign exchange value in a few weeks.

It is just as hard to make a strong case about the ability to predict runs on currencies, or an impeding collapse. On and off, there were plenty of warnings about Thailand in 1997 but nobody predicted a calamity. 'Nothing in my 26 years on Wall Street or my 6 years in government suggests that there is any predictive capability even remotely reliable enough for such a system', Treasury Secretary Robert Rubin commented in early 1999.

Uncertainty about what is next does not move into action global institutions and people that count. The IMF notes that it often detects signs a crisis is brewing 'here' or 'there', but later finds out this crisis never arrives. 'We've successfully predicted 14 of the past 6 financial crises,' said Stanley Fischer of IMF (*Herald Tribune*, 1 March 1999).

The fallout from the global crisis of 1997 and 1998 has inevitably created setbacks in the movement towards globalisation. At the same time, there is always a tendency when things go wrong to blame the free market for the evils – as if command economies produced better results. The centralised command economy of the Soviet Union has crashed in a big way, and none of the resulting states can even crawl in a financial sense. Meanwhile, the planned economy of Japan, which searched for a third way, has damaged itself beyond repair, yet there was a time when Japan could do nothing wrong.

This does not mean that liberal economic principles work in the best possible manner. In mid-1998, the 1997 BIS annual report had been critical of the conventional wisdom on a number of issues: 'This [the 1997 events] was the first crisis in the post-war period featuring the combination of banks as the principal international creditors, and private sector entities as the principal debtors.'

These 'private sector entities' have largely been in that part of the world which counts little in terms of total global economic weight, the so-called emerging markets where private and sovereign interests intermingle in a curious form known as 'crony capitalism'. Here is encapsulated the *Who's Who* of economic power:

- European Union (EU), with 31 per cent of global GDP (but Euroland has a lower annual growth rate than the USA);
- the USA, with 27 per cent of global GDP;
- Japan, with 16 per cent to 17 per cent of global GDP, in spite of lack of natural resources;
- Asia Pacific (where crony capitalism has taken residence), with 11 per cent of global GDP;

- Latin America with 6 per cent of global GDP;
- Russia (another bastion of crony capitalism), with 1 to 2 per cent of global GDP;
- rest of the world with the remaining 6.5 per cent or so of global GDP.

If any evidence were necessary, these statistics leave little doubt that the parties who should care most about global financial stability are the USA, the EU and Japan. Between them they wield 75 per cent of the world's economic power. Their central bankers and finance ministers are paid to worry about the systemic meltdown.

It has therefore been disappointing to see that when the finance ministers and central bankers from the G-7 met on 20 February 1999, in Bonn, what they produced is best described through Gottfried Benn's phrase 'Nothing and over it enamel.' (See sections 6 and 7 on what is required for a rigorous solution.)

The goal of that meeting was to establish the outline of a new global financial architecture, an urgent task since the world economy has continued to deteriorate. Instead, they only agreed on the much narrower scope of a Financial Stability Forum. The good news is that it will be headquartered at BIS in Basle, and chaired by Andrew Crocket, general manager of BIS. The bad news is that this Forum is too little, too late.

The Financial Stability Forum is expected to meet twice a year which, to say the least, is too seldom. In essence what this new organ will be doing is to formalise the *ad hoc* consultation among policy makers. The finance ministers of the G-7, IMF, World Bank, Organisation for Economic Co-operation and Development (OECD) and other international bodies are members. This sets the Forum apart from the Basle Committee on Banking Supervision whose members are the G-10 central bankers.

According to Dr Hans Tietmeyer, president of the Bundesbank who drafted the 11-page proposal to create the Forum, the new body's main function will be pooling information on the markets and on reserves, as well as acting as a warning system on potential economic and financial shocks. This fills a gap in surveillance, because no central bank has the breadth of information to formulate a complete assessment of evolving risk, but it is a far cry from the necessary modernisation and revamping of the word's financial and commercial architecture conceived in the 1940s in Bretton Woods.

During that same meeting in February 1999, Robert Rubin suggested that the USA cannot remain the 'importer of last resort', acting as the primary engine to support recovery in emerging markets (*Herald Tribune*, 22 February 1999). And it was also discussed that the 'emerging markets' themselves are not happy with globalisation, although this is due to other reasons.

Egypt's president, Hosni Mubarak, for instance says: 'In the emerging world there is a bitter sentiment of injustice. There is a sense that there must be something wrong with a system that wipes out years of hard-won development because of changes in market sentiments.' This argument forgets some basic facts characterising globalisation and money flows: contrary to the post-Second World War financial assistance programmes, put up mainly by the USA, globalisation switches around private money, and this is not government aid in disguise. Private money goes where it can make fat profits and it rushes out of the door when the perceived risks exceed returns. But without this private money, the so-called emerging markets would never have emerged, and there would have been no 'years of hard-won development'.

A better way to explain this is through a joke which was heard around in the 1980s: 'What's worse than being exploited by multinationals?' The answer is, 'Not being exploited by them.' It is no less true, nevertheless, that global markets do not have the social cohesiveness which sometimes, though by no means always, characterises national and local markets.

A new financial architecture is necessary exactly because global markets lack government supervision, shared values and social responsibility. A quotation of a recent statement by Kofi Annan, the Secretary-General of the UN, explains this issue: 'National markets are held together by shared values and confidence in certain minimum standards. But in the new global market, people do not yet have that confidence.'

In a nutshell, this is an environment characterised by some significant doubts arising from disfunctioning rules and markets. Not everything, however, is to be thrown out. As Henri Poincaré once suggested: 'To doubt everything or to believe everything are two equally convenient solutions; both dispense with the need for reflection.'

3 Reflections on a new global financial architecture

The Great Depression of 1929–32 helped to put in place a national system of regulation and financial disclosure. It also set the stage for government safety nets, at least in some parts of the world, such as North America and Western Europe. But it did not weed greed out of the financial system. It is simply impossible to regulate human nature.

I consider the safety nets provided by governments to be a milestone in national regulation (see section 7). That point has not yet been reached in the emerging countries, or in a global sense. In fact, many sovereigns are still far even from appreciating that it is necessary to head in that direction because the risks of the market place are not going to go away by decree. They will be around as long as there are business opportunities. A safety net implies responsibilities, because first and foremost it is a cultural and legal issue rather than just a financial solution, and to avoid inconsistencies a new global approach to regulation should address all entities, big and small, whether private companies or sovereigns (see Chapter 15).

In the context of a global market, at an equal level of priority to a safety net is the issue of business financing. Since the merchant bankers in

Table 2.1 Percentage of company financing done by commercial banks, early 1990s

Country	(%)
United States	30
Germany, France, Italy	70
Japan	80

London and the development of intermediation by commerical banks, credit institutions have been the main providers of capital to business and industry. During the last 15 years, however, this has significantly changed, and its aftermath should be counted in any new financial architecture.

In America, the early 1990s have seen two different populations: entrepreneurial start-ups in technology and a host of AAA businesses, moving away from traditional bank borrowing. They are raising capital by issuing stocks and bonds. So far, this process has not had much momentum in continental Europe or in Asia. Table 2.1 dramatises the percentage of company financing done by the banking sector in the US, Germany, France, Italy and Japan.

There is plenty of documentation that, today, company financing through the banking system is highest in lesser developed countries. Many economists now believe that overdependence on intermediation by domestic banks is a basic reason why a financial system is unable to efficiently allocate available monetary resources. Statistics support this hypotheses:

- In East Asia (including Japan) bank assets are larger than those of stock markets and bond markets combined.
- By contrast, in the US this relationship is reversed. Stock and bond markets are four times larger than bank assets.

But, capital markets would not grow, the public would not trust them and the markets themselves would not trust the companies – their equity and their obligations – unless there is a proven amount of transparency as well as evidence of accountability throughout the financial system. Both are in short supply in most of the world's capital markets where banks still have a lock on intermediation.

The call for accountability, transparency and prudence made by clear-eyed economists, global institutions, regional development banks and what Ben Graham called 'Mr Market', has consistently met with resistance by domestic players who profit from secrecy and the crony capitalism it breeds. Resistance also comes from foreign investors who hope for a quick buck followed by 12th-hour IMF bailout, which creates moral hazard.

Governments as well as regulators should be aware that this state of affairs leads to a dysfunctional economy. Local investors are put off by inflexible, arteriosclerotic government regulations, high walls raised by embedded interests, inadequate or non-existent transparency and disregard for shareholder value and bondholder interests.

When capital markets mistrust those who are in charge of the economy their instinct is to favour the relative security of savings accounts rather than the greater risk and return found in more complex financial instruments. To make matters worse, savings accounts are often taxed by the government further reducing their appeal. In Japan, for instance, $10 trillion is locked up in local savings institutions, earning a negative real rate of return.

The new financial architecture for the global system which is now contemplated must serve (as well as control) both the old and new economy – as well as both the giants and the dwarfs. Because the current system is far from being perfect, few would question the need for a change in the financial architecture which dates back to Bretton Woods. Essentially, what is needed is a fundamental restructuring of international finance. The East Asian, Russian and Brazilian crises revealed deep underlying flaws in the world's financial system, but there exist remarkably few new ideas on how the global economy and its regulators could do better.

The search for a better solution has been hindered by the fact that, unfortunately, many international bankers worked on the belief that sustained high earnings were not a hype but a new economic reality. As a result, they saw themselves compelled to take ever greater risks, overstuffing their institutions with securitised liabilities and engaging in high-stakes transborder capital flows.

Against all evidence, investors too have come to believe that sovereigns or private companies under the sovereigns' wings are obligors who will never default on their credit, and therefore counterparties will face no liquidity or solvency risks. With this sort of surrealistic thinking, it is no surprise that the global economy is now so highly geared and so prone to crash.

Not everybody, however, has been taken in by this hype. The more clear-eyed regulators think that the restructuring of global finance is an issue which cannot be, and should not be, delayed because major problems in the USA and in Europe may soon follow. Even tier-1 economies face near-crisis conditions, as the fate of Japan documents. In other continents, Europe is mired in over 10 per cent unemployment, and the USA's trade balance continues to deteriorate.

As Figure 2.1 demonstrates, trends which started in 1980 with current account deficits continue to decimate the US export trade. The situation is characterised by an overall decline of US exports to the rest of the world, coupled with rising imports, particularly from countries offering no reciprocity in free trade.

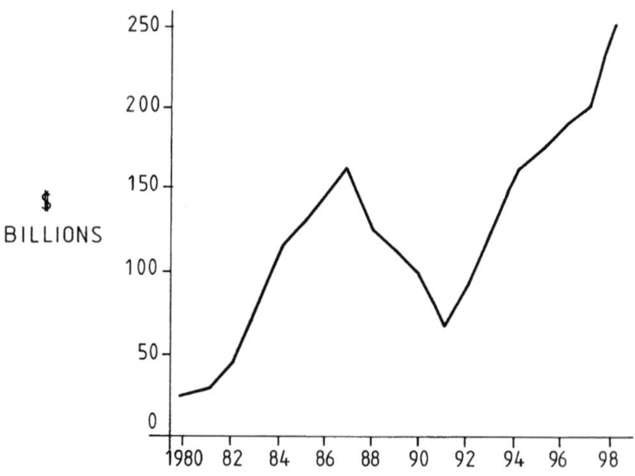

Figure 2.1 Trade deficit in American physical goods, 1980–98

Persistent current account deficits are a complex worry, all the more so when an economy depends on exports for over 10 per cent of its GNP. Back in the early 1950s, exports represented only 5 per cent of US GNP. Today, in the American economy, one in five goods-producing jobs depends on exports. How complex the rules of a global financial architecture for the new millennium could be is dramatised by the fact that, in 1998, the USA registered a trade deficit which is 50 per cent greater than in 1997, and the highest America has ever had (see Figure 2.1). For physical goods alone, the picture is even worse. A nation that depends on a quarter of a trillion dollars of goods imports per year is below break-even.

From current account deficits to an imbalance in global finance there is only a small step. Huge current account deficits by major industrial nations add to international capital flows; indeed, they accelerate them. Belatedly we have come to realise that not only the institutions we rely on to facilitate the international exchange of capital, but also our trade practices and systems of payments, are deeply flawed.

Not only are the balances in merchandise goods lopsided, but the capital markets themselves have been defective, leading to overleveraging and galloping speculation. This is the sort of trouble that led to the failure of LTCM (see Chapter 1), which revealed the price of miscalculating risk.

In principle, the 1944 Bretton Woods agreement was established to remedy international speculation, stop the export of deflation, and correct capital distortions that plagued the pre-Second World War world. Under the Bretton Woods agreement, central banks made occasional changes in parities but their common goal was stability, not profiteering from chaos. Credits from the IMF and the World Bank were meant to help nations recover by resuming expansion, rather than by exporting deflation.

Things, however, have changed. In the USA, George Shultz (the former secretary of state and treasury secretary), Anna Schwartz (an economic historian) and editorial writers on the Wall Street Journal argue that today's financial woes are caused by bailouts of countries and investors by the IMF, hence public money. Investors and borrowers behave recklessly because they believe they will be able to pull out of the mess they have created when trouble hits. The IMF, these experts argue, creates moral hazard in two ways:

- by rescuing governments from the consequences of rotten policies, thereby encouraging them to repeat their poor judgement or deliberate mistakes; and
- by rescuing greedy investors by rewarding their recklessness.

This criticism has gained considerable momentum because of the frequency and size of IMF support packages in 1997 and 1998. Another frequently heard criticism is that today's World Bank and IMF are just a shadow of their originals, which were anchored by a more powerful US dollar and a US government more activist as a world stabiliser.

When the first major post-Second World War Mexican crisis exploded in 1982 the Federal Reserve, not the IMF, rushed to the rescue to avoid an avalanche. But by mid-1997, this role of global financial stabiliser was taken over by IMF with huge loans to Thailand, Indonesia and South Korea. With these loans, the East Asian economies were salvaged up to a point, but in August 1998 the Russian crisis added to the market's problems. The *de facto* default increased the riskiness of emerging sovereign debt. Investors who had until then assumed that foreign debts would at worst be rescheduled, and that the IMF would bail out the Russian government, found that the assets they had recklessly lent had suddenly become much more risky, if not altogether worthless. As Western banks and hedge funds lost plenty of money in Russia (see Chapter 1), they needed to reduce risks in other markets to reflect their diminished equity. This led to sell-offs such as those in the American and European stock markets, which superficially were unrelated to the Russian crisis.

Another consequence has been that, as was the practice in East Asia, after the meltdown some Russian investment banks refused to honour derivatives contracts sold over the counter to counterparties. They argued that the Russian government default was a case of *force majeure*, freeing them from the obligation. This is a case study in unwillingness to perform. The OCC and its derivative instruments aggravated the crisis by magnifying the players' financial losses to such a degree that no fire-brigade approach could cope with them.

4 The moral hazard posed by a fire-brigade approach

To appreciate the situation in which the global financial system currently finds itself, and its gravity, we must start by understanding what has happened with the current financial architecture, and why. The first big issue is the long-term weakness of a system which over the years got into the habit of misallocating its resources and of underweighting its risks. This drifting has been promoted through crony capitalism, as is the case in East Asia and Russia, and by means of an ever-growing financial speculation, characterising the USA and Europe.

Washing crony capitalism out of the system is no simple matter even if the economic size of 'emerging markets', including Russia, is not that big. Paul Volcker, the former chairman of the Federal Reserve, points out that the entire banking system of many an emerging country is no bigger than a typical regional bank in the USA or Europe. That is the size now considered too small for global financial markets.

For many 'emerging' economies, small financial markets mean that exchange-rate volatility will be a structural problem rather than a temporary one, and it will haunt them for many years to come. If a hedge fund decides to play in its stock exchange or buy and sell its assets, or if a couple of mutual funds decide to make a serious investment, the country's exchange rate could rocket. This would start an unsustainable boom in real estate and banking, causing havoc for exporters. The opposite scenario would be that a currency collapse will take place the moment the financial invaders went home, as shown in Thailand, Indonesia, South Korea, Russia and Brazil.

On several occasions during the last couple of years, Dr Alan Greenspan, the chairman of the Federal Reserve, has stressed the issues underpinning the problems facing emerging countries, concluding that the countries whose economies went down the drain should move as fast as possible towards standards of:

- market liberalisation;
- transparency in financial reporting; and
- a more rigorous financial regulation.

All three points are valid. However, we should not forget the impact of the ever-growing financial speculation by hedge funds and other institutions (see Chapter 8), because it is a major determinant of future financial health. Experience acquired during the last quarter of a century demonstrates two issues which have grown out of proportion to the real economy of the world, as outlined below.

1. International currency exchange transactions grew, in 1999, to $2 billion per day. This corresponds to slightly less than a quarter of the USA's GNP, as Chapter 1 has explained.

2. Financial institutions, and other companies, found their way out of regulation. The more global they are, the less they are supervised and controlled, and hence the more vulnerable to self-inflicted damage.

Another crucial issue making the current financial environment so risky is the great change which has come into the interaction between the implicit and explicit guarantees to the financial system of the capital-importing countries. Largely because of the timely intervention by IMF through a fire-brigade approach, there has developed a credo among international lenders that no matter what blunders they commit they will be helped to get their money out.

This is the sense of *moral hazard*, a term coined to express the investors' and traders' disregard of information about nearly bankrupt nations and corporations to whom they lend, or the stress their deals create to the banking system. Because of moral hazard, hedge funds as well as other investors and speculators end by acting more recklessly since 'they know' that they will be bailed out if things go wrong.

Some analysts and quite a few bankers say that it does not really matter if the global financial duties are out of reach of the classical regulatory authorities because the markets have become the new regulators, and so far they have done this job in a fairly efficient way. But avoiding scrutiny by prudential supervisors is counterproductive and it becomes a big negative in the longer term.

During his lecture at the First International Conference on Risk Management in Banking (London, 17–21 March 1997), Jean-Pierre Paelinck, the secretary general of the European Federation of Stock Exchanges, made a reference which is worth recording. The executive in charge of listing at the London Stock Exchange (LSE), who had a solid background in accounting, asked Robert Maxwell some sharp questions when the wheeler-dealer wanted to register his firm at LSE.

Upon hearing these questions which, depending on the evidence being provided, might have blocked his registration at LSE, Maxwell became angry and arrogant. Finally he used political pressure to bypass the listing obstacle. Yet the registration executive was right in being inquisitive. What happened afterwards proved that there were good reasons to pose rigorous queries. The registration official had asked the right questions and if these had been answered there might have been no Maxwell scandal.

A surprisingly large number of people who think of themselves as experts in global finance tend to forget that analysing the prospect's ability and willingness to pay is a matter of investigating, respectively, his economic prospects and his character. In part, this absentmindedness comes from the fact that in the 1980s and 1990s there have been two kinds of capital:

- bank capital; and
- market capital.

Market capital is stocks and bonds. Investors who put money into Asian stocks have been severely punished by the markets. Peregrine Investments went bust and most stock exchanges took a nose dive. Bangkok, for instance, dropped 78 per cent to an 11-year low.

For all their blunders in South Korea, Indonesia and Thailand, however, banks have escaped without much pain. An ever increasing size of IMF loans became the rule. And when, six months after the late 1997 crisis, international banks were pressured to roll over their private loans, they persuaded the Korean government to transform them into national obligations.

The case of Brazil, Mexico, Argentina, Thailand, Indonesia, South Korea and Russia is that of investors demanding a bailout. While the governments of these countries also profit, it is essentially the foreign investors who are salvaged when the IMF acts as lender of last resort, with all this means in terms of moral hazard.

Until Russia was left to stew in its own juice, in August 1998, access to this rapid-deployment of funds rewarded misbehaviour, yet it has been promoted by the Western nations. Now it is suggested that preventive measures are preferable to the fire brigade. But what will be the criteria? Will the Fund maintain a public list of countries that pre-qualify? Will all this be handled centrally by bureaucrats who think that they are the experts?

Floating ideas about new solutions without thoroughly studying them and their aftermath is part of the problem, rather than of the solution. What if IMF takes a country which shows signs of improvement off its pre-approved list, thereby precipitating capital flight? Will this country be obliged to seek assistance through one of the Fund's other facilities? And then what will become of the moral hazard?

There are also other critical questions to be addressed by the new financial architecture which is currently contemplated. Because transborder flows are so big, both exchange rates and interest rates have become a sort of moving target. What about the interaction between:

- pegged exchange-rate regimes in a number of countries;
- floating exchange rates in other countries; and
- the unstable global macroeconomic environment?

Just a few years ago currency boards were saluted as the saviour, and pegging the Argentine peso and the Brazil real to the dollar was seen as a brilliant idea. Little thought was given to the fact that weak economies cannot offer themselves that luxury, and when the protective wall implodes the currency can get devalued by a hefty 31 per cent, as happened to the real in January 1999.

The catch is that keeping the currencies fixed requires importing lots of money from abroad. That could work as long as international investors are willing to pour cash into emerging market stocks, bonds, direct investments and plain loans. But when business confidence wanes, the system of artificially supported high exchange rates comes undone.

There are, however, more constructive ways of looking at these challenges. What about taxing the larger transborder capital movements not to finance the underdeveloped countries, as has already been proposed, but to create a *deposit insurance* for coverage of losses up to a certain level? This can be done in a manner similar to the policy followed in the USA by FDIC (see section 6).

A thorough study of a new global financial architecture would address capital flows, current account deficits and exchange rate problems. Even First World countries are not immune to them. Particularly important are fluctuations in the dollar–yen exchange rate in the 1990s, and the aftershock, throughout the Asian economies, of a possible devaluation of Chinese renmimbi.

5 There is a synergy between monetary policy, exchange rates and bank supervision

What many governments and their short-sighted politicians fail to appreciate is that the international capital markets have an unerring ability to detect weaknesses. Sometimes they capitalise on them; in other cases they run away. Either way, through their actions they significantly affect what lies ahead.

Take, for instance, the silly idea of tying together the euro, the dollar and the yen (as well as their respective currency blocks). It has been proposed by some finance ministers of the G-7 as the cornerstone of a new global financial order. Those promoting it fail to appreciate this will be a huge mistake as well as an unsustainable policy. It would be a mistake because, if currencies are frozen, then interest-rate movements would have to take up the slack. That would not be a problem if America, Europe and Japan were on the same economic and financial wavelength, but they are not. (See Chapter 5 on the responsibilities of the European System of Central Banks.) Tying the three main currencies together will be unsustainable because the global financial landscape would become a speculators' paradise. With huge transborder money flows, hedge funds and other speculators would massively attack the weakest of the three currencies, while the central banks of the G-7 do not have the funds necessary to provide efficient and believable support when confronted with an onslaught. Behind the reasons why fixed dollar–euro–yen parities are unwise and unsustainable lie of course the fundamentals: the USA is running a surplus of 1 per cent of GDP. By contrast, Europe and Japan are running deficits of 3–4 per cent.

The opposite is true of current account surpluses and deficits: Europe and Japan have trade surpluses that amount to about 1 per cent of their GDP, while the USA has a mounting trade deficit that stands at about 3 per cent of its GDP.

A third fundamental difference concerns economic prosperity, employment and growth. All diverge widely in the three monetary regions: the USA features a fast-moving information economy, growing at nearly 4 per cent annually, with unemployment down to 4.3 per cent; but Japan is stuck in recession, unemployment is rising and future prospects are grim, while Europe is an also-ran in economic issues, with double digit unemployment persisting.

The bottom line is that there are neither the necessary conditions nor a compelling reason for currency linkages, even if the mathematics might look interesting. As of mid-February 1999, if the euro dropped 11 per cent in value against the dollar and if the yen rose 18 per cent, all three currencies would easily reach parity. The eggheads who suggest this scenario forget that currencies often move more than 10 per cent or even 20 per cent in a single year.

The algorithm $=€=¥ will not stand the test of currency volatility that melted Asia, decimated the LTCM hedge fund, defaulted Russia, and nearly brought the world's financial house down. Those who think in terms of resurrecting the fixed parities of Bretton Woods have not learned that a fixed exchange rate is like a tall, rigid ill-structured building that can crumble under hurricane conditions. Therefore, rather than stumbling backwards into the past, the contemplated new financial architecture should get on with building structures that can weather the financial storms of the next decades and contain their effects on monetary policy. To a significant extent this can be achieved through two measures which performed well in the USA: deposit insurance and a federated system of regulators.

Rather than building a huge new bureaucracy, this federal system of regulators can effectively use the services of independent rating agencies such as Standard & Poor's, Moody's Investors Service, and Fitch IBCA. Indeed, my research documents that regulators are increasingly interested in rating.

So far, in the G-10 countries the policy of the regulators has been that the market dictates the rating system. But in developing countries, particularly in Latin America, rating has become obligatory. Major rating agencies now expect that this may also happen in Eastern Europe, but not in Asia where financial reports are less reliable and more secretive.

The new global financial architecture should also address monetary issues. As we will see in section 7, a policy of bank regulation cannot be effectively separated from monetary policy. Because of its own excesses and for other reasons, the banking system can be hurt by lack of liquidity. When liquidity is low, many financial intermediaries find themselves with liabilities equal to or greater than their assets, and what follows is a credit crunch.

Monetary policy impacts on the markets in many ways. For instance, monetary authorities influence the behaviour of bankers and investors by shifting their focus from controlling inflation to reviving confidence in financial markets and economies. This has happened in the USA in September to December 1998, with three successive interest rate cuts by the Federal Reserve.

As monetary policy can be so much more effective when co-ordinated with bank supervision, in Europe many cognisant people regret that the European Central Bank (ECB) has not been given regulatory powers over the banking system, but its role is limited to monetary matters. The Maastricht Treaty confers upon ECB more power over monetary policy than any other central bank has had, but the authority of bank supervision remains diffused. Financial analysts now comment that because of the lack of bank supervisory duties, ECB could be ill-equipped to handle a major financial crisis. A polycentric structure of bank supervision left in the hands of existing national bodies is considered to be a source of weakness, as banks merge and become more pan-European.

The fear is that the ongoing integration of financial markets will make it more difficult for national supervisors, such as national central banks, special supervisory authorities and/or the Ministry of Finance, to monitor and assess the commercial and investment banks' overall risks. It will become harder to judge accurately the health of the banking system as a whole, and of each institution individually.

In the background of these worries is the fact that every significant domain of bank regulation and supervision tends to include several factors whose synergy is instrumental to the development and maintenance of a sound policy. The same is true of monetary policy. The ECB, for instance, has designed a business architecture for the euro which is shown in Figure 2.2. The serious reader will appreciate the synergies which come into play.

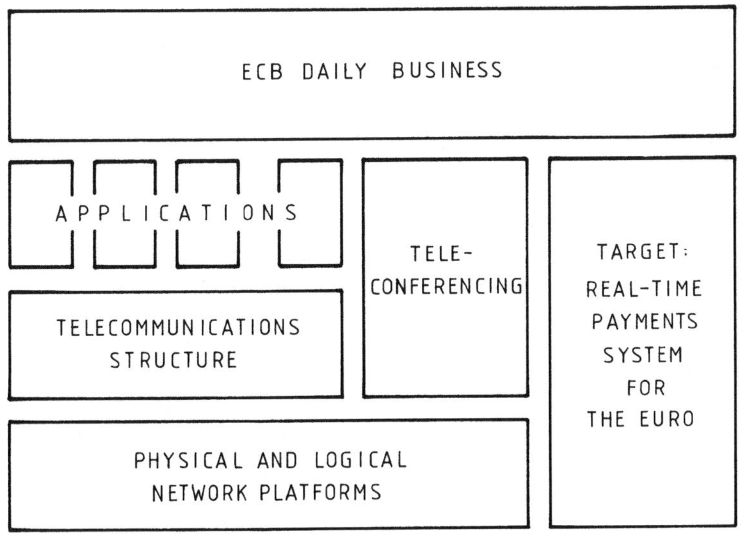

Figure 2.2 The business architecture implemented by the European Central Bank for the euro

The reference to the need for an association between monetary policy and regulatory authority is most pertinent to the search for a new global financial architecture. The debate over the policies which will replace Bretton Woods, and the associated organisation of the new duties, should begin and end with the issue of risk. The new structure must be able both to identify and to price correctly credit risk and market risk.

This need is further underlined by the fact that the requirements for rigorous risk management are not yet generally recognised. To many Asian bankers, for instance, risk was not even an issue as connections to politicians and well-placed family members determined capital and patronage flows. When the notion of risk slipped in after the 1997 meltdown, it was followed by a credit crunch.

One should learn from failure. The concept now taking shape is that of global markets tempered by regulation but helped by the synergy between monetary policy, bank supervision and a greater appreciation of risks by the financial industry. This synergy can help economies which find themselves in a classic liquidity trap. Short of a system approach, the scenario will be no different from what happens today: the more countries try to stimulate spending, the more their nervous consumers keep out of the high street. The more shy they are in facing their structural problems, the more they suffer from imported financial speculation. Because of globalisation, no solution can afford to disregard the market forces. The builders of the new financial architecture should remember that right after the Second World War the case for free markets and market economies was put by only a very small minority of economists who were looked upon as outliers, because the large majority believed in Keynesian economics. Today the majority believes in competition but finds it more painful than was first expected.

6 The deposit insurance solution in America which could serve as a model

No part of America's financial system is more encumbered with regulatory agencies than banking. Apart from the four main federal bank regulators (the Federal Reserve, FDIC, OCC and OTS), there is a regulator of the country's credit unions, plus regulatory agencies at state level. There is some overlap in supervisory functions, though each agency has specific objectives. But there are also bright spots in this constellation of regulatory agencies.

The FDIC, for example, supervises banks whose deposits it insures. Deposit insurance is typically regarded as one of the American banking industry's most powerful competitive edges, as well as a government subsidy to the industry that is costing some $20 billion a year. FDIC was born as a result of a crisis. It was set up under President Roosevelt's 1933 Banking Act to run the then innovative *federal insurance* scheme for bank deposits, which aimed to revive the public's confidence in the banking system after the run on the banks of 1932. All national, and virtually all state, banks are required to have federal deposit insurance.

FDIC got an act of its own in the 1950s. By then it was deep into bank supervision. Based in Washington, DC, FDIC now has 13 regional offices and receives no budget allocation from Congress. It finances itself through running its insurance system on bank deposits. That is the model I suggest for global insurance covering the financial industry.

In the USA, when deposit insurance was first introduced, coverage was limited to \$2500 per depositor. When coverage widened to deposits of \$100000, it caused many problems. For instance, a growing number of depositors felt that they could put their funds into the highest interest-paying and thus riskiest institutions, letting the insurers pay for collapses. Also, having so much money insured per personal deposit per credit institution is a drain on FDIC resources.

There is no reason why a global deposit insurance should be at the \$100000 level. The British model of £20000 (\$32400) coverage may be fine for the EU, while in Asia, Latin America and other regions the level may be less, in a way being commensurate with the cost of living and size of bank deposits per individual account.

It is the principle of FDIC, not the exact amounts, that I consider an excellent example. There is also the fact that for 56 consecutive years FDIC has been profitable. Only in 1988 did it make its first operating loss. Since then, premiums have risen, and FDIC has survived the test of time.

Better managed than one of its peers, the FDIC has not followed the example of the Federal Savings and Loan Insurance Corporation (FSLIC), which provided deposit insurance for thrifts but went bust. The irony is that FDIC gained new power from the changes the collapse of the FSLIC brought about. These are useful lessons for a global deposit insurance scheme.

Let me repeat this reference to make sure it is understood. Non-existent in many countries, the safety net provided by deposit insurance has been instrumental in shielding depositors from the uncertainties of credit institutions' bankruptcy. Critics say it also shields the banking industry from market discipline, and they add that since for up to \$100000 depositors have no incentive to favour one bank over another, badly managed banks, even some near insolvency, have been able to attract deposits. They do so as easily as healthy, well-run institutions, by paying much higher interest rates which they know leave no profit margins in the longer run. These critics forget the fact that FDIC is not the Salvation Army; it is a regulator which inspects the banks through its own examiners, and the penalties it applies are hefty. In other terms, it carries both a carrot and a stick.

As it proved to be a success story, deposit insurance is a good idea which, as cannot be repeated too often, should be adopted on a global scale. Banks and non-banks trading, investing and lending money abroad should be contributing a small percentage of their cross-border deals to a deposit insurance scheme which can come to the rescue in cases of legitimate bankruptcy. This will significantly improve on the current fire-brigade approach of the IMF, which recently has become chronically short of money.

Let us also recall that the OCC was also born out of crisis. It was established in 1863 to help finance the American Civil War. The North wanted a bond-secured national currency which it hoped would give the country common banknotes and stimulate the sale of national bonds.

The National Currency Act of 1863 created a currency bureau in the Treasury to be run by a comptroller. A year later, the National Banking Act authorised the comptroller to supervise national banks, and gave him a staff of bank examiners. Regulating national banks is now the OCC's main job. The comptroller has the power of reporting directly to Congress, over the head of the Treasury Secretary. The comptroller is appointed by the president of the USA and confirmed by the Senate. His term of office is five years, and he can be sacked only by the president, but typically the appointment runs the full 5-year term.

The OCC uses its routine examinations of each bank's books to learn a lot about bank management, in order to stop what the comptroller considers to be unsound banking practices. Federal banking law gives the OCC wide discretionary authority which strengthens the banking system by making controls much more rigorous. The problem is that these controls might overlap with those of the Federal Reserve. In the USA there is a need for interagency co-ordination. But in a global setting, an FDIC–OCC frame of reference could well be the infrastructure of the new financial architecture.

7 The Federal Reserve System provides a good background for restructuring the IMF

Another model which could help as a blueprint of a transnational supervisory agency for banks and non-banks is the US Federal Reserve System. The 'Fed' was created by Congress in 1913 after a run of bank panics over the previous century, with a nasty one in 1907, and soon became a powerful central bank. It conducts America's monetary policy and supervises the nationally chartered commercial banks through its 12 regional Federal Reserve Banks, which themselves are audited by the Fed.

A little known fact about the Fed is that it was designed by Paul Warburg based on his experience with the German Reichsbank. In turn, after the end of the Second World War, the concepts underpinning the Fed helped to structure the powerful Bundesbank of the German Federal Republic and more recently the ECB, although, unlike the Fed, the ECB and the Bundesbank have mainly monetary policy rather than supervisory duties. (The Bundesbank has some examiners, but in Germany bank supervision is the responsibility of the Federal Banking Supervision Bureau.)

If these are good precedents which, with some modifications, could provide a valid blueprint for a global bank supervisory solution, it is because the Reichsbank and the reserve institutions which followed its model have not been centralised entities. To operate, they depend on a network of banks just as a new IMF might depend on an East Asian, South Asian, Latin American, East European and other regional reserve banks.

Regional reserve institutions and a global bank supervision system proves the fact that today's capital market is world-wide: therefore it should not be supervised and regulated strictly on a national basis. The two structures of Bretton Woods, the IMF and the World Bank, have slowly drifted into being bureaucracies doling out public money. They are not regulators of banks, non-banks, and other hedge funds moving colossal amounts of money at a key-stroke.

The current system has been shattered by the turbulence of the last years; hence the search for radical reform leading to a new global financial architecture. The big question is 'which'. Though most people agree that in, say, 10 years' time the financial architecture will look substantially different from today's, few people have come up with novel ideas, and even these do not achieve consensus. The regional integration I am suggesting is a distinct possibility for still another reason.

Eventually we will see a few big regional currency blocks tying together as trading partners. This, too, will require both global and regional regulatory standards on supervision and crisis management. For this to happen a compromise will have to be found in what has become known as 'the impossible trinity':

- continuing national sovereignty on money supply and bank supervision;
- financial markets that are effectively regulated, supervised and cushioned; and
- the benefits of global trade, capital markets and money flows which created the prosperity of the last 20 years.

Many people are suggesting that the incompatibility among these three propositions comes from the fact that it is not possible to maintain sovereignty and yet allow capital markets to integrate. When this happens, we get the distortions of the 1980s and 1990s because capital-market integration, free trade and global regulation work against national sovereignty, or do they?

They do not. National sovereignty has been eroded in so many aspects that one more would not make a big difference. What is basically important is to redefine sovereignty in a way which does not contradict globalisation. In the short term, the best hope lies in improving the trade-offs between conflicting aims. This is what the 11 countries of Euroland have done, albeit in a half-baked way. They gave up some national sovereignty not because they wanted to but because they appreciate that once a global crisis strikes, the reaction of today's interconnected financial markets is vehement, and because their ills in economic and financial terms prove highly contagious for everybody.

To better explain how this system of regional monetary policy and bank supervision could work, let me briefly review the Fed's structure. Headquartered in Washington, the Federal Reserve System is run by a seven-member board of governors and works closely with 12 Federal Reserve Banks representing the regions. Governors are appointed for non-renewable 14-year terms of office by the US president, and are confirmed by Congress.

The Fed's chairman is confirmed for four years, but his term may be renewed. US law requires that appointments to the board must provide a fair representation of the financial, agricultural, industrial and commercial interests and geographical divisions of the country. This, too, is a sound principle for a global central bank and supervisory authority.

As a bank regulator, the Fed is responsible for controlling bank holding companies, state-registered banks that are members of the Federal Reserve System, many bank mergers, the foreign activities of American banks, the American activities of foreign banks and federal consumer-credit laws. That being said, monetary policy is still the Fed's prime concern, and the Federal Open Market Committee its means of execution.

The day-to-day operations of the Fed are carried out by its 12 regional banks. The regional reserve banks test the chartered member banks and bank holding companies for soundness using their own examiners, but also depend on audits by internal auditors and certified public accountants. In 1980 the Fed's responsibility for setting reserve requirements was extended to all depository institutions.

Perhaps the greatest contribution the Fed, the old Reichsbank and the Bundesbank can make to a global financial architecture is the *federated* concept. A federal structure is very different from typical decentralisation. As seen in Figure 2.3, autonomous though indirectly subordinate units within an organisation grant certain powers to the centre, but also retain certain essential powers which allow them to act as local conditions warrant. By contrast, the majority of 'decentralised' divisions have little practical autonomy.

Let us cast for a moment this concept of 12 regional banks into a global setting. Under each of the regional banks would be the national reserve institutions and bank regulators of each country. Can this approach instil a greater market discipline? Can it limit, if not avoid outright the current pouring of big money into emerging markets to the point of no return?

In my judgement, both queries should be given a positive answer. In the background of the current global financial crises is the breakdown of pricing discipline in the world's markets, as well as of self-discipline in big money transfers. Capital is thrown into emerging economies with little attention

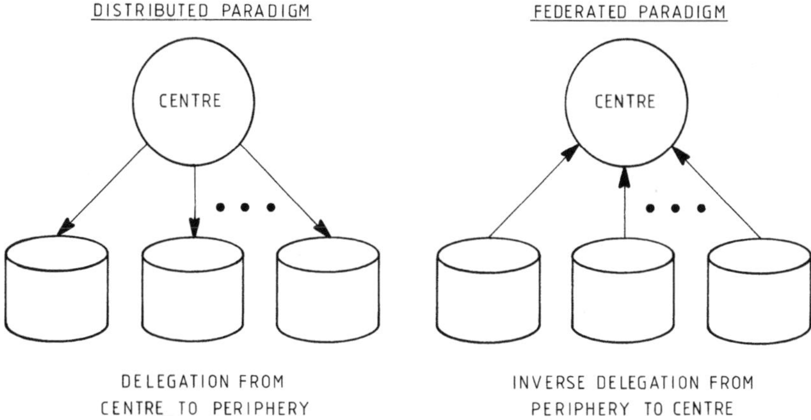

Figure 2.3 There is an essential difference between distributed and federated concepts

to either the creditworthiness of the borrowers, or the prevailing financial fundamentals.

Companies with political connections in countries such as Thailand, Indonesia, South Korea, Brazil and many others were able to borrow in dollars at far lower interest rates than they would be required to pay at home. This encouraged the countries themselves and individual big business borrowers to take on far more foreign debt than they could possibly handle.

The lack of market discipline also had another effect. When problems arose, everyone tried to get their money out as quickly as possible, which only made the crisis worse. Neither were there clear guidelines that leaders in the private sector had to share the cost of cleaning up the financial mess they had created. A regional reserve bank and regulator, along the Fed's model, could correct this imbalance.

Regional central banks would see to it that such events do not recur. Their examiners would closely look into the books of the borrowers and their leverage, applying penalties where they are due and diffusing the coming crisis before the bubble bursts. This might help to avoid a repetition of what happened in July to December 1997 in East Asia, in August 1998 in Russia and in January 1999 in Brazil.

Once that kind of supervisory system is launched, there is no turning back. Let us also recall that, as Chapter 1 has explained, the greater freedom to communicate promoted by the spread of the Internet can be used as a competitive advantage. The builders of the new financial architecture should fully appreciate the Internet's implications for policy which could be profound, because they are leading to greater competition and market liberalisation. The Internet will also impact in a significant way on both public opinion and public behaviour. The networked economy is here to stay. Under no condition can this fact be left out from the elaboration of global, financial rules and regulations. Failure to give IBC its due weight in the new financial architecture will eventually lead to anarchy. For a global economy to function without networked swindles, far greater disclosure is needed of:

- usable bank reserves, and outstanding liabilities;
- forward liabilities of corporations; and
- Foreign-currency liabilities of banks and states.

In order to enhance information transparency pertaining to each subject identified by the three bullets, intraday bulletins can be effectively posted on the Internet, the way NASDAQ carries intraday security prices. An example is shown in Figure 2.4. In matters of public information, particular emphasis must be placed on leveraging through derivatives and other off-balance-sheet financing, with accurate real-time data made available for oversight.

Not only banks but also hedge funds should reveal their positions, indicating gearing to regulators, as mutual funds already do in the USA. Allowing different financial players to go unregulated is a huge mistake. Closing one's eyes to exponential growth in the size, leverage and power of financial transactions is synonymous with building a financial atomic bomb.

Finally, the governors of the global reserve bank and the regional entities of bank supervision must have independence and they should show full accountability. Independence of means and of opinion would be a new culture in many parts of the world. For the outlined policy to be effectively

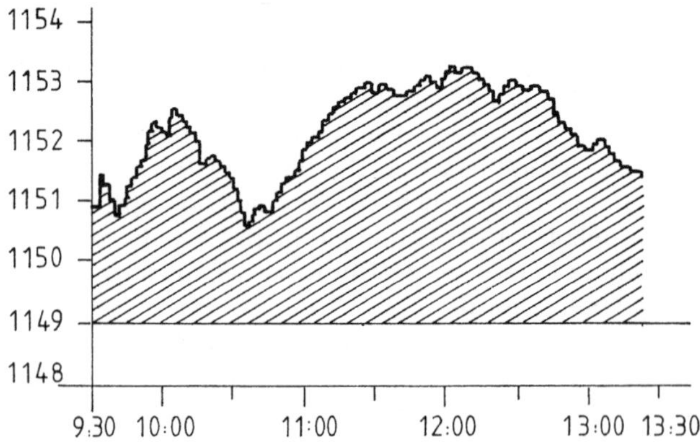

Figure 2.4 After four hours of trading, NASDAQ composite +2.49, but volatility has been high

implemented, the governors of regional banks have to be given a long-term status, like the governors of the Federal Reserve System. They should be free of political pressures and of crony capitalism, and they should be able to stand by their opinion against all odds.

'It is not an easy thing to vote against the president's wishes', Henry Wallick, a member of the Federal Reserve Board of Governors, said:

> But what are we appointed for? Why are we given these long terms in office? Presumably, it is that not only the present but the past and the future have some weight in our decisions. In the end, it may be helpful to remind the president that it is not only his present concerns that matter. (William Greider, *Secrets of the Temple. How the Federal Reserve Runs the Country*, Touchstone/Simon Schuster, New York, 1987. The quotation relates to the inflation of the late 1970s and the Carter presidency.)

* * *

As of September 1999, there are three issues independent expert opinion considers as critical to a new financial architecture.

- Whether the Basle Committee, the IMF or somebody else should take on itself the role of coordinating private sector responses to a global financial crisis.
- Whether greater public resources should be made available through the IMF to manage financial panics.
- Whether curbs on capital flows are necessary or are a deeply bad and dangerous idea.

Neither of these three key questions has been answered by G-7 governments and the G-10 regulators as this book goes to press. Till valid answers are given, no new financial architecture can be made to work.

3
Systemic Risk, Bank Supervision and Follow-the-Sun Overdraft

1 Introduction

What makes regulators nervous with *systemic risk* is the likelihood that failure in one big financial institution, or a segment of the economy, may trigger failure in other banks or industrial sectors. When such failures snowball through the global financial market, there is a domino effect. In September 1998, a LTCM-type bankruptcy would have led to such an avalanche world-wide.

Precisely because of the risk of a domino effect in the global capital market, Chapter 2 has underlined the need for a federated supranational authority which is able to influence economic policy in all countries, supervise transnational banks, provide conditional support to insolvent countries and credit institutions, and manage the international response to systemic emergencies in a proactive way (for instance, the Latin American debt crisis of the early 1980s, the Asian meltdown of 1997, the Russian bankruptcy of 1998, the Brazilian crisis of 1999 and the looming derivatives crisis).

Since the time of the oil earthquake of the 1970s and the piles of debt which followed the recycling of oil money, successive crises have been close calls whose resolution has required fire-brigade approaches first by the G-7 governments and then by the IMF. The careful reader will observe that in the 1990s their frequency has increased. One of the first close calls among private institutions was the liquidity problems which affected Salomon Brothers at the time of its Treasury bond scandal in 1991. Salomon had more than $600 billion in derivative contracts on its books which, if suddenly unloaded, would have had the potential of a global systemic risk. A supranational reserve institution and regulatory authority along the lines outlined in Chapter 2 has a major role to play in managing systemic risk, because private capital markets cannot deal well with the major challenges which today happen on a global scale. Managing systemic risk in a proactive manner is a new task, made that much more urgent as the exposure of the banking system mounts into trillions of dollars. Experience from salvage operations at the national level can effectively help as a reference but, as we have already seen, the system must be modernised to account for global networking.

Other references from the US also help in understanding how transnational regulation may work. When two American derivatives dealers – the Bank of New England and Drexel Burnham – failed, the damage was successfully walled off by the Federal Reserve. However, in notional principal amounts the exposure of these companies was relatively small. Each had 'only' $30 billion to $60 billion of contracts outstanding when the crash came.

Today global players are much more exposed. LTCM had debts of about $200 billion against a capital base of only $4 billion, and a Treasury barely left with $400 million which was below the level of liquidity needed in one week. As leveraging grows and grows, it brings into play a follow-the-sun overdraft (see section 3) with the financial crisis being exported from one country to another according to the law of unintended consequences.

2 Reasons underpinning systemic risk

A systemic crisis is a disturbance that severely impairs the working of the financial system and may eventually cause its complete breakdown. Systemic risks may originate because of a variety of reasons. What they have in common is that ultimately they will impair at least one of the key functions of the financial system:

- deposit of funds;
- credit allocation;
- pricing of financial assets;
- payment methods; and
- business confidence.

Uncertainty in terms of the ability to avoid systemic risk becomes greater as the number of unknowns increases. So far, the derivatives industry has not been tested by a giant failure. This would have been the case if serious problems affected J.P. Morgan, Chase Manhattan or United Bank of Switzerland (UBS), each with over $6 trillion in derivatives exposure in notional principal amount; even Société Générale (now SG Paribas) or Tokyo-Mitsubishi who are at the $3.5 trillion level in notional principal have their flanks exposed to all sorts of adverse conditions.

Based on BIS 1998 statistics, some of them adjusted as of 30 June 1998, Table 3.1 shows the top eight derivatives exposures, in notional principal amounts, among money centre banks. Even demodulated by a factor of 20 to reduce the notional principal to a level close to that of credit risk, this exposure is mind boggling, and way in excess of the capital reserves of these banks (see D.N. Chorafas, *Derivative Financial Instruments. Strategies for*

Table 3.1 The top eight derivatives exposures by money centre banks based on BIS statistics as of 30 June 1998

	Market risk (Notional principal in $ trillion)	*Credit risk (demodulated by 20 in $ billion)*
Chase Manhattan	8.5	425
J.P. Morgan	7.5	375
CitiGroup**	7.1	355
Deutsche Bank**	6.7	335
UBS**	6.3	315
Bank America**	3.7	185
NatWest*	3.7	185
Société Generale*	3.6	180
Tokyo-Mitsubishi*	3.4	170

* Adjusted by 12.5% over 31 December 1997.
** Idem as *, after the merger.
*** Idem as *, after the merger with Bankers Trust is consumed.

Management Risk and Return in Banking, Lafferty Publications, London and Dublin, 1995).

To help the reader appreciate what this exposure means, Figure 3.1 takes as an example a money centre bank with $7 trillion worth of derivatives exposure in notional principal. Demodulated by 20, this represents $350 billion. This institution, however, has $22 billion in capital and $350 billion in assets. Therefore, its credit risk equivalent derivatives exposure is sixteen times its capital, and equal to all of its assets.

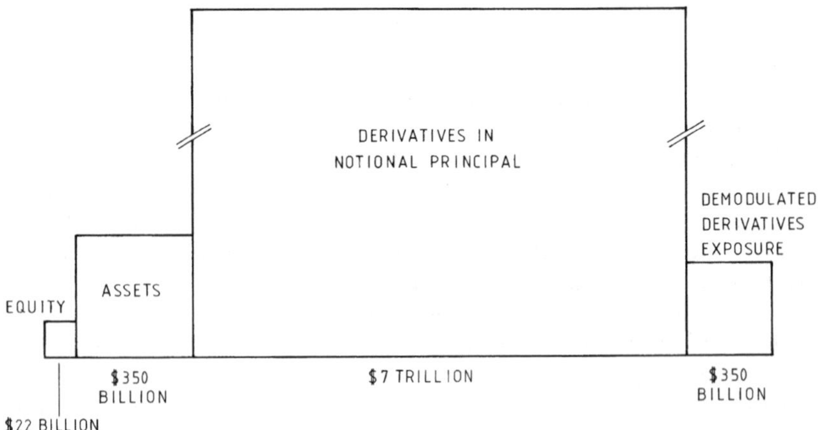

Figure 3.1 Some frightening statistics on equity, assets and derivatives exposure

A great deal of systemic risk comes from the fact that nobody really knows how this fast expanding interlocked business of global capital flows, loans given without collateral, and off-balance-sheet financing would come through a really severe crisis. As we will see in section 3, the problem is amplified because the overdraft of each credit institution is carried through networks around the globe in real-time.

When financial activity reaches the edge of chaos and tends to get out of control, a disturbance can grow into a systemic crisis influencing, and being influenced by, the prevailing economic circumstances. Such shocks have a nasty habit of occurring when the degree of confidence which exists in the market is at its lowest: hence at the worst possible moment.

The reasons underpinning a systemic risk are usually complex and many of them have not been that well understood until today. The growing activity in derivatives may not, *per se*, result in increased threats to systematic stability, but this statement is not valid in regard to the aftermath of an off-balance-sheet meltdown because derivative instruments strengthen linkages between counterparties across a spectrum of financial activities. The banks which lent money to LTCM to speculate with highly geared products were some of the institutions which entered into big derivatives contracts with LTCM. In addition, disruptions or increased uncertainty in one market have shown their ability rapidly to affect other markets.

As I have already explained, networks, computers and software which made derivatives possible also help to disseminate news, rumours and misunderstandings at speeds that leave market participants and central banks very little time to react in the event of a crisis. This instantaneousness of financial news showers can also greatly affect liquidity in markets, because business confidence has always been an important ingredient in any trade.

With derivative products, for example, some market players have exploited what they considered to be a 'modest risk correlation' across market segments. But this hypothesis of modesty in correlation is rarely sustained by the facts. In the case of interest rate products, certain banks have found that the significant offsets on which they were betting by hedging the risks embedded in the books have not materialised.

Even more complex is the case of hypothetical risk offsets arising from relationships between exposures in foreign exchange, interest rate and equity markets at the same time. LTCM bet on such an assumption of risk offsets to make money until it turned belly up. The most commonly cited events capable of triggering systemic problems are the:

- defaults of financial institutions; and
- major settlements failures propagating through the system.

Because both these reasons for systemic risk are feasible and global trading activity increases their likelihood, central banks, supervisors, clearers and several commercial banks believe that over the years systemic risk has increased. Such recognition seems to be instrumental in shaking the classical degree of complacency fostered by a more or less firmly held belief that the G-10 central banks and/or the IMF would act to prevent any disruptions from reaching systemic proportions.

Corruption amplifies the risks suggested by the preceding paragraphs. An article in *The Economist* (13 February 1999) commented as follows on the challenges facing the Chinese regulators: 'There is no doubt that China is stuck with a cluster of financial time-bombs. Its state banks are insolvent, and they have few reliable borrowers. The competence and power of financial supervisors are stretched too thin, while mismanagement and fraud are stripping state assets.' (See also in Chapter 6 another reference to the Chinese Securities Regulatory Commission.)

The same article went on to say that the discovery of large unreported and unpayable debts at Guangnan Holdings, a food-distribution giant, has cast a shadow over the shares of all *red-chip* companies. These are the shares controlled by a Chinese entity, such as a provincial government, but registered and listed in Hong Kong. In early February 1999 auditors reported that they had uncovered 'irregularities' at Guangnan, but insiders told analysts of:

- fraudulent letters of credit;
- inflated asset values; and
- stock market speculation.

This example is relevant to our discussion because, after the twelfth-hour rescue of Brazil, many investors said: 'Happily there is no big country left whose default can create havoc.' This statement of relief from stress has forgotten China, the most populous country in the world, even if its economy (like that of Russia) is a small fraction of its size.

In China's case the most important aftermath may be psychological. Chapter 2 has explained the major problems involved in stabilising markets after the crisis hits. The collapse of Barings in February 1995 demonstrated that both cash and derivatives positions can move instantly from country to country leaving nation-bound national overseers without the means of control.

While a number of international agreements for co-operation in prudential supervision were forged in the Barings aftermath, these mainly centred on information exchange. They have been voluntary and primarily deal with priorities and contacts in the event of a full-blown derivatives crisis. They do not include either a global prudential supervision of institutions operating transborder, or the sort of severe penalties which must be available to sanction management for taking excessive risk.

Furthermore, while the fear of systemic risk sees to it that Western bank supervisors collaborate with one another, this collaboration is not the case in a global sense. True enough, the British, American, German and French bank supervisors do hold hands. But other central bankers and regulators keep their distance and keep their findings close to their chest, which leads to systemic risk.

The Asian authorities, for example, are not forthcoming, and this includes the Japanese. When the SEC in New York informed the Bank of Japan about the wrongdoings of the New York-based senior executive of a major Japanese institution, the only response was to repatriate this executive back to Tokyo, replacing him with somebody else.

Solutions to systemic risk must not only be rigorous but also proactive. In his keynote presentation to the 1997 Bürgenstock conference, attended by some 300 of the world's leading bankers, derivatives exchange heads, fund managers and government officials, Urban Bäckström, governor of Riksbank (the Swedish central bank), chose to focus on *crisis prevention*. This was a very timely speech.

'Each crisis is unique', said Bäckström. 'Each one is different, but steps can be taken to try to prevent or contain them before they come. In Thailand, the macroeconomic policies were clearly wrong. Governments need to follow price stability and stable economic policy.' Thailand, of course, is just an example. A dozen others can be added today to that list.

'Disruptions are inevitable', the head of Riksbank further advised. He ticked off a list of such disruptions in the past, like the bursting of the 'tulip mania' which in fact proved that financial crashes are older than we might think. He then cited the crash of the South Sea Bubble in 1720, the failure of the French Union Générale in 1881, Barings Bank in 1890, various US banking panics, the collapse of the Austrian Kreditanstalt in 1931, and Black Thursday in October 1929.

3 The follow-the-sun overdraft

International financial conferences tend to be a favoured place by experts for discussions concerning systemic risk. The point was made during the 1997 debates at Davos that none of the leading features of the present international financial order offered any serious remedy to a global system so obviously teetering on the brink of catastrophe. This absence of an alternative was underscored by Howard Davies, deputy governor of the Bank of England, who proposed instituting 'stress tests' on such areas as Japanese banking, and the European Monetary System to determine possible systemic threats (EIR, 21 February 1997). The same Davos meeting also examined possible systemic triggers in the global interbank payments network, as well as hidden risks not yet seen. Andrew Crocket, General Manager of the BIS, defined the risk to the global interbank payments and settlements network as a major worry: 'Twenty years after the Herstatt Bank crisis, little has been done... when Drexel Burnham went under [in 1991], we were very close to a global system freeze.'

Andrew Crocket's emphasis on a possible crisis which can hit payments and settlements on a global scale comes none too soon. Compared to other crises which are national or local, like the December 1994/January 1995 Mexican peso crisis, the Banesto Bank crisis in Spain and the Metallgesellschaft crisis in the USA and Germany, a world-wide collapse of payments and settlements can immediately lead to a snowball effect. The magnitude of some payments orders would contribute to the meltdown: less than 1 per cent of orders going through the London Clearing House and Payments System (CHAPS) represents 95 per cent of the value. The financial risk involved in this and similar statistics also prevails within each bank in connection to the exposure it takes towards its most important clients.

In a meeting I had with Manufacturers Hanover Trust just prior to its merger with Chemical Banking, it was said that day-in and day-out the institution had a $2.0 billion to $2.5 billion exposure with General Motors. Interestingly enough, this statistic became known to Manufacturers Hanover management only after major financial institutions implemented solutions to monitor daylight overdraft following the failure of Herstatt Bank.

No matter why big money orders originate, their pending execution sees to it that a *follow-the-sun overdraft* exists in the global securities market and in capital flows. Whether these flows come from hot money, legitimate securities, trading, loans, derivatives or any other origin, the risk associated with them is being exported and imported. This leads to a critical query: 'In the event that something goes wrong, who is liable?'

To better define financial responsibility, it is wise to look at this issue from a technical perspective. Interconnected networks are so complex that, without appropriate means for analysis of journals and a great deal of homework, it is extremely difficult to know when a settlement has taken place. This leads to the need for re-evaluating and re-establishing:

- network-based payments and settlements, whether the systems are public (such as Swift, ACH, CHAPS, and so on) or private, belonging to this or that money centre bank, and
- the concept and practice of financial integrity in the wholesale banking trade, taking into full account not just management accountability but also network dependability.

Real-time timestamps and database mining are not among the current features of payment systems. Because a specific preparation in risk containment is wanting, it is nearly impossible to untangle completed settlements, or to rollback a complex transaction (see D.N. Chorafas, *Transaction Management*, Macmillan, London, 1998). This is, however, part of the mission and duty of the new global financial architecture currently being projected (see Chapter 2).

Financial, managerial and technological failures which may lead to exporting and importing systemic risk must be analysed in a factual and documented manner. Global institutions should be subject to more rigorous regulations than national ones, well beyond the 8 per cent capital requirement. In a 1997 study by the Group of 30, survey correspondents listed three likely causes of failure of a financial institution:

- inadequate management procedures;
- breakdown of internal controls; and
- the actions of rogue employees.

The Group of 30 added to this finding the concept that it is unreasonable to expect supervisors alone to keep global institutions from mishaps: 'The speed and complexity of innovation in the markets, the supervisors' position 'behind the curve', and their real handicaps in competing for talented staffers, all argue for private institutions to take on greater responsibility' (*Global Institutions, National Supervision and Systemic Risk*, Group of 30, Washington, DC, 1997).

While one has to agree in general with this statement, I would take exception to the reference to supervisors being behind the curve. In the research meetings which I held in Washington, New York, Boston, London, Frankfurt, Berlin, Zurich, Bern, Basle and Paris, I found the bank supervisors most alert to the challenges of internal control, risk management and technology although only in the USA are the supervisory authorities supported by a sizeable body of examiners who perform on-site investigations in the commercial banks, savings and loans, investments banks and mutual funds which they control. Rather than the supervisors, it is the current rules of supervision which do not permit the effective capture and control of follow-the-sun overdrafts. Furthermore, the problem-solving process is more drawn-out than should have been the case, and this must be corrected by the new global financial architecture.

The Group of 30 is right in underlining the fact that external supervision alone, though necessary, is not enough. Comprehensive and effective controls must cover an institution's audit committee, the internal audit function, risk management and compliance, including legal, regulatory and ethical issues. Let me close this section by quoting a statement John Walsh, of the Group of 30, made during our meeting: 'Understanding the intricacies of internal control systems requires a high level of skill.'

4 Systemic risk as a result of subprime lending by financial markets

Section 2 has explained that the interdependence of banks and dealers in derivatives trades is much closer than that of participants in more classical banking chores, even in syndicated loans. Even if on the surface the off-balance-sheet risk might seem to be contained in the institution going belly up, in reality derivatives tie together the counterparties so effectively that even minor shocks in one bank lead to ripples.

Not only individual counterparties get unbalanced: a whole market may be upset. A shock wave can spread to other markets with such speed that regulators do not have time to manage the situation, particularly so as few checks and balances are in place world-wide as regards derivative instruments.

Overgearing in the global financial environment started in 1986 with the creation of an important junk bond market which exploited the rather benevolent statistics of 'fallen angels': that is, firms which could no longer qualify for bank credit and based their financing on junk bonds offering in high interest rates. At the peak of Drexel Burnham Lambert's and Michael Milken's power, billions of dollars in low grade BB bonds were issued. During the 1980s, a total of some $150 billion in junk bonds saw the light of day, and this was considered to be a big number. But subsequently, in the first eight years of the 1990s, nearly $500 billion in junk bonds have been issued.

Year after the market's bonds exposure to subinvestment level bonds has increased. The year 1998 was on track to smash the 1997 record with $117 billion in junk bonds being issued during the first seven months until August when, with the Russian default, the market for junk abruptly dried up. In September 'only' $2.7 billion in bonds rated BB or lower saw the day, but exposure is not removed from the books that easily. Today, there are about $30 billion worth in the vaults of Wall Street firms, gathering dust.

Almost ten times larger has been the market for asset-backed securities, therefore derivatives. There are some $2.5 trillion outstanding today, of which $2 trillion are mortgage-backed financing (MBF) issued by Fannie Mae, Freddie Mac, or Ginnie Mae (see Chapter 15, section 5). MBF is created by pooling residential mortgages, then issuing securities backed by the income from the mortgages in the pool. Smaller than the residential MBF market, but growing, are the markets for securities backed by:

- consumer debt;
- commercial real estate; and
- corporate loans or business loans.

Issuing securities based upon credit card receivables has become big business for US banks which, as of 30 June 1998, had sold $239 billion in credit card securities, more than the amount of credit card debt carried on their balance sheets ($217 billion). Debt financing is not by itself a negative: the problem is that nobody knows where lies the safety threshold.

The $200 billion commercial mortgage-backed securities (CMBS) market suffered a major hit on 5 October 1998 with the bankruptcy filing of Ginnie Mae, which had bought nearly half of the CMBS bonds issued in recent years. But there is also the *subprime lending market*, in which people whose credit ratings prevent them from getting regular loans can get loans at exorbitant rates of interest.

Let me briefly explain 'subprime' as a term. Independent agencies such as Moody's Investors Service and Standard & Poor's make both long-term ratings and short-term ratings. As shown in Table 3.2, Moody's uses different symbols for the short-term and long-term classes.

1. Not only 'triple A' but also A1 is Prime-1 in short-term rating, qualifying for prime rate.
2. Some long-term ratings, such as A2, A3 and Baa2 belong to more than one Prime subclass.
3. But everything below Ba1, which corresponds to BB+ in Standard & Poor's classification, is Not Prime.

Not Prime, or subprime is essentially junk bond level. But there is a difference. While the junk bonds promoted by Michael Milken were mainly Ba1 or Ba2, subprime may be anything, all the way to Ca or C. These are bankruptcy or default levels, barely for credit.

Table 3.2 Moody's long-term and short-term ratings

Long term	*Short term*
Aaa, Aa1, Aa2 Aa3, A1, A2, A3	Prime-1
A2, A3, Baa1, Baa2	Prime-2
Baa2, Baa3	Prime-3
Ba1, Ba2, Ba3 B&, B2, B3, Caa1, Caa2, Caa3 Ca, C	Not Prime

The subprime market has exploded in recent years, with some $250 billion in subprime loans outstanding today in the USA alone. According to the FDIC, subprime loans secured by residences, both home equity and mortgage loans, amounted to between $120 billion and $150 billion or nearly 20 per cent of the estimated $800 billion in origination of conventional mortgages.

Another growing practice is the so-called high-loan-to-value home mortgage, in which the homeowner is typically lent 25 per cent more than the value of the mortgage, using the extra cash to consolidate credit card and related debt. In short, virtually any income stream which can be turned into securities is speculated upon and sold to the junk bond fans, who take inordinate risks for higher yields.

While these are American statistics and in other markets the figures are not yet that big, they are growing. This poses systemic risk problems because the global capital markets have become more closely linked with the rise of cross-border capital flows. The synergy is further promoted through efforts by governments to open national borders in the hope of attracting mobile capital. Derivatives are part of this larger phenomenon and there is reason to believe that dynamic hedging could produce overwhelming pressures because:

- many of the institutions who write options do not understand options pricing; and
- very few banks prudently limit their short options positions to avoid snowball effects.

Systemic risk cannot be faced by central banks alone. Every player in the derivatives business must be part of the effort to avoid it. This means that commercial banks and investment banks should strengthen their risk management practices as an essential first line of defence against possible systemic problems.

Timely and factual risk control calls for a top management policy able to guarantee that each individual and each department in the bank is steadily improving their practices. Analytical risk management systems operating in real-time are most essential to conducting business in the financial markets generally, not just in derivatives. They must address credit risk, market risk and liquidity risk, as well as operational and legal risks.

This leads to another question regarding the adequacy of internal controls and of risk management systems. Efficient risk control cannot be done through the legacy software, the mainframes and the batch processing still used by most banks. It requires knowledge engineering, agents and advanced techniques for managing risk: a technology possessed today only by tier-1 institutions.

5 Coping with liquidity risks without igniting inflation

Liquid assets include cash, balances due from banks and short-term investments. Typically, liquid assets mature within the next three months and should be presented in the balance sheet at fair value. A payment and settlement system is based on liquid assets, but because sometimes liquidity is wanting payment systems involve risks. If they are not properly managed, liquidity risks can lead to serious disruption in the markets because of the critical role liquidity plays in modern economies.

Liquidity risk due to a temporary default by a single participant in the payment system can be the aftermath of credit risk or market risk; but systemic risk might result from a chain reaction in settlement failures that sends shock waves through the world's financial system. For instance, systemic risk might come about if one or more big banks failed to honour their obligations triggering a domino effect. That would cause a further series of failures by other member banks of the settlement system, ultimately spreading to most institutions world-wide. A snowball from derivatives failures would have the same effect.

As they appreciate the aftermath of a wave of bankruptcies due to liquidity risk, over the years governments and central banks have developed different strategies to deal with troubled banks. None is fail-safe. The most evident way is liquidation. Insolvent banks are placed in receivership, with insured depositors paid off and residual assets being sold. The bank's owners lose their equity as happened in the 1980s with Continental Illinois, and holders of debt also lose some, or all, of their money.

Drastic measures such as closing a bank are taken after due consideration of clearing systems implications. As an alternative, the regulators might choose to keep the fallen bank alive. The government sees to it that good money runs after bad money by injecting fresh capital (taxpayers' money) into the defunct institution. Usually, this is done over a limited period of time to close those positions which might create systemic risk. This has been the case for the Bank of New England. But the injection of taxpayers' money might also be done over the long run, as in the case of Credit Lyonnais (to the tune of nearly $45 billion).

The artificial survival of a badly wounded credit institution is usually ensured through government loans intended to clean up the defunct bank's balance sheet by transferring its worst assets to the government, or by getting the state to guarantee them. The simplest form of intervention in this case involves a guarantee that the government will act as a lender of last resort should bad loans threaten to swamp the bank.

If the global derivatives markets were to go bust and each of the governments of the G-10 countries came to the rescue of the home-grown banks, how much would it cost the taxpayer? The answer depends on the cumulative derivatives exposure by the country's own banks, the population in that country which will ultimately pay the bill, and the time this question is being asked. As the careful reader will see in Table 3.3, between 1995 and 1997, the derivatives exposure of the banking system in the G-10 countries increased by more than 50 per cent. Because its population is less than 6 million people but its big banks are overexposed, the heaviest capital burden from a salvage operation is in Switzerland.

It has already been mentioned in the Introduction that the notional principal amounts in derivatives exposure are not a good measure of real risk. To convert notional principal to real money it is necessary to use a demodulator. In Table 3.1 a factor of 20 was employed to convert the notional principal to an equivalent credit risk. In Table 3.3, the demodulator is 30 because the real money being targeted is connected more to market risk. If

Table 3.3 The heavy per capita burden of some countries because of derivatives' overexposure by their banks

	1995 notional amount of derivatives holdings ($ billions)	*1995 derivatives holdings per capita ($ thousands)*	*1997 derivatives holdings per capita ($ thousands)*	*1997 real money per capita ($)*
Switzerland	6.321	877.7	1.316.5	43.883
France	9.374	161.7	242.5	8.087
Sweden	1.278	145.6	218.4	7.280
UK	7.367	126.5	189.8	6.327
Canada	3.321	112.7	169.0	5.633
Netherlands	1.596	102.9	154.4	5.147
Japan	11.532	92.2	138.8	4.610
USA	23.129	87.9	131.9	4.397
Belgium	0.689	68.1	103.4	3.447
Germany	4.258	52.2	78.3	2.610

20 were used rather than 30, then the per capita cost of a derivatives meltdown should be increased by 50 per cent across the board.

These figures are most relevant if the government decides to follow the old strategy of nationalisation as a way out of the mess. Nationalisation was popular in Europe during the crisis of 1929–32. It is adopted when a government believes that there is significant danger that the problems of a single bad bank could spread, leading to the collapse of the entire financial system, especially if numerous other banks experience the same problems at the same time, or there are no takers for the falling institutions or no assets to turn around.

Today, a salvage operation of money centre banks is very costly to the taxpayer because the stakes are so high in derivatives exposure. A different form of liquidation of the bankrupt institution(s) is closure by merger. This involves handing over the sick bank to a healthy one to which regulators offer an incentive, such as making a payment to insured depositors or creditors (see Chapter 2 on FDIC).

A better solution than outright loans, nationalisation or closure by merger is to mine the defunct institution for assets which may still be worth a lot or at least stand a good chance of being turned around. These assets can be ingeniously exploited through the creation of a new agency with ample powers, such as:

- Sweden's Securum;
- America's Resolution Trust Corporation (RTC, see section 6); and
- Japan's Financial Restoration Commission (FRC).

At the time Securum was instituted a fire sale would have given less than 40 cents to the dollar for Nordbanken's assets, the only Swedish bank where the government was a major shareholder. But five years down the line Securum had recovered better than 75 cents to the dollar. Similarly, RTC faced total potential losses of $800 billion, but patient unwinding of assets and liabilities reduced losses to the American taxpayer to between $160 and $180 billion (plus some more billions, as we will see in Chapter 14).

Not only ample powers are necessary for a Securum/RTC/FRC sort of solution, but also a tough boss who does not bend under political pressure is required. As head of Japan's FRC, Hakuo Yanagisawa has an army of lawyers, accountants and bank examiners: these examiners are given the authority to grill bank presidents about the extent of their liabilities. While Yanagisawa is making rescue money contingent on internal information, no other Japanese regulator is ever asked.

FRC's policy seems to be to cut the number of city banks (money centre banks) from 19 to 9. To reach this objective, the new regulatory agency pressures each bank it rescues to form alliances. These alliances involve such big names as Sakura, Sanwa, and Tokyo-Mitsubishi. One of the problems is that Japan's banking sector disaster is much larger than the savings and loan crisis. Cleaning it up will be a painful and lengthy experience, rather than a source of instant gratification.

While this text was being written the credit collapse in Japan – the world's largest credit nation – continued and the withdrawal of Japanese banks from the global market accelerated. The bad news is that the intensification of the credit crunch in Japan could lead to a surge in capital repatriation, a development which clearly has negative implications for global credit markets, and most particularly for the dollar.

'If the banks don't change, they will lose their competitiveness', says Hakuo Yanagisawa (*Business Week*, 22 February 1999), also signalling that foreign experts and foreign capital should lend him a hand. Long-Term Credit Bank of Japan has hired Goldman Sachs to ofter it around. It is wiser to depend on the global capital market rather than only on the Japanese taxpayers' contribution to the salvage.

Finally, let us take notice of the FRC's broader aim: to tear down the walls separating Japan's traditional long-term credit, commercial and trust banks. The new authority hopes that mergers and alliances will produce institutions that offer clients a mix of traditional retail banking, insurance, brokerage and investment banking services; and, above all, better financial staying power.

6 The model of the Resolution Trust Corporation and the avoidance of systemic risk

As we have seen in section 5, governments have frequently come to the rescue of insolvent banks, particularly if they are of a certain size or of significant importance to the economy. This is the 'too big to fail' syndrome. Most politicians and many bank regulators seem to think that big banks must be kept afloat at all costs, in order to avoid the financial instability which invariably results from systemic risk.

Increasingly, however, this belief has proved both costly and controversial. On some estimates, between 1989 and 1992 Scandinavian governments spent $16 billion shoring up the region's insolvent banks. During the last 15 years, bank rescues have multiplied because the financial bubbles that characterised the 1980s and 1990s led to painful and long-lasting shocks. When interest rates rise and economies slow, banks suddenly find a large number of loans turning sour, while the collateral they thought was sound proves to be worthless as real-estate markets and stock exchanges plunge.

In principle, governments and reserve institutions are right to worry about the fate of commercial banks because of their role as providers of business confidence, issuers of credit and agents of the economy's payments system. The sure bet is that a run on one bank will probably infect others; hence the concept of deposit insurance schemes to reassure banks' customers that their money is safe in the event of a collapse.

Deposit insurance, however, is not exactly the same thing as bailouts. As Chapter 2 underlined, deposit insurance should be self-financing and it should mainly address depositors at the lower end of the food chain. That is why FDIC may be a perfect model for the global financial system. Salvage through huge capital injection is a totally different game, and there is a growing belief among economists that most big bank rescues are unnecessary because ultimately they cost more than they are worth, and also that bailouts have become mechanisms for delaying a needed deflation, whether of a financial system as a whole or of an individual bank's assets.

The main problem with bailouts, as the contrary opinion states, is not their high cost but the fact that there is often nothing to be gained by the delay in cleaning up the mess, which increases the cost of a rescue. Unless regulators punish a bank that comes to it for help at the twelfth hour, the moral hazard will stay around. Punishment can take three forms:

- ensuring the responsible managers are sacked, if not prosecuted;
- shareholders' equity is partially or totally wiped out; and
- if it survives at all the bankrupt institution is forced to shrink.

A growing number of analysts now believe that a salvage operation orchestrated by the government or the central bank may aggravate the exposure of the banking system rather than provide for financial stability. When bank managers think that the government will step in if there is an impending collapse, they become risk-prone and they turn into mismanagers.

Greater risk aside, other arguments against bailouts draw on real cases. Continental Illinois, for instance, suffered a disastrous run on its wholesale deposits in 1984. Its bailout was justified by regulators on the ground that there was a systemic risk that other banks which had lent it money might themselves be caught short. Some 65 banks had uninsured exposures to Continental, equivalent to more than 100 per cent of their capital, while a further 100 banks had exposures of between 50 per cent and 100 per cent of their capital. The twelfth-hour salvage by the Federal Reserve did away with stockholders' equity and washed clean the top management ranks, but ultimately it did not save the bank. Ten years after the rescue, Continental went under, being bought at a bargain-basement price by Bank of America which in 1998 was itself absorbed by NationsBank. Today, several US bank regulators privately say that Continental should not have been rescued.

Contrary to Continental Illinois, the RTC, which was put together to face the acute US savings and loan crisis, provides a better example of ways and means for rescuing institutions. The American government created RTC in 1989, and employed it until it was shut down in 1995. RTC spent an estimated up to $180 billion to bail out the US thrifts.

The thrifts were not the only banking sector under stress in the USA in 1988–93. During this period, the USA experienced a breakdown not just of its savings and loans but of its entire banking system. In fact, the most bankrupt institutions were the major money centre commercial banks, led by Citibank (which was then the largest). To avoid systemic risk, the US government engaged in a bailout of the whole banking system with its $5 trillion in assets; the RTC salvage-or-liquidation of the thrifts was one important piece of this effort but, as the numbers show, it was only part of the act. In a way similar to the action by Sweden's Securum in connection with Nordbanken, RTC took over the non-performing loans of the failing savings and loan sector as well as the assets underlying the bad loans. Post-mortem, however, analysts think that without the manipulation of the real estate market to support prices, the thrifts real estate asset sales would have been a failure, and thus the RTC strategy would have collapsed.

The RTC cost chapter is not totally closed, as far as the American taxpayer is concerned, as we will see in Chapter 14. Because of a US Supreme Court decision which found wrongdoings in the way the government manipulated the write-offs of thrifts assets – particularly a loophole which permitted the writing-down of liabilities *as if* they were assets – a number of investors and speculators are now in court asking for extra money which may amount to several billion dollars.

The careful reader will also notice that five years elapsed between the establishment of the RTC to deal with the thrifts crisis and a return to robust economic growth in the USA. In the early 1990s, Fed chairman Alan Greenspan repeatedly spoke about the fierce headwinds the US economy faced as the debt resolution process went forward. But there was a happy ending as the US economy was able to come through and land softly.

Contrary to the piecemeal Japanese solution, which finally crystallised into FRC, and the delayed action because of political brinkmanship, the Fed approached the problem of bank insolvency in a broader manner, and the Fed also engaged commercial and investment bankers. The solution was not to reflate one sector at a time but to pump up the entire economy, thereby reflating real estate, the stock market, and off-balance-sheet deals. With this, the use of derivatives exploded – which has dangers of its own as we have seen on repeated occasions in this and the preceding chapters.

To make a similar approach work today, Japan would require Weimar-style hyperinflation. This the Japanese government cannot afford to do. Leaving aside the fact that the will to make radical moves is lacking, Japan Inc. knows quite well that any major U-turn has to be approved by the G-7 and the G-10, because once hyperinflation starts in one of the major countries it will spread like brush fire, posing a most acute type of systemic risk.

4

Structuring the Regulatory Environment: Examples from the United States

1 Introduction

Chapter 3 pressed the point that one of the major goals of regulatory authorities is to preserve business confidence and to promote financial stability. The question then arises: who will benefit from this? And the answer is everybody: consumers as well as the business enterprises and the public authorities. Most of the benefits, however, go to those who are able to learn from every experience.

While inflation taught consumers to be more price conscious, it was deregulation that forced banks, airlines and other industries to streamline their services so they could survive intensified competition. Locked in an expensive battle to offer the highest interest rates for savers, many institutions found they could no longer afford to provide cheap or free services to small-account holders. Neither could they depend for their survival solely on the established, time-honoured product lines. By raising service charges dramatically, some banks actively discourage small accounts, because the profits involved are slim or non-existent. Then, by making trading the main pillar of their profit and loss account, most institutions found themselves behind the curve or out in *terra incognita*.

Regulators now appreciate that numerous unregulated competitors such as General Electric Capital, General Motors Insurance Corporation and American Express are able to offer a wide array of bank-like services. Corporations, aided by Wall Street, are selling ever-greater volumes of commercial paper, which has cut into banks' short-term corporate borrowing business.

Commercial credit firms and insurance companies are actively providing long-term financing. Money market funds offer better yields than certificates of deposit. Formidable rivals such as the Teachers Insurance & Annuity Association (TIAA), America's largest private pension fund, lent nearly a quarter of their multibillion portfolio directly to corporations. All this has an evident impact on the evolving new regulatory environment.

Another matter of importance is that the issue of risk and the need for its management finally slips down the organisational ladders. Risk does not only relate to finance. As Dr Max Planck, the great physicist, once said: 'Without occasional venture or risk, no genuine invention can be accomplished even in the most exact sciences.'

This message is vital in regard to finance and the economy. On the one hand, regulators must ensure that there is free competition and special interests do not stifle the market. On the other, they must see to it that the risks being taken with globalisation, innovation and stiffening competition do not run wild, do not defraud the users of financial instruments, and do not end up as Ponzi games.

2 From the Sherman Act for free trade to rules targeting the control of risk

Enacted in 1890, the US Sherman Act contains two broadly worded provisions which have kept even today the same actuality as they did when the act was originally passed. Section 1 makes unlawful every 'contract, combination, or conspiracy in restraint of trade'. Section 2 prohibits business conduct from 'monopolising, or attempt to monopolise' any market.

The language used in these statements is laconic, and over the last 110 years the courts have developed their own jurisprudence to distinguish between lawful and unlawful business practices. First and foremost of the rules guiding the hand of the courts is that the Sherman Act is to be applied to protect competition, *not* the competitors.

Anti-trust law is indifferent to the success or failure of individual firms as long as competition in the market place is not harmed. Competition is harmed when, and only when, some identifiable group of providers of products and services or other agents acting in the market place are likely to confront customers and potential customers with:

- higher prices;
- lower product or service quality;
- a reduced rate of innovation; or
- persistent lack of product quality improvement.

When a company has the ability to harm competition by itself, it is said to have market power which can be censured by the Sherman Act. Companies can also act in collusion among themselves or with the government. However, abusive market power must be proven by the prosecutors. Basically, antitrust offences address conduct, not status.

The Sherman Act does not make a dominant position in the market *per se* illegal; what matters is whether a bank or any other firm has gained or maintained its dominant position through conduct that harms competition. If, for example, all New York banks merged into one, then competition would be harmed, but in fact the merger between Chemical Banking, Manufacturers Hanover and Chase Manhattan has had no such effect.

Restricting the ability of a supplier or a distributor to deal with a third party, limiting the freedom of purchasers or licensees to modify or change a product, or requiring a purchaser or licensee to obtain one product in order to obtain another product, are not by their very nature illegal even though they may in some sense restrain trade. Such contracts must be anti-competitive to be unlawful and, as long as competition is not constrained, they are not necessarily unlawful.

The Sherman Act should not be confused, as is sometimes done, with the Glass–Steagall Act of the early 1930s. Glass–Steagall did not address competition. What it did, in the aftermath of the Great Depression, was to separate commercial banking from investment banking. During the last couple of decades Glass–Steagall reform has become a soap opera that has put countless sons and daughters of Washington lawyers and lobbyists through college.

The irony about this legislation is that, for any practical purpose, Glass–Steagall barriers between commercial and investment banking have already been obliterated. A turf battle between the Federal Reserve Board and the Comptroller of the Currency blew the Glass–Steagall wall wide open in late 1996. Securities firms such as Alex Brown, Montgomery Securities, Robertson Stephens, First Wheat Securities, and others were acquired by banks and operated through bank holding company subsidiaries.

At the same time, however, mega mergers such as Citicorp–Travelers signified that size matters. This forced Washington to acknowledge that the depression-era banking laws were overdue for an overhaul. Subsequently, the US House of Representatives passed its controversial reform bill, HR 10, by one vote in early May 1998. Experts say that the next big step beyond that would be to allow a big industrial company, say Microsoft or Ford, to own a large bank, and for Citigroup, Chase or BankAmerica to control more than $1 out of every $10 of deposits nation-wide. There is no legislation, however, which targets the control of global risk. Yet ways and means for keeping exposure at reasonable levels are important as banks are trying harder than ever to push into foreign markets, and they are racing to expand their private network which is evolving into a global system.

As Chapter 1 has demonstrated, the Internet and private financial networks virtually eliminate the boundaries of time and distance. They permit institutions to expand their vital space, enter into agreements with distant entities and aggressively market their services, but thus do not by themselves contribute to global risk control. A sound global risk management policy should underline the need to map the whole market into the system, proceeding with experimentation on exposure under different hypotheses. This is the next frontier in the effective management of financial institutions, whether or not there is legislation to that effect, and it goes way beyond the 1996 Market Risk Amendment.

The regulators are aware of the need to move towards establishing a risk management structure, but this happens at a slow pace. Therefore, the prudent thing for *our* bank is to determine whether it has a comprehensive risk management strategy of its own, and then to identify key risk categories and take steps to clarify which risks apply to its operations. To safeguard *our* bank's survival, top management should be keen to analyse existing internal controls, and their ability to capture exposure; and also to judge in a factual and documented manner whether it has available the necessary skills and effective tools to assess and control its risks.

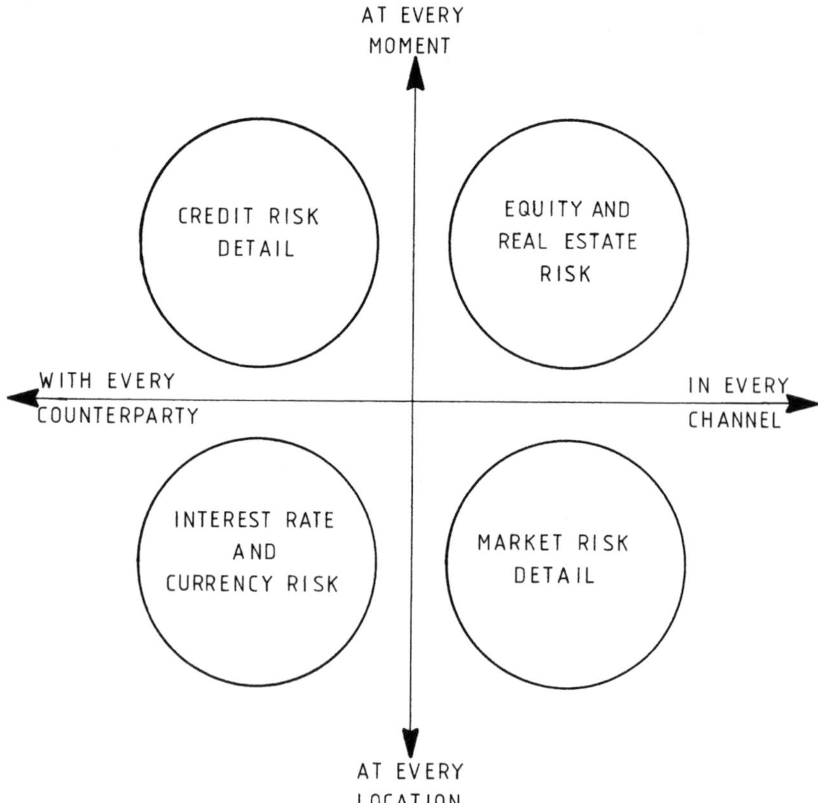

Figure 4.1 A four-dimensional system is necessary for effective risk management

Risk management is not a one-off business but a steady effort to be maintained over every moment, in every channel, for every location, and for every counterparty. Figure 4.1 brings into perspective this four-dimensional approach to the control of exposure an institution takes in its transactions and has embedded in its portfolio.

Another top management responsibility is to study the existing information system and communications channels, establishing a real-time IT structure with mathematical models and risk visualisation facilities. Top management should also assess the adequacy of *our* bank's overall risk management culture, identify necessary changes and implement them.

3 Establishing rigorous rules for risk disclosure

An example of rules and regulations for internal control and financial reporting has been given in Chapter 1 with COSO. Tighter regulatory controls help to deflate the greed mentality which sometimes dominates the financial industry. By so doing, they help to avert the dangerous fallout which will occur when the highly geared assets bubble bursts. Usually, those caught in a spate of company collapses are the victims of their own delusions plus some bystanders who thought they could make a fast buck.

Regulators should want all the executives of the financial industry to feel the urgency of risk control and to appreciate that whatever they have done so far has not been nearly enough. Traders, investors, speculators, shareholders, directors and the institutions themselves all share excessive expectations about the trades they make and their future returns. But one day they all come to grief. In principle, regulation and supervision should not be forbidding but should aim to justify and control exposure. No government can legislate against unrealistic expectations which have to do with human nature.

During the 1990s proactive shareholders, particularly institutional investors, have supplemented the watchful eye of regulators. But if ownership is going to be in charge, then we should never forget that shareholders can only act on information the companies have disclosed. This means that risks should not be hidden behind a wall of secrecy, as so often happens.

With balance sheet products, some of the information gaps are filled by the Stock Exchange's listing rules, but off-balance-sheet, with OTC traded derivatives and other instruments, there is the complication that so far there exist no clear-cut guidelines on standard metrics for risk disclosure which are meaningful to all concerned. This is now changing, but not fast enough or in a way commensurate to outstanding risks.

In other terms, both standards for risk management and norms for financial reporting practices need to be significantly improved so that banks and other companies are made to fully report cash flow, related party transactions, notional principal amounts and fair value of their trading book and banking book. If the standards are fully defined, then companies will not be able to cook their books quite so much as some of them are doing. Indeed, if exposure is properly measured, the banks will have to back it up with assets and cash flow to avoid following in the footsteps of LTCM. Also, a sound risk control system must give greater discretion to the regulatory bodies to improve the quality of information which they get and to remedy defective reports by means of better focused interventional powers. COSO is the right move in this direction. Another case will be made in section 4 with the OTC trades.

Limited or ambiguous disclosure rules, such as those existing in several countries, create a major risk by themselves. Many investors are uninformed when they put their money in funds that play with risky financial instruments or participate in unpredictable emerging country markets. The same is true when investors buy equities in companies which aggressively use their treasury operations for profits. Limited disclosure rules raise the risk that downturns in markets could send shareholders and bondholders scrambling to sell, further pushing values down; in addition, when players in the derivatives markets cut a major deal, it is hard to know how much exposure has been assumed and whether it is time to buy or sell.

The stock of the UBS, and therefore the bank's capitalisation, halved in price after it was disclosed that the institution lost nearly a $1 billion in the near-bankruptcy of LTCM. Even the VAR models (see D.N. Chorafas, *The 1996 Market Risk Amendment. Understanding the Marking-to-Model and Value-at-Risk*, McGraw-Hill Burr Ridge, IL, 1998) did not disclose that exposure because they were 'updated' with obsolete data and used hypotheses which were patently wrong.

It all boils down to the fact that by and large current accounting rules relating to disclosure are inadequate. The VAR model brought forward by the 1996 Market Risk Amendment is not providing the crucial information it was supposed to give. Therefore, it is not surprising that problems with disclosure are now attracting great attention on a global scale.

Besides COSO, accounting groups are working on an international scale to develop rules that would require standard and comprehensive disclosure of risks stemming from major movements in financial markets. It would then be up to the regulators to see to it that these financial reporting rules are observed by every corporation exposed to those shifts, whether a financial institution, a manufacturing, merchandising or other company.

For instance, the SEC is working with mutual fund companies to develop one-page summaries for mutual-fund prospectuses that lay out clearly a fund's riskiness. For the time being, however, neither in the USA nor anywhere else is it possible to gauge the probability that a large problem could occur in an institution's assets because vast sections of the global financial market remain largely invisible.

Similarly, to avoid a repetition of the thrifts débâcle of the late 1980s (see Chapter 3) the OTS has developed an ingenious system of reporting which is now religiously observed on a daily basis by some 1100 supervised savings and loans. This system requires that each savings and loans communicates to the regulators their current exposure:

- at prevailing interest rates; and
- at interest rates up and down from the current rate by 100, 200, 300 and 400 basis points.

This gives regulators the time to respond most rapidly to interest rate mismatches which hit not just the savings and loan industry but also other institutions. Such action is the key to effective supervision and the management of risk, whereas the lack of analytical disclosures made available to supervisors practically at real-time, permits large structural defects to develop undetected eventually leading to a bubble.

While some people assume that 'the chance a major economic shock would result in the domino failure of major financial institutions has declined', in reality there is no other basis than undocumented optimism on which to make such assertions. Experience teaches that when adversity hits there is a flight to quality, but few really sound investments remain as practically everybody runs to the exit through the same door.

4 The difficult act of regulating the over-the-counter market

In early May 1998, the US Commodity Futures Trading Commission (CFTC), the regulatory agency for the American futures markets, decided to go ahead with its plan to review the huge and largely unregulated OTC market (see also section 5 on CFTC). This has been a piece of long overdue regulation because during the last 10 years the level of trades relative to the economy has soared, and so have the risks.

CFTC stated as its goal the maintenance of adequate safeguards without impairing the ability of the market to grow. Its chairman stressed that the commission was not approaching the OTC review with any preconceived results in mind. But she added that: 'The OTC derivatives market over the past few years requires the commission to review its regulations' (*Financial Times*, 8 May 1998).

To some extent, this initiative by the CFTC runs contrary to a 17 March 1997 US House of Representatives' version of a bill targeting the deregulation of the derivatives markets. This was supposed to give American futures exchanges the right to open their own version of unregulated markets for institutional customers, indirectly suggesting that the vast OTC derivatives trades would be exempt from the US Commodity Exchange Act which regulates listed futures markets. The derivatives deregulation bill had the support of the exchanges and global securities firms that deal in swaps and other OTC financial instruments; but the CFTC objected to this swingeing measure, saying that it would curtail the government's ability to detect and deter fraud.

In CFTC's opinion, which I fully endorse, the explosive growth in the OTC market in the 1990s has been accompanied by an increase in the number and size of losses even among sophisticated users who claim to be hedging price risk in the underlying cash market, while in reality they are assuming an even greater amount of exposure.

What is meant by the statement that the OTC business has grown most rapidly in recent years? Released on 30 November 1998, a BIS report offers illuminating statistics on the derivatives exposure of the world's major banks and securities firms. BIS said that they held more than $103.5 trillion in notional principal with derivatives contracts at the end of 1997, and that this represents a $21 trillion (25 per cent) increase over the $82.6 trillion featured at the end of 1996. While statistics as of 31 December 1998, will not be available till the end of 1999, one can use the 1997/1996 percentage increase in derivatives exposure as the best available estimate for the 1998/1997 period. If one does so, the number at the end of 1998 stands at $129.4 trillion.

Notice that the BIS survey, conducted jointly by the Basle Committee on Banking Supervision and the technical committee of the International Organisation of Securities Commissions (IOSCO), limits itself to 67 banks and 11 securities firms headquartered in the G-10 countries. While it includes the bulk of the world's derivatives activity, it provides neither national nor world totals.

How much is left out? An educated guess would use Pareto's law: these 78 transnational institutions represent among themselves about 80 per cent of derivatives trades. Therefore, in notional principal amounts, the 31 December 1997 derivatives exposure stands at $129.4 trillion, and the 31 December 1998 at $161.7 trillion; of these, US institutions held about $32 billion.

Forex exposure provides a good example of the notional principal amount of outstanding contracts because since the early 1970s, when fixed interest rates were abandoned, it has mushroomed. By now, however, currency exchange trades have very little to do with the real economy they are supposed to serve. No better reference exists on this statement than American import–export trade as percentage of forex turnover, as shown in Figure 4.2.

Notice that during the last 20 years American export trade largely expanded, but derivatives grew exponentially. With futures and forwards, deals involve notional principal amounts. But with spot transactions foreign exchange exposures are real, not nominal. There are, however, accounting constraints in effectively estimating the risk, because the accounting framework in most companies ensures that management follows a simplistic paper trail approach. Yet the need for an accurate appreciation of real currency exchange exposure is confirmed by the fact that many banks market off-the-shelf forex hedging products which are inappropriate for the specific problems faced by their clients.

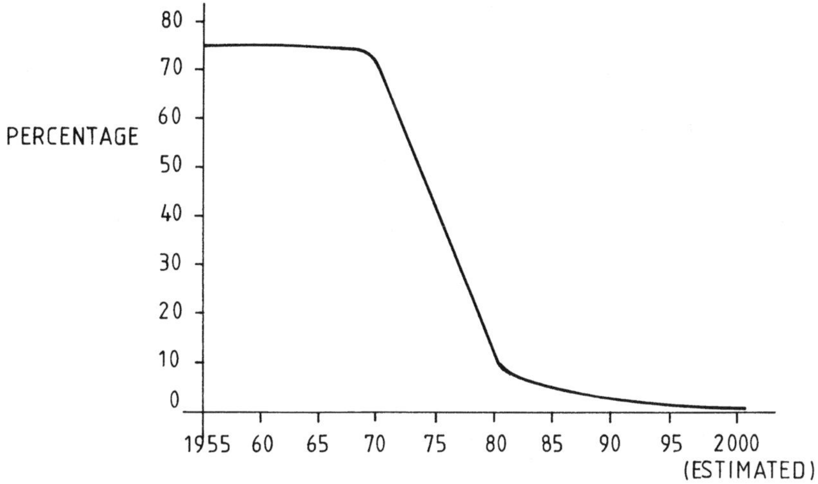

Figure 4.2 American import–export trade as a percentage of currency exchange turnover

Such off-the-shelf hedges break down when host governments adopt policies that interfere with the smooth functioning of the market, as Malaysia did in the wake of the 1997 East Asia meltdown. The imposition of forex controls and price controls in a foreign country are examples of moves which can destroy the local cost–revenue balance, turning the global earnings picture on its head.

An important issue embedded in these examples is the fact that, coinciding with that zero-balance which the US economy reached in 1970–71, the world's financial and monetary system underwent a fundamental phase-shift in its functional characteristics. This change is reflected most simply in the aforementioned decline of total currency exchange turnover attributable to combined imports and exports.

The decoupling of the real economy from the virtual economy by means of the financial system is not limited to forex. It has also manifested itself in other domains such as junk bonds (see Chapter 3). One of the reasons CFTC feels obliged to come forward with regulation is that it largely exempted swaps and other hybrid products from regulatory supervision in 1993. But it now claims that:

- circumstances have changed;
- the market has expanded;
- some products have become standardised; and
- there are proposals put forward for centralised clearing of contracts such as swaps.

The regulators finally appreciate that as the OTC market has mushroomed, players such as mutual funds, and countries have been affected by derivatives losses, in addition to the losses sustained by corporate shareholders. Banks have also been burned by huge derivatives losses, as has already been discussed in Chapters 1 and 2.

The bankers are particularly worried about the new CFTC regulation because it may cast new light on the red ink in their books. For this reason, the CFTC stresses that any rule changes resulting from the new measures would be applied prospectively only. This means it will be impact on contracts struck after the changes are made.

5 The changing regulatory landscape in the USA

Section 4 has explained that the role of the CFTC in America is to oversee the futures market. Can CFTC be out of a job? A first attempt took place on 15 October 1995, when members of the House of Representatives' Banking Committee held a hearing by the larger SEC. Instituted in the 1930s, SEC regulates the securities markets.

The view that CFTC's responsibilities should be transferred to SEC were supported by a study prepared by the General Accounting Office (GAO), the auditor of the US government, which pointed to 'serious deficiencies' in the CFTC's enforcement record. GAO's words have much weight because it acts as the audit arm of the US Congress. The GAO study noted that the CFTC had organisational and training problems, and that it has been often slow to subpoena its targets.

CFTC answers that its record might not always have been perfect, but things have changed. Recently wrongdoers have been brought to book, including Bankers Trust and MGRM, the subsidiary of Germany's Metallgesellschaft which made spectacular losses in oil futures. CFTC also says that it is working with the exchanges to improve their own self-regulation by strengthening their trading audit trails.

The risk that the much tougher SEC may take over regulatory and supervisory duties has moved some of the exchanges into a self-policing action. In December 1995, at the Chicago Mercantile Exchange (CME) a group of 21 members, calling themselves' the CME Equity Owners' Association', signed and circulated a letter to other traders and brokers, arguing that something was amiss at the exchange. Their fear was that the exchange was drifting without strategic direction and they were worried about:

- the lack of new products with significant potential;
- the plunge in the price of seats on the exchange; and
- the delays in bringing technological innovations on to the trading floor.

Also in direct response to the Gibson Greetings and Procter & Gamble versus Bankers Trust cases, OTC derivatives dealers cobbled together an extensive document of voluntary conduct guidelines. Dubbed 'Principles and Practices for Wholesale Financial Market Transactions', this code has been criticised for its bias towards the dealer community and its assumption that dealers and endusers enter trades on an equal footing as counterparties.

Critics say that rather than being concerned about self-policing in the broker community, the dealer group which drafted the guidelines wanted an iron-clad protection from a client returning after a losing trade and saying it had been put in an unsuitable transaction. Principles and Practices recommends its subscribers agree in writing, ahead of a trade, if one counterparty feels it is relying solely on the other for information or advice.

Principles and Practices is, however, controversial as attested to by the fact that the National Association of State Treasurers in the USA has warned its members that by doing business with a company that uses the voluntary pact they may be waiving valuable legal rights. Such differences of opinion are instructive because they show that there is significant divergence in appreciating:

- the amount of risk taken with OTC transactions by the counterparties; and
- the responsibilities assumed by either party entering into a bilateral agreement.

For their part, America's exchanges have been up in arms against the idea that the SEC may be the vehicle for their supervision and control, because they understand the risks involved with exchange-traded derivatives and the need for control action. Although the SEC may serve many public interests, they say, no one would claim that its long suit is fostering innovation and reducing onerous regulation. This statement is wrong.

To the exchanges, CFTC seems to be the lesser evil as a regulator. There are many members of the trader community who suggest that with derivatives taking centre-stage on the world financial markets, eliminating the CFTC seems to be an inappropriate prescription. Instead, they would like to reduce federal regulation of futures markets to allow OTC futures to trade without fear of legal enforceability. Also, concerned that many American banks are overexposed in derivatives, the Federal Reserve is not coming down on derivatives risk with the same force as the SEC.

However, those who think of reducing the transparency of exposure would be wrong to calculate without the heavy hand of the GAO, and its expertise in unearthing and bringing to light inefficiencies. Since the early 1990s GAO has been ringing the alarm bell, warning that the growth of derivatives markets could endanger the stability of the financial system, and that rigorous risk controls are long overdue. The increase in the use of options, futures, swaps, and the new generation of complex derivatives has led to high gearing in financial markets, while the exposure inherent in derivative instruments and the effects of global networking have made the markets more vulnerable to a crisis, as has been often underlined in this book.

While recognising the positive aspects of derivatives (they can be used to hedge risks and allow banks and companies more flexibility), for more than six years GAO has warned that the collapse of a leading market participant or extreme market turbulence could set off a chain reaction. The case of LTCM fully justified the position taken by GAO and the SEC.

GAO has also pointed out that one of the leading challenges is that problems in the derivatives markets could prompt a liquidity crisis in the cash markets and endanger the whole financial fabric. Such developments can only be avoided if market participants in any country where they may be based are aware:

- of all the ways in which derivatives instruments can be deployed; and
- the risks attached to using them, including the fine-tuning of control mechanisms.

As the critiques made about the dangers of a soft regulatory position in futures, swaps and options are not new, since 1995 CFTC has upgraded its enforcement staff. It has also tried to promote enforcement actions by instituting fire drills at America's three largest futures exchanges to see if the existing supervisory framework could deal with a large-scale default. Such exercises, CFTC officials say, invariably expose issues that had not been anticipated. Following on from such findings, the regulations are being upgraded and new norms are coming to light.

American financial exchanges are also constructing some trigger mechanisms that allow wider information-sharing between agencies when a company's market position becomes large in relation to its capital and also when that position comprises a significant percentage of open trades in a particular market. These triggers have been presented to international regulators, to see if they would be useful globally, but a global regulatory framework based on the findings of drills and of stress testing has not yet been enacted.

6 Private Securities Litigation Reform Act of 1995

A milestone in American regulation has been the Private Securities Litigation Reform Act of 1995 which provides a safe harbour for forward-looking statements made by public firms. A company and its representatives make, from time to time, written or verbal forward-looking statements, including those contained in the company's filings with the SEC and in the annual and quarterly reports to shareholders. The question is what sort of commitment such statements represent.

According to this relatively new regulation, all statements which address operating performance, events or developments that management expects or anticipates will occur in the future are basically commitments. Within the meaning of the 1995 Reform Act they are not historical references but forward-looking statements relating, for instance, to:

- volume growth;
- share of sales; and
- earnings per share growth.

They may also be expressing general optimism about future operating results at a given level of certainty. Such forward-looking statements are based on management's current views and assumptions regarding future events and operating performance which, short of very adverse conditions, are expected to occur.

A number of factors, however, could cause actual results to differ materially from estimates contained in such forward-looking statements. If so, such factors must be identified and documented by management. Examples are changes in laws and regulations (including changes in accounting standards), and tax rates, or new tax laws and revised tax law interpretations.

Other changes regard competitive product and pricing pressures, and the likelihood of gaining or maintaining a share of sales in the global market as a result of actions by competitors as well as in the aftermath of extreme events. Also, changes may happen in connection to the ability to generate sufficient cash flows to support:

- capital expansion plans;
- share repurchase programmes; and
- general operating activities.

Forward-looking statements may also be affected by fluctuations in the cost and availability of raw materials; the ability to maintain favourable supplier arrangements and relationships (the so-called 'supply chain'); or the possibility of achieving earnings forecasts based on projected volumes and sales of different product types, some of which are more profitable than others. Because costs matter, changes in the cost structure also affect forward-looking statements.

Banks point to the deteriorating creditworthiness of some borrowers and reduced demand for credit during the period as reasons for deviations from plans, or note that a slowdown in lending was also evident in other regions (for instance, across Continental Europe and Japan). While the extent of linkage may be open to debate, there is no denying that such factors do impact upon actual results, making them deviate from projections.

Other reasons why there may be differences between forward-looking statements and actual results are economic and political conditions in international markets, including civil unrest, governmental changes and restrictions on the ability to transfer capital across borders. Equally important is the ability to penetrate emerging markets, which also depends on:

- prevailing economic and political conditions, including shifts in this environment; and
- how well a firm is able to form strategic business alliances with local companies to get market clout.

Differences between intended results described in forward-looking statements and actual results might also be due to advertising failures, particularly for companies which depend on intensive advertising campaigns. The effectiveness of their advertising, marketing and promotional programmes can contribute to a switch between profit and losses, particularly when margins are thin.

Similarly, companies facing litigation problems will add into their reporting the uncertainties of litigation. Often litigation proves a handicap because it diverts management attention or results in outright constraints. These and other risks are detailed from time to time by firms in their SEC filings.

Still other reasons which can mean that actual results deviate from those projected are interest rate volatility and other capital market conditions, including significant changes in foreign currency rates. When these factors have been accounted for, but none really fluctuated so much as to justify major derivatives from forward-looking statements, what really counts is management's efficiency or inefficiency.

Given the aforementioned factors, the Private Securities Reform Act of 1995 is essentially a way of gauging *management intent*, and adherence to the intended line. The Act takes account of the fact that most of the exposures a global company has to capital markets, including interest rates and foreign currencies, are managed on a consolidated basis. For certain exposures, this allows them to bet, taking advantage of any offsets.

The Act also reflects the fact that today most firms use derivative financial instruments to reduce net exposure to financial risks. But as every management should know there can be no assurance that hedging programmes will be successful in minimising foreign currency and interest rate exposures. In fact, some currency exchange hedges can backfire, as happened with Mitsubishi Motors when the yen went from 80 to the dollar to 115, instead of going 'as expected' to 70.

5
Changes in Bank Legislation: Examples from Germany

1 Introduction

In mid-1997, the German Parliament passed the Sixth Act Amending the Banking Act. This amendment came into force at the beginning of 1998, its prime objective being to implement three directives of the EU: the Investment Services Directive, the Capital Adequacy Directive, and the Post-BCCI Directive.

Through the implementation of the Investment Services Directive, investment banks will be supervised according to the same rules as credit institutions (commercial banks). To the regulators this change to the Banking Act means a level playing field for all banks, but it also revolutionises the established German supervisory practices.

Until the 1997 amendment came into effect, on 1 January 1998, the supervisory regulations in Germany did not apply to investment firms even though they were in direct competition with commercial banks. This also happens in other EU countries. Therefore, the EU Investment Services Directive laid down minimum requirements for both the authorisation and the supervision of companies which carry on the business of providing investment advice and related trading or asset management services. Investment banks can opt to confine themselves to providing national services, or they can set up or provide cross-border services through correspondent bank branch(es) in other contracting countries. In either case, the institution's home country is responsible for the core part of supervision.

The Capital Adequacy Directive (CAD) of the EU will not interest us in this chapter, as it is reviewed in Part Three in conjunction with the discussion on the 1988 Capital Accord and more generally on capital adequacy. But brief reference should be made to the aftermath of BCCI on the regulation of financial institutions.

In response to the 1991 closure of the Bank for Credit and Commerce International (BCCI), authorities in all the G-10 countries launched inquiries to learn more about what went wrong with bank supervision. Particularly intense has been the investigation in Britain and Luxembourg, the two European countries where the BCCI buck stopped.

In London the inquiry was conducted under the chairmanship of Lord Justice Bingham, and it explored several issues related to the role of external auditors and the reliance by supervisory authorities on the reports by certified public accountants. The Bingham inquiry recommended that, as contrasted to the earlier *right* to communicate, external auditors should be placed under the *statutory duty* to communicate directly with the Bank of England – as a necessary measure to safeguard the audited bank's depositors.

2 Changes to the German Banking Act and their consequences

The Introduction made reference to the three reasons underpinning the Sixth Act Amending the German Banking Act, which came into effect on 1 January 1998. It also explained that one of these reasons, the Post-BCCI Directive, carried with it a significant change in external auditors' responsibilities. This affected the manner of supervision not only in Germany, but also in Switzerland and Austria where the authorities also depend on reports by certified public accountants.

Another basic reason for the adoption of the Sixth Act Amendment has been the preparations for the introduction of the euro. German central banking legislation had to be adapted to the requirements under European Community law for the participation of the Federal Republic in Stage Three of monetary union. Concomitant to this was the opportunity to amend:

- the regulations governing the Bundesbank's capital and reserves; and
- the accounting principles characterising financial reporting by the reserve bank.

To better appreciate the meaning of the changes brought about by the Sixth Act Amendment, it is necessary briefly to turn back the clock to previous amendments to the German Banking Act. A basic objective of three amendments (the Fourth, Fifth and Sixth) has been to bring the provisions governing reporting requirements into line with developments in the credit markets.

Until mid-1993, in the German Federal Republic, the reporting threshold to the Bundesbank was DM1 million. This level had remained unchanged since the currency reform in 1948. But owing to economic growth and price increases, the number of reportable loans rose considerably over the years. Therefore Parliament responded by raising the threshold in mid-1993 from DM1 million to DM3 million through the Fourth Act Amending the Banking Act.

With this change of threshold, the number of financial reports went down by about half, a fact reflecting the relatively large percentage of loans between DM1 million and DM3 million. On the other hand, the aggregate volume of the reported loans did not decline perceptibly. As a result, the raising of the reporting threshold did not seriously diminish the banking information gained for supervisory reasons from the banking industry's financial reports (see also section 4).

One of the changes introduced by the Fifth Act Amending the Banking Act, which came into force at the end of 1995, was that the concept of *exposure* – which is relevant to defining loans but also derivatives and other transactions – was substantially expanded. Its scope has become broader and it now comprises:

- risk assets;
- securitised claims; and
- off-balance-sheet derivatives.

For ascertaining the level of indebtedness in the case of derivatives business, the Fifth Act Amendment introduces the concept of a *credit equivalent* amount. This is generally in line with marking to market. The notional principal amount of the derivatives transactions, which must also be reported, serves as additional information but is not added to a borrower's overall indebtedness. The Fifth Act Amending the Banking Act also included:

- a watch over short-term interbank loans with maturities of up to 90 days, which often filter to hedge funds; and
- loans to public credit institutions falling within the reporting requirement for DM3 million or more.

Equities and other participating interests, as well as securities held in the trading portfolio, continue to be exempt from reporting requirements. Also exempt from financial reporting are some lending commitments, such as loans to the public sector of the Federal Republic and loans to the European Community.

The Fifth Act also expanded the definition of concepts underpinning a single borrower unit. In the past, the reporting system for loans of DM3 million or more had required all companies belonging to the same group (or affiliated through profit transfer agreements as well as majority-owned enterprises) to form a single borrower unit. The same has been applicable to:

- partnerships and their general partners; and
- nominee loans (that is, companies on whose account loans are raised).

These are treated as a single borrower when applying the regulation governing large exposures and loans of DM3 million or more. But, in addition to such criteria, the Fifth Act makes it possible for borrowers to be considered a single borrower unit, or *risk unit,* even if no dominant financial influence is involved.

An equally important change to basic financial reporting concepts connected with the Fifth Act is that, following the translation of the EU netting directive into German law in October 1996, offsetting of positions is permitted in the reports of loans of DM3 million or more. This is, however, subject to conditions laid down in the regulation governing large exposures.

Whether we talk of regulators or of commercial bankers, *netting* has not been an easy topic because it has so many ramifications. In finance, netting is the practice of offsetting payments in one direction (for instance, liabilities) against those in the opposite direction (assets). This is done algorithmically, but it involves major risks. Theoretically, netting enables market players to compensate assets and liabilities on-balance-sheet and off-balance-sheet. Practically, this theory is junior high school stuff because one leg of the netting transaction (particularly the gains) rarely follows in a way which compensates the other leg. The way to bet is that the money flows – in and out – across the balance sheet and through an institution are not even. Only up to a point do counterparties feel comfortable in accepting each other's credit and assurances. Beyond that, they want some sort of reassurance because the accounts shown as netting out can implode.

What the reader should retain from this section is that the examples of the Fourth, Fifth and Sixth Acts (see section 3) amending the Banking Act of the German Federal Republic demonstrate that bank legislation and regulation are not static but can evolve fairly rapidly. These three amendments took place in the short span of four years, from 1993 to 1997, whereas the previous three amendments had taken 45 years (from 1948 to 1993).

3 The redefinition of specific duties through the Sixth Act Amendment

The contribution of the Sixth Act Amending the Banking Act is that of defining specific organisational and behavioural duties for financial institutions. Banks must have in place appropriate internal control and information systems for managing, monitoring and controlling the risks they incur. Short of this, their risks may be ballooning. Internal controls and management information must ensure that risk can be determined with sufficient accuracy, at any time.

The banking supervisory authorities have been given the power to issue instructions to an institution and its managers to prevent or remedy irregularities which may jeopardise the safety of the assets with which it has been entrusted, or impair the orderly execution of business. The process of correcting irregularities includes dismissing the managers. Besides organising their business properly, and establishing an effective internal surveillance, banks are also required to take safety precautions in the use of IT. If areas of work which are fundamental to carrying on banking and financial services are outsourced to another enterprise, this outsourcing should not impair the orderly execution of the institution's and of senior management's ability to direct and control operations, or the auditing rights of the Federal Banking Supervisory Bureau which is directly responsible for bank supervision.

Let me take an example with new financial instruments. There are several conditions to be fulfilled for credit derivatives, said the German Federal Banking Supervisory Bureau. The first directives were issued in 1997. New rules now specify:

- the fine print of regulatory aspects; and
- how banks should recognise credit derivatives.

This is the right time for regulation because up until late 1998 German banks had not been big players in credit derivatives. They are getting started, but also think these instruments have a good future, although much depends on how the market develops in terms of liquidity. Another problem is cultural.

'We are a user of credit derivatives', said Hans Voit of Deutsche Bank. 'We trade in credit derivatives but, like any other bank, we are still in a learning curve.' 'Credit derivatives will bring market risk and credit risk closer together', suggested Peter Bürger of Commerzbank. In terms of responsibilities, the credit derivatives team at Commerzbank is part of Global Bond operations.

Since the regulatory authorities press the need for rigorous control by senior management, at Commerzbank credit derivatives are evaluated by the New Product Committee, which meets weekly and brings every single product through the treadmill of:

- internal controls;
- legal counsel;
- marketing expertise;
- accounting; and
- information technology.

The German Ministry of Justice, which has responsibility for accounting standards in the Federal Republic, seems concerned about the risk involved with credit derivatives. Therefore it is doing its own research to establish advantages, problems and pitfalls.

Prodded by the regulators, in a growing number of German institutions top management now asks for more powerful measurement methods and solutions for reporting risk. 'Classically the banker managed risk without instruments', said a senior German banker. 'Therefore complexity was hidden. Now we appreciate that we need both instruments and transparency.'

Another development of which the reader should take note is that with the implementation of the Investment Services Directive of the EU, German legislation now distinguishes between banking *per se* and the more general context of financial services. The concept of a financial services institution, of an investment bank and of a commercial bank are not identical. However, the notion of brokerage is extended beyond the previous securities-based confines to include other financial instruments handled for the account of third parties. Indeed, some of the most important parts of the Sixth Act are that:

- it made jobbers and factoring firms subject to reporting requirement; and
- the regulatory changes tighten supervisory control over different forms of financial transactions.

The Sixth Act Amending the banking Act has also changed the provisions governing consolidation of financial statements, making them better focused although somewhat simpler. For instance, the lenders subject to financial reporting requirements now only need one reporting form to submit their exposure and their loans of DM3 million or more.

Since the beginning of 1998, prior to granting a loan lenders may also ask the Bundesbank to inform them of the cumulative debt level of a potential customer, as recorded in its credit register. The conditions for this are that the envisaged loan to the customer amounts to DM3 million or more, and that the customer has agreed to the advance inquiry.

One more significant change with the Sixth Act is that it is now possible for a financial institution to be the parent firm of a group of other institutions, something practised, for instance, in the USA for several years. The definition of a financial holding group no longer requires that a deposit-taking credit institution is a constituent part of the group; it suffices that a securities trading house is part of the group.

To simplify the task of supervision, the mandatory consolidation of a company in which the parent institution holds a direct or indirect participation of at least 40 per cent has been abolished. In principle, the only units that now have to be consolidated are subsidiaries. By this is meant firms:

- in which the parent institution holds a majority participating interest; or
- over which it can exercise a dominant influence.

Subconsolidation in the case of cross-holdings, or participating interests of less than 75 per cent, is no longer a reporting threshold as it used to be. For the purpose of market risk, the netting of long and short positions within a group is permissible *if*, and only if, companies belonging to the group are included in the central risk management activity of the parent firm.

The careful reader will detect in this connection a certain effect of the post-BCCI Directive. This is more explicitly shown through the fact that the authorisation of companies wishing to conduct banking business or provide financial services is to be refused (or withdrawn) if the structure of the enterprise, or the relationships between it and other entities, make effective supervision impossible. In a way, the regulatory rules have been tightened.

4 The prudential value of information on loans

Section 3 made the point that information on loans of DM3 million or more is available in the Bundesbank's database and it can be mined and then communicated to commercial banks under certain conditions. This most valuable information serves two purposes:

- to provide banking supervisory bodies with data which can support regulatory activities; and
- to inform lenders of the overall indebtedness of their borrowers, and therefore outstanding risks.

The requirement to submit quarterly reports on loans of DM3 million or more meant that during the 1997/98 Asian meltdown banking supervisors had up-to-date information on the exposure of German financial institutions to borrowers in East Asian countries. In compiling and evaluating the information on loans above the aforementioned threshold, the Bundesbank's credit register classifies loans according to the legal domicile of the borrower. Hence, as the ultimate risk bearer the commercial bank can find out if beside credit risk it also takes currency exchange risk.

By evaluating this information, the Deutsche Bundesbank and the Federal Banking Supervisory Bureau can gain an up-to-date insight into the credit commitments of the major lenders and borrowers. When big debtors become insolvent, the banking supervisory authorities are able to quickly obtain a current overview of:

- exposure of individual institutions; and
- the overall burden on the banking industry.

By including derivatives with the associated notional principal and credit equivalent amounts in their monitoring of loans of DM3 million or more, since mid-1996 banking supervisors have been able to gain an additional insight into gearing by commercial and investment banks and leveraged financial instruments. They can also experiment with the possible consequences of gearing.

Timely and accurate information is that much more important as derivatives regulation in Germany makes it mandatory to inform the supervisory authorities about counterparty large exposure. This is true not only of loans but of all risk assets. Underpinning such an approach is the ability to integrate credit risk and market risk by major counterparties. The Bundesbank also uses expert systems to help in the evaluation.

Starting on 1 July 1998, the German central bank introduced a new credit assessment procedure for its tier-2 collateral in the form of bills and loan claims to meet the higher demands on creditworthiness. This is an improvement over the previous credit assessment procedures, which required non-banks posting collateral for loans to present detailed annual accounts.

The new credit assessment system focuses not only on quantitative annual account data but also on analytical techniques such as sector-specific discriminants and knowledge engineering constructs. To appreciate the improvements featured by the new method, let me add that under the old procedure a standard treatment was applied solely to annual account data in the form of:

- the funds statement;
- individual economic ratios;
- discriminant analysis; and
- a process of corporate comparison.

The improved method goes beyond classical ratio analysis by subjecting both quantitative and qualitative information about an entity to rigorous tests, whose output is processed by the expert system. The knowledge artefact produces a computer-based credit assessment. Each entity is examined to see whether its use of available accounting options differs significantly from the other firms with which the Bundesbank deals. If there is a deviation from the norm, the entity's accounting practice is categorised as conservative or progressive, in which case it is investigated further.

An important point which the reader may wish to remember is that in the analysis of financial statements the Bundesbank is using operating characteristics (OC) curves, permitting the testing of classification errors within the same industrial sector and the same accounting year. An OC curve is shown in Figure 5.1: α indicates the share of solvent enterprises classified as insolvent (this is known as producer's risk, rejecting a good item), and β is the proportion of insolvent enterprises classified as solvent (consumer's risk, accepting a bad item).

Bankers familiar with VAR will appreciate that α is the level of confidence set by the 1996 Market Risk Amendment. The Basle Committee did not say so, but in every OC curve α has associated with it a β. Correctly, the rocket scientists of the Bundesbank have accounted for this risk. (Do not confuse *this* β with volatility. They have nothing in common.)

While expert systems are a new and valuable addition to the armoury of inspection, in legal terms the new regulation has been an extension of

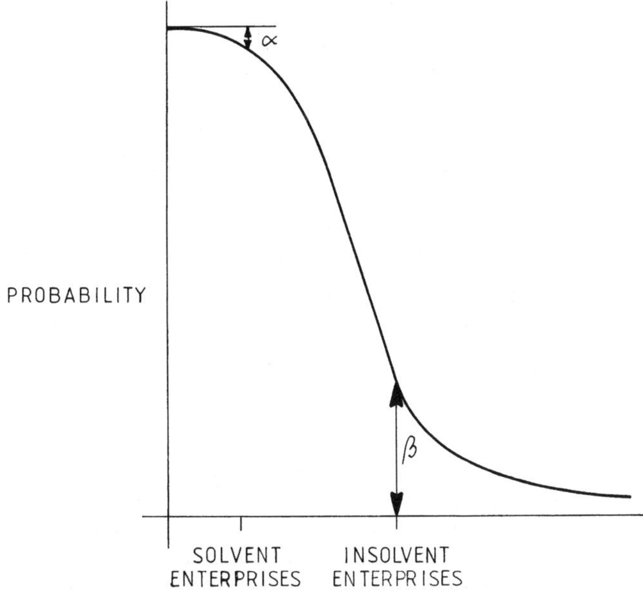

Figure 5.1 Operating characteristics curve and level of confidence

paragraph 13 of the Banking Act of the Federal Republic. It obliges a commercial bank to report on counterparty exposure when the business relation involves an amount equal to 10 per cent or more of its own capital. Because this is a rather high threshold, the board of commercial banks would be well advised to apply a threshold step of 1 per cent, as far as the internal accounting management information system (IAMIS) is concerned. Information on all types of exposure, from loans to derivatives, is a crucial tool for timely and rigorous regulatory action.

Banking supervisors in Germany now have information on the counterparties with whom institutions have concluded major transactions, with the credit equivalent amount of derivatives included in the total indebtedness (see Chapter 3). Through this policy, the quality of supervision has improved, since the risks stemming from derivatives have become transparent.

By steadily updating the credit register, it has become possible for the Bundesbank to inform financial institutions about exposure at their request. In this manner, senior management can make factual and documented credit risk decisions, and take measures to avert a crisis or at least bend the exposure curve.

The contents of the Bundesbank's database are dynamic and some of the results of datamining worth recording. For instance, over the last few years the shares of the various groups of borrowers in the overall volume of

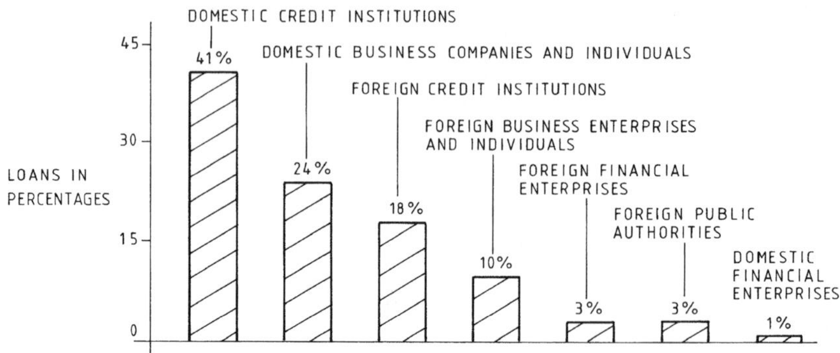

Figure 5.2 Loans of DM3 million or more by major groups of borrowers

exposure in the German financial landscape have undergone a distinct shift. In the early to mid-1990s, about half the total number of reported loans have been granted to domestic business firms and individuals and only around 15 per cent to domestic credit institutions; but in 1997 and 1998 domestic credit institutions constituted the largest group of borrowers, with a share of about 41 per cent, with all that this entails in gearing.

Figure 5.2 reflects these statistics. In what seems to be a significant change in trend, domestic industrial companies and individuals make up only one-quarter of the total. The rest is taken by foreign borrowers, with the larger share going to other credit institutions.

From mid-1996, when the Fifth Act Amendment came into effect, until the end of 1997, the volume of exposure and the number of individual loans of DM3 million or more rose by some 30 per cent (to around DM8.5 trillion) and by 12 per cent (to around 460000 loans) respectively. In other terms, the loans got bigger. The number of reported borrowers increased by about 9 per cent to some 300000 during that period.

Other statistics regard financial reporting. Through modification of the concept of exposure, the number of lenders required to submit reports has risen by more than 2000 to over 5000. If the overall volume of exposure is divided between balance-sheet and off-balance-sheet business, following the incorporation of derivatives into reporting requirements, off-balance-sheet trades now represent little more than 10 per cent of the total. In my book this means Germany is not yet as highly geared as some of its neighbour.

5 The contribution of the Sixth Act Amendment to the introduction of the euro

It is proper to bring into perspective the contribution by the Sixth Act Amending the Banking Act to the preparatory steps for the introduction of the euro. Under Article 108 of the European Community Treaty, each member state has been required to ensure, at the latest by the time of the establishment of the European System of Central Banks (ESCB) and the ECB (which has already taken place), that its national legislation is compatible with the Treaty and the statute of the ESCB. This requirement addresses:

- the statutes of the member country's national central bank; and
- the provisions for the independence of the ESCB.

As is the case with all member states which participate in the euro and their central banks, the integration of the Bundesbank into the ESCB required the adaptation or repeal of several of the original Bundesbank Act provisions. The national central banks remain in operation as an integral part of the ESCB, rather than independent entities as before.

This leads to certain important changes. For instance, in the era of the Deutschemark it was the explicit responsibility of the Bundesbank to keep inflation under lock and key. On the contrary, price stability is now a key objective of the ESCB. This is the primary mission of its Governing Council, comprising the members of the Executive Board of the ECB and the governors of the national central banks of the participating member states (currently numbering 11).

Since 1 January 1999, the Governing Council has been responsible for taking the key monetary policy decisions, as well as adopting the guidelines and putting into effect the actions necessary to discharge the duties conferred upon the ESCB. Basically, the tasks of the ESCB are primarily to:

- define and implement the monetary policy of the EU;
- conduct foreign exchange operations (see also Chapter 2);
- hold and manage the official foreign reserves of the member states; and
- promote the smooth operation of payment systems.

As has already been noted, a very important duty is missing from this list. The ECB is responsible for monetary policy, but it has only an advisory function in bank supervision. It can make proposals. Banking legislation, however, is the province of the European Commission (see Chapter 11), and not of the ECB which has no such powers given by the Treaty.

The transfer of responsibility for monetary policy to the Community level means that key monetary policy decisions are taken centrally in the Governing Council of the ECB. Following this co-ordinated level of decision making, the monetary policy will be implemented in a decentralised manner by the national central banks. The refinancing of credit institutions, however, will continue to be undertaken by each national central bank (see Chapter 12 on repos). The ESCB Statutes contain no detailed provisions regarding an own set of monetary policy instruments.

The main preoccupations of the ESCB, as well as of the ECB, being monetary policy, financial stability and the value of the euro, an important question is how major central banks outside Euroland (for instance, the Federal Reserve, the Bank of England and the Bank of Japan) look at the euro. What is known is that they make base line reviews of the euro's impact, as well as taking the necessary steps to ensure that the payment and settlement system operates efficiently.

During our meeting, a senior commercial banker was to comment that the introduction of the euro has influenced both liquidity management and collateral. Eventually, it will probably transfer liquidity around the global financial market intraday and will do so by means of networks (see Chapter 1). There will be, as well, other changes in payments systems. Rather than keep on moving mainly cash, through dematerialisation, networked payments solutions will also move government bonds and other debt around the globe. This concept can be instrumental in establishing a new relationship between cash and bonds, and in all probability it will be very relevant to the policy of central banks.

Will the euro be successful? To this query the US rating agencies have responded from the sovereign standpoint. Moody's is more generous; it has upgraded all 11 countries which entered the first round of the euro into AAA status. Standard & Poor's is more concerned about the rating of some of the countries because there is no exit strategy, but basically it is also positive.

Let me add that though on 1 January 1999 the introduction of the euro was generally flawless, the ECB, ESCB and the central banks of the 11 EU countries had a lot of homework to do to prepare for the euro's evolution. Some commercial and investment banks, however, did not effect the change-over so smoothly. One major broker, for example, cancelled as of 2 January 1999 the DM accounts of his client and opened a euro account. As a result, the transfer of DM by a Swiss bank found no corresponding account to credit. It took weeks to solve this problem.

Technical failures can happen both with the mechanics and with the dynamics of the system. In terms of dynamics, technical adjustments were made by altering existing regulations and by concluding or amending individual contracts with business partners. More is, however, necessary in terms of reorganisation of the capital and reserves structures and the incorporation of ESCB's accounting rules throughout Euroland's landscape.

6 Other challenges connected to the euro, the *ins* and the *pre-ins*

The first day of January 1999, marked the start of Stage Three of the European economic and monetary union (EMU). On that date the currencies of eleven EU member states merged into the euro, forming a common currency which superseded the European Currency Unit (ECU) in a ratio of 1:1.

Capitalising on the background gained with the old European Monetary System (EMS), which on 1 January 1999 ceased to exist in the form with which the financial markets were familiar, the new exchange-rate mechanism was designed to be more flexible. The underlying objective is that price stability, which is given priority by the ESCB and the ECB, must in no circumstances be jeopardised; but there is a hint that this may be allowed to happen if a conflict develops with the other primary objectives of the EU, such as reducing the level of unemployment.

Unlike the situation in the former EMS, which provided for reciprocal central and intervention rates in the form of a parity grid for all the participating currencies, in the new exchange-rate mechanism the euro has expressly been given the role of anchor currency. Central and intervention rates are all defined in terms of the euro.

To avoid settlement risk posed by compulsory intervention, a procedure known as *payment after payment* has been introduced. In the event of intervention, the *in* central bank being concerned, or the ECB, would not authorise payment for a given transaction until it had received confirmation that the amount due had been credited to its account.

In this context, the central banks of those countries which are not yet in Euroland but which plan to enter, known as *pre-in*, act as correspondent banks of the ECB and of the *in* central banks. Note should also be taken of the intramarginal support operations which may be conducted within the margins of fluctuation of exchange rates, either unilaterally or by means of co-ordinated action on the part of the ECB and the *pre-in* central bank(s) concerned.

In the event of shifts in economic fundamentals between participants in the system (for instance, changes in the purchasing-power parities applying pressure to the currencies participating in ERM Two), central rates are to be adjusted to the new economic situation faster than has been the case in the EMS. There is a new procedure for granting initiator rights to the ECB and national central banks. This is designed to:

- de-politicise central rate adjustments; and
- accelerate procedures, which in the past have occasionally been sluggish.

Attention has also been paid to very short-term financing. To enhance the credibility of the intervention commitments assumed, there is a provision for automatically accessing very short-term financing facilities. Those are worked out between the ECB and the central banks of the *pre-ins* participating in the exchange-rate mechanism.

Central banks which seek recourse to short-term financing are required to make appropriate use of their own foreign reserve holdings for their support operations before taking up such loans. In the event of compulsory intervention, the financing is in principle unlimited in amount and it has an initial maturity of three months. However, at the request of the debtor central bank, the maturity is automatically extended once for another three months on due date, within the limits of agreed ceilings.

Loans under very short-term financing facilities are remunerated at a representative three-month money market rate of the creditor's currency, prevailing on the date when the facility is drawn on or is renewed. As far as private firms are concerned, at least theoretically, the arrival of the euro should make little difference to a company's legal obligations on contracts. Two regulations adopted by the Amsterdam summit, in June 1997, set the legal framework for the new currency.

1. These regulations should ensure the continuity of contracts, making clear that references to national currencies in legal instruments are references to the euro.
2. A principle of international law, *Lex monetae*, should ensure that European contracts will continue to be valid in other countries.

Several American states that do a lot of international business have enacted legislation recognising the euro and ensuring the continuity of contracts during the transition period. This, however, does not mean that non-enforceable contracts cannot be drawn up. In any major transition there is plenty of opportunity for all kinds of fraud. British experts point out a number of fraudulent contracts which were uncovered after decimalisation in the UK in 1971.

Other problems will emerge in 2002, when the euro moves beyond a mere existence in accounting systems and is used in the form of notes and coins. Already a quantity of euro coins has had to be scrapped because they were designed and produced in a way which would have confused users regarding their value. The Mafia also played its part as the plates of some of the euro notes were stolen from the briefcase of a Banque de France executive during his trip to Munich in late 1998.

As costs matter, it is correct to mention their incidence. Both banks and merchants will have to carry the cost of handling multiple currencies between 1999 and 2002. Banks must exchange any currency issued by the 11 euro countries, but they will no longer be allowed to charge commission. Instead, they must pay a low interest rate for euro deposits.

The euro will also do away with some important bank revenues, such as the profits from foreign-exchange charges. According to one estimate, foreign-exchange revenues for EU banks are expected to drop by about 70 per cent. It is likely, however, that the most important aftermath will be the element of competition.

The most aggressive, best organised and best managed firms in Euroland will treat the single currency as an opportunity to gain a strategic edge. This will unleash competitive forces which may eventually constitute the greatest gain to be derived from the single European currency, making the euro a *de facto* deregulator of chronically ossified labour markets.

Part Two

The Many Aspects of Bank Supervision

6 Hands-On Experience with Bank Supervision

1 Introduction

The three most important reasons for effective supervision of financial institutions are assurance of business confidence, protection of the investors and the prevention of a systemic meltdown. That much has been discussed in Chapter 1. Subsequently, Chapter 2 made the point that prudential regulation and supervision must rest on a solid framework; it also explained that because of globalisation and technology, this requires a new financial architecture.

As was shown in Chapter 3, historically the prevention of systemic risk is done through effective follow-up of the banking system's exposure all the way to the individual banks. When necessary, the supervisors wind down a business rather than risking a crash which can tear apart the financial fabric because of overleveraging, too many bad loans or other clear signs of mismanagement.

More complex is the protection of the investors because this, in many countries, is not the chief goal of supervisors, or even of legislators. One of the reasons as well as one of the consequences of this is that in some countries, particularly in Asia and Latin America, private participation in the stock market is at a very low level. Even in Continental Europe the general public does not trust its savings to the stock market.

However, it is not difficult to appreciate that all users of the financial system must have confidence in the banks, the brokers, the exchanges and the other companies with which they are working. Confidence underpins any profitable business, but without a strong supervisory system accidents in the financial industry will multiply, further reducing confidence and leaving investors confused as well as unprotected. What has happened in 1997 in East Asia and in 1998 in Russia documents this point.

Who should exercise the duties of bank supervision? If the G-10 countries are taken as a frame of reference, it must be admitted that there is no one answer to this query. Table 6.1 gives a bird's eye view of the differences which exist among the G-10 countries in regard to:

- responsible supervisory authority;
- the institution failing banks; and
- reliance on in-house examiners.

One of the major differences is that most European supervisory authorities rely in varying degrees on internal audit, and on external audit by certified public accountants, but there are exceptions: the Auditing Division of the

Table 6.1 Supervisory responsibility and the effective handling of failing banks

Country	*Responsible supervisor*	*Institution responsible for failing banks*	*Reliance on own examiners*
Belgium	Commission for Banking and Finance	Commission for Banking and Finance	No
Canada	Superintendent of Financial Institutions	Superintendent; Canada Deposit Insurance Corporation; and Department of Finance	Yes
France	Banking Commission*	Banque de France, and Ministry of Finance	Partially
Germany	Federal Banking Supervisory Bureau	Deutsche Bundesbank; Federal Banking Supervisory Bureau	Partially
Italy	Bank of Italy	Bank of Italy	Yes
Japan	Financial Supervisory Agency	Financial Supervisory Agency; Ministry of Finance; Bank of Japan	Partially
Luxembourg	Monetary Institute	Monetary Institute	No
Netherlands	Netherlands Bank	Netherlands Bank	Partially
Sweden	Financial Inspection Authority	Financial Inspection Authority; Riksbank	No
Switzerland	Federal Banking Commission	Federal Banking Commission	Partially
UK	Financial Services Authority	Financial Services Authority; Bank of England	No
USA	Federal Reserve, OCC, OTS, FDIC	FDIC	Yes

* The Banking Commission reports to the Bank of France, but its authority is shared with the Ministry of Finance.

Bank of Italy has its own examiners, and recently the Swiss Federal Banking Commission appointed its own examiners for big banks. This is the policy in the USA where the four major supervisory authorities (see Table 6.1) rely upon the findings of their own examiners. The same is true of the SEC.

2 A closer look at the different supervisory models in G-10 countries

In the UK, the Bank of England did not carry out on-site examinations, supervision being based on financial reports which relayed critical aspects of a bank's business and largely reflected the analysis of financial data. Since the mid-1980s these reports have been provided by external auditors. Prior to that date the Bank relied primarily on internal audits and statistics provided by the individual banks as well as interviews with senior management.

In all probability, the new FSA – which took over the bank supervision functions of the Bank of England and integrated them with those of the old FSA – will continue on the same path. The information external auditors provide includes an annual report on whether the Bank's accounting and financial records have been maintained adequately, as well as the status of internal controls.

The fact that British and other supervisory authorities do not use their own examiners in no way waives the responsibility of the bank's management for accuracy of financial statements and for the information provided to external auditors who report directly to supervisors. This practice, however, contrasts with that of the American supervisors who primarily rely on their own examiners (see Chapter 4).

In a way similar to the American practice, in Canada the Superintendent of Financial Institutions faces a legal obligation to conduct on-site examinations at least annually. In both the USA and in Canada such examinations are conducted primarily at the head office of the institution and focus on:

- financial reporting;
- capital adequacy;
- cash flow and liquidity;
- asset quality; and
- management quality.

North American examiners have full access to bank documents, receive both the internal and external audits, and maintain close contact with senior management. Supervisory authorities have the power to revoke the appointment of an external auditor if they are not satisfied with the results, and may require the certified public accountants to report on bank procedures affecting critical issues, which essentially amounts to a special examination.

In Germany, the Federal Banking Supervisory Bureau, which reports to the Ministry of Finance, primarily relies on annual financial statements for accuracy and observance of legal requirements. The external auditor is appointed by the bank but the Bureau may require appointment of another auditor if necessary for the purposes of prudential bank regulation.

As in most other European countries, while external auditors report to bank management, and have a professional duty of confidentiality, a copy of the annual auditing of the institution's financial reports must be sent directly to the supervisors (in this case to the Bureau and the local office of the central bank). The external auditor is under a legal obligation to inform the regulatory authority directly of serious problems found in an audit, or violations of legal or fiduciary responsibilities by management.

In Switzerland, the Federal Banking Commission licenses certified banking auditors. While each credit institution's board of directors appoints its public auditor from the list of licensed bank audit firms, the external auditor may only be confirmed or changed with Banking Commission's approval.

As in Germany, in Switzerland the Federal Banking Commission is an independent body directly appointed by the government and indirectly reporting to the Ministry of Finance. The Swiss National Bank addresses itself to monetary policy; it does not enter into matters of inspection and control of the banking industry.

Flexibility and adaptation are very important in fine-tuning the supervisory duties, and Switzerland provides a good example. Until recently the Federal Banking Commission, which has under its responsibility also brokers/dealers, investment funds and securities exchanges, consisted of five departments: Authorisations/Investment Funds; Supervision; Securities Markets; Legal Service; and Central Services. In July 1998 a new department was added entitled Big Banks, with its own examiners for auditing the UBS and Credit Suisse.

The careful reader will notice that with the institution of the Big Banks department there has been a change in supervisory policy. While regulation and supervision had previously depended on the report of external auditors, the new department will use its examiners to audit the big banks' books, as the Federal Reserve does with all commercial banks under its jurisdiction.

Until July 1998, the Federal Banking Commission used examiners only in connection with the control of mathematical models, developed and used by Swiss banks. This, too, was recent, following the 1996 Market Risk Amendment by the Basle Committee and the adoption of VAR models by the banking industry.

It is interesting to note that the first supervisory authority in Europe to take a rigorous look at the information technology of commercial banks under its jurisdiction has been the Audit Division of the Bank of Italy. Since the early 1970s, the Audit Division has sent its data processors to a credit institution to take control of the computer over a long weekend. This inspection has been polyvalent, not only controlling the files and the functioning of the centre, but also analysing the software in search for computer crime or other misdemeanours.

In France, the Commission Bancaire supervises both banks and securities firms. It also covers non-banks engaging in financial business. This integration of responsibilities, which is found in the UK's new FSA, highlights the current supervisory trend. Regulatory bodies try to keep pace with financial instrument innovators, which is indeed a challenging job requiring a special focus on both risk management standards, and sustained market transparency.

In Japan, bank supervision is the responsibility of the Financial Supervisory Agency, under the Ministry of Finance. The Supervisory Agency conducts on-site inspections in accordance with legal authority provided in the bank law and other legislation. The Bank of Japan also proceeds with examinations in accordance with contracts concluded with banks and other financial institutions that maintain accounts with the Bank. Such examinations are pursuant to its responsibility for the maintenance and strengthening of the credit system.

As in practically all other countries, beyond these on-site inspections of financial statements and other issues, Japanese banks that are publicly quoted are required to have external audits. Generally, however, in a policy similar to that prevailing in North America, Japanese supervisors rely upon their own examinations rather than financial reports audited by certified public accountants.

Whether the bank supervisor is the central bank, the Ministry of Finance or an independent authority, to perform its duties in an able manner it must be endowed with wide powers by the law of the land. Paper tigers do not go far in their control activities, as many countries such as South Korea, Indonesia, Thailand and Russia have recently found.

Take China as an example. Following years of fighting bureaucratic turf battles, the China Securities Regulatory Commission, the country's stock market watchdog, has finally got some real power. From 1 July 1999, the Securities Regulatory Commission is allowed to:

- control rampant insider trading;
- tighten listing requirements; and
- enforce big fines and prison terms on crooked brokers and company managers.

Theodore Roosevelt used to say: 'Speak softly and carry a big stick.' This is the best advice to be given to bank supervisors no matter what the authority for which they work is called or to which country it belongs. Rigorous action is not just the best way; it is the only way that can bring results.

3 Common elements in the supervision of banks and public companies

Banks must be supervised not only because they deal with financial instruments which are inherently risky, but also because they bear a maturity exposure by taking time deposits and issuing short-, medium- and long-term credit. The mismatch in fixed interest rates between deposits and loans sees to it that the institution can go under, as happened with the US savings and loans in the late 1980s.

There are of course other reasons for bank supervision, such as the risk of fraudulent financial reporting (see Chapter 1 on COSO), but most of these other reasons are also present with all publicly quoted companies. In some countries, one example being the USA, a special authority watches over companies which issue stock and are quoted in the exchange. This is the role of the SEC, to which reference has often been made in Part One and in the Introduction to this chapter. As its name implies, the role of a securities and exchange commission is to regulate, supervise and license the operators in the securities and exchange business. Basically, such a commission does not decide whether or not a company is financially solid; it simply ensures that everything is disclosed in the proper manner, and that there is transparency in the industry, permitting investors to make informed decisions. For instance, registered brokers/dealers must comply with SEC rules regarding customer reserve requirements and net capital computation. These rules oblige a firm to calculate and set aside the amount of funds needed to protect its clients' assets. Another SEC rule requires that the broker physically counts and confirms all client securities at least once a quarter, including all fully paid for and excess margin securities. Still another obliges the broker to disclose whether he has a vested interest, such as making an active trade, in some of the stocks his analysts recommend to his clients as 'buys'.

Whether we talk of the Fed or the SEC, whether the inspection is on-site or through external auditors, and whether the rules concern commercial banks, investment banks or other companies, there exist some basic principles which transcend the dichotomies and basically apply to every sort of supervision. These are principles of *accountability*, and their impact begins at the level of the board of directors.

Personal accountability should characterise the mission a bank's board of directors and senior management gives to itself. Every board should be alert in protecting the company's and shareholders' assets and value, and also in building public confidence in the bank and in complying with regulations. They should:

- avoid extraordinary risks with systemic implications;
- ensure financial reporting is truthful and correct; and
- wind down parts of the business when they are severely impaired.

For its part, to perform its duties in an able manner, the supervisory staff (internal auditors, external auditors, and the authority own examiners) must be well-trained. If even a few of its members lack the skills to exercise effective supervision, neither the public nor businesses will look at it with confidence. Nepotism has no place in prudential supervision. Supervisors must also have available the appropriate information technology and rocket science skills. Because a growing amount of supervisory know-how depends on state-of-the-art systems, methods and tools, falling behind in technology works to the detriment of regulatory functions. I would go a step further here: regulators should not only equip themselves with the best tools and systems available in the market, but also aim to bring the banks under their authority to a state-of-the-art level.

This was not part of the mission of regulatory bodies until quite recently, but because of the Basle Committee of Banking Supervision, EU directives and – most importantly – because of market forces, the frame of reference has changed. Technology is today the core business of any financial institution. Failure to control the banks' technology creates loopholes which are exploited by different banks to gain undue advantages and to bend the rules of competition. Supervision in a globalised market is only then effective if it can be exercised on a steadily maintained basis in terms of policies, systems, methods and tools.

Globalisation also poses other requirements. Though the supervisory authorities in each country may establish their own priorities in the light of the prevailing local economic, financial, social and political realities, they should not lose sight of the international regulatory prerequisites. Major discrepancies in rules of regulation (and also in technology) between one country and the next increase systemic risk.

In my view, among supervisory rules transcending national borders and local conditions is that external auditors should be required to report to the supervisors directly; regulatory authorities must be informed of a change in external auditors; if they do not have their own examiners, supervisors should have the authority to appoint extraordinary auditors to carry out specific investigations on their behalf; and in addition to the requirements of the annual audit, external auditors must be responsible for reporting on:

- the reliability of internal controls;
- the adequacy of information technology;
- large credits, and credit limits which might be violated;
- money laundering and insider trading.

External auditors should also be required to provide a description of, or opinion on, the bank's OTC trading practices as compared to the use of established exchanges; exposure to credit, liquidity and market risks; their approach to monitoring risk; and the adequacy of the bank's risk assessment systems and procedures.

A vital issue of supervision is the detection of irregularities. Both internal and external auditors must be responsible for informing the authorities of irregularities found in the course of their work. For instance, the law in France says that the public prosecutor must be informed of *serious* infringements, while in Switzerland, the external auditor has to inform the Banking Commission of *any* violation of law or any irregularity, along with the deadlines set for corrective action.

4 Financial examination programmes: on-site auditing versus monitoring

In its *Overview of Financial Examination Program Objectives* the Federal Reserve directs its examiners to evaluate compliance with rules and guidelines established by the Committee of Sponsoring Organisations of the Treadway Commission (see Chapter 1). The COSO framework against fraudulent financial reporting should guide their hand while reviewing the effectiveness of management, staffing, training, productivity and work flow, and also the computers and communications support systems, forms, files and records storage.

The COSO guidelines also dictate that internal control should be examined in a rigorous manner, to ensure proper maintenance of the depository institution's accounts. There are both requirements and penalties associated with internal controls, the most important rule being that the chairman of the board is personally accountable for the proper functioning of the bank's internal control system. Examiners are directed to review the appropriateness of the internal controls, and to undertake an assessment of current status, as well as to recommend improvements.

Recently this issue has also been raised in Europe. Among other authorities the Bank of England and the Bundesbank – as well as the Financial Services Authority and the Federal Supervisory Bureau – now require an audit of internal control. The difference is that in Europe this is to be performed by external auditors, which raises certain problems.

On-site examination carried out by the supervisory bodies' own examiners, conducted in accordance with North American regulatory rules, evaluates in greater depth (and as frequently as it is necessary) a number of channels which indirectly provide information on the adequacy of internal control, such as:

- counterparty risks;
- loan portfolio management;
- mismatch in interest rates;
- adequacy of loan loss reserves;

- credit underwriting;
- OTC and derivatives exposure;
- foreign currency exposure;
- other market risks taken with financial instruments.

Information obtained from these channels is enriched by other subjects coming under scrutiny: capital adequacy; quality of earnings; liquidity management; risk control; compliance with laws, rules and regulations; accuracy of financial reporting; and also quality of board supervision and quality of senior management.

While theoretically external auditors could perform this range of functions, practically this is not feasible. First and foremost, external auditors are third parties essentially outsourcing some of the bank's internal audit function. They also work in a certified public accountant relationship which imposes confidentiality requirements, and they are in competition with one another.

There is a human factor in terms of the confidentiality of information which enters the equation, and the risk of conflict of interest increases as the number of major external audit firms shrinks. Furthermore, the mammoth international accounting firms working as chartered accountants have been subject to prosecution for negligence during recent years, as the case of the Barings liquidators against Coopers & Lybrand (now Price Waterhouse Coopers) and several similar cases document.

Certified public accountants, therefore, are very reluctant to take on new responsibilities which involve subjective judgements and human error, such as the audit of internal controls demanded by European regulators. They prefer to keep to what they know best, and what is more objective: that is, auditing the books.

The interface of external auditors reduces the role of European regulators to *monitoring* – which is a lighter duty than examining – although they may get involved in periodic review of financial and other reports prepared by the bank. A main goal of monitoring is that of obtaining a pattern regarding regulatory compliance and financial reporting, though this might be extended into issues such as:

- fair lending;
- conflicts of interest;
- insider trading; or
- money laundering.

In contrast to monitoring, on-site inspections carried out by examiners working for the regulators pay attention to the qualifications of the bank's internal audit staff as well as the critical mass permitting it to perform its tasks adequately. Is the staff experienced in auditing and banking? Is a training programme in effect? Are members of the staff experienced in specialised areas such as information technology, currency exchange trading, interest rate decisions, loans and trust? Above all, has the audit function the full support of top management?

On-site examiners can perform a more rigorous analysis: for instance, the personality traits and responsibilities of the bank's chief auditor might be called into question. COSO questions include: is the chief auditor preparing a *time budget* for his people? Is the *best technology* used to assist the auditing function? Are plan (as opposed to actual time) analyses used as a guide in planning? Furthermore, is there an Audit Committee, whose authority also incorporates the supervision of the board? Does the depth coverage of the audits sufficient? Should there be greater detail?

Examiners who work for the regulatory authority also bring under a magnifying glass the auditing procedures. Do these procedures employ statistically valid sampling techniques? Is there an acceptable level of reliability and precision? Is the nature of the auditing policies and procedures independent of adverse influences or conflicts of interest? Have changes in auditing procedure been approved by the board of directors? Other possible questions include the following:

1. Do current procedures provide for resolution of exceptions and deficiencies?
2. Have the results of audits been promptly communicated to senior management and the board?
3. Has the Audit Committee been meticulous in investigating whether there is fraud?

In the course of their work, on-site examiners focus on whether the board and the Audit Committee promote internal (and external) auditors' impartiality and independence. Other critical queries address the soundness of risk assessment plans, policies and results, including whether or not they are appropriate for the bank's activities.

Examiners working for the supervisory authorities have statutory full and timely access to the supervised bank's internal audit resources. This includes personnel, reports, work papers as well as programmes and budgets. Based on these elements and on interviews, they assess the quality and scope of internal audit regardless of whether it is performed internally or outsourced. What I am writing is part and parcel of COSO.

The analysis of feedback and corrective action is just as important. Has the bank promptly responded to weaknesses identified? How many of these weaknesses concerned internal control? Are the board and senior management using valid standards when assessing the performance of internal audit? How good is the effectiveness of the bank's technological infrastructure? Are the audit activities consistent with the long range goals of the bank, with its globalisation, and/or with its latest new product offerings?

Finally, a significant advantage of on-site examination programmes is their timing flexibility. Monitoring through external auditors is usually done once per year, but on-site examinations can be annual, quarterly or more frequent: whatever the situation warrants. In mid-1998, for instance, the Federal Reserve Bank of Boston had on the critical list a one-digit number of commercial banks which were under frequent scrutiny because of their financial condition.

5 Benefits derived from a collaborative effort in banking supervision

Much of the effort in a prudential supervision is focused on investigating ways in which regulations can be used to promote sustainable financial well-being, which is able to serve a growing segment of the population and also to capitalise on technological innovation. The application of regulations should not be prescriptive but creative, and centre on:

- the banking industry's capacity for change;
- risk and return with new financial instruments;
- rigorous internal controls and audits;
- the kinds of technological responses that provide a cutting edge; and
- the form of rules that bring to bear desired results in swamping systemic risk.

Regulation should be designed to encourage new product and process development rather than to snow under initiative, or be used as an excuse for perpetuating the diffusion of a suboptimal technology into the banking industry. Regulation should also be instrumental in bending resistance to change. I personally look at regulation as a problem-solving process rather than as a constraint.

It is absolutely evident that an effective system of regulation requires standards. The Washington-based Group of 30 has proposed an industry forum able to come forward with a suggested set of standards which could become universally applicable through the G-10 countries. The concept is that supervisors ask the commercial and investment banks to develop the proposals themselves; these proposals would be amended or approved by supervisory authorities which would subsequently control the banks on the basis of such standards.

A procedure by which commercial and investment banks as well as other institutions participated in standards-setting should not be considered as self regulation. On the contrary, the supervisors need to be, and to be seen to be, in the driving seat. But several creative ideas can come out of such collaboration, particularly concepts which are based on common sense.

A major benefit could be a global normalisation of supervisory procedures which should, to my mind, lead regulators towards the use of their own examiners, as happens in Canada and in the USA. Supervisory standards should be like a good system of laws: few but unambiguous. Let me outline six core values in standards-setting.

1. *A change in the institution's management increases the risks taken by the bank.* The people composing the bank's senior management establish through their decisions and their actions a certain pattern. A new management usually alters that pattern and, typically exposure increases until the new executive committee finds its balance.

2. *Capital is no substitute for effective risk management.* Unless the bank's senior management knows what the risks are, and unless it has in place a system to capture exposure and act upon this information, it cannot control the risks being taken in the four corners of the organisation. Capital adequacy is necessary, but it is no substitute for effective risk control.

3. *Financial institutions are responsible for their own health.* It is not the supervisors' duty to hold up the bank. This is the job of its own board and senior management. Neither is bank supervision meant to be finding no failures: a certain failure rate is unavoidable. Leaving aside the fact that zero failures are neither sustainable nor realistic, such a policy would lead to immobility.

4. *Statistical quality control is a good method for assessing management quality and for studying decision patterns.* The financial industry has been too slow to adopt and implement statistical quality control charts by variables, by attributes and by the percentage which is defective (see D.N. Chorafas, *Statistical Processes and Reliability Engineering*, D. Van Nostrand, Princeton, NJ, 1960); yet such methods have given first-class results in the manufacturing industry for over 55 years. Only when we measure the quality of services and plot the resulting pattern are we able to judge the outgoing quality level.

5. *Very detailed rules and/or complex standards provide an unsatisfactory regime.* Rule-books with 1000 pages typically include too many opportunities to turn the rules around. The more complex are the supervisory standards and directives or the clauses, the better is the chance given to the different parties to find their way out of them.

6. *Level playing fields are an unnecessary impediment to effective supervision.* Level playing fields are something industry wants rather than something the regulator needs for the effective performance of his duties. Banks should have the freedom to use the resources at their disposition in the best possible manner in order to gain competitive advantages. What the regulator is interested in seeing is the system of checks and balances which gives the message that senior management is in charge.

Between the lines of these half-dozen core values, the careful reader will detect a great deal of the benefits brought to the banking industry through effective supervision. The basic concept underpinning these values is the steady and orderly management of change. Over the years, few banks have indeed succeeded in managing change, and these are today the leading institutions.

6 The risk of conflicting rules and regulations

Jacques Chirac once said that too many taxes kill the state's tax intake. The same is true of regulations. There are five different regulators supervising a money centre bank in the USA: for example, J.P. Morgan is inspected by the Fed, OCC, FDIC, SEC and CFTC. Not only does this take time but it also creates a risk of conflicting rules. Even more serious is the problem of conflicting regulations which, to a large extent, have been an outgrowth of globalisation.

A money centre bank operating in, say, 30 countries has to cope with an equal number of rule-books (which sometimes conflict with one another), and with an even bigger number of regulators and supervisors. In the end this is counterproductive, because global banks have the lawyers and the experts who know how to circumvent, or even optimise, the bewildering arrangement of conflicting rules.

Let me repeat the sense of this statement: both internally in one nation and in a global sense, regulatory rules and the means for prudential supervision need streamlining. This starts happening in the national landscape. Until the early 1998 reorganisation of the authorities supervising financial institutions (see Chapter 7 on the new FSA), in London prudential supervision was exercised by the Bank of England, the Securities and Futures Authority (the old FSA), the Personal Investment Authority (PIA), the Investment Management Regulatory Organisation (IMRO), and other entities.

As we will see in Chapter 7, with an example from the UK, the need for an integrated approach to supervision is promoted by the fact that the financial services industry has evolved rapidly over the last few decades and has grown in complexity. Distinctions between the various types of financial institution (commercial banks, brokers, investment firms, insurance companies and so on) have blurred. A recent survey in Europe suggested the existence of 800 financial conglomerates in that continent alone.

The challenge is even greater in the global landscape where the financial industry is confronted by an overlap of different regulations, some of which are a subset of another while others are complementary, but there is also a good deal of contradiction between these different rules. Figure 6.1 gives a bird's eye view of the set of rules facing the European universal bank and its activities, from loans to securities, and to derivative financial instruments.

Some of the reasons are historical as every country classically had its own regulations and accounting standards. If this country is a member state of the EU, its banks must also observe the CAD and other rules from Brussels

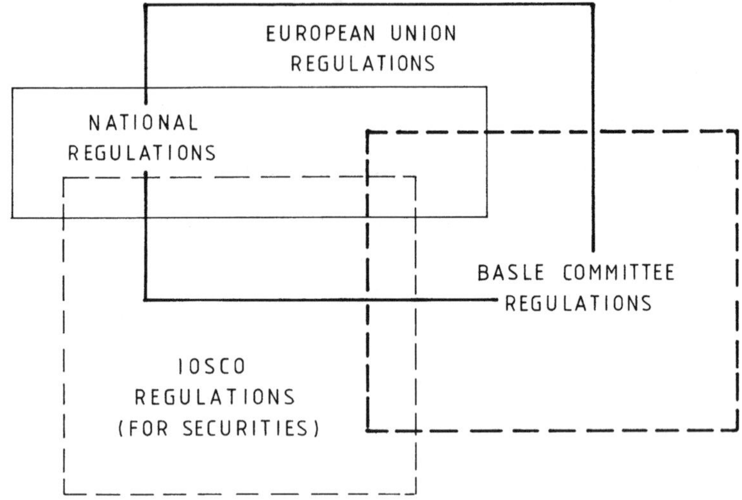

Figure 6.1 Partly overlapping regulations do not provide a crisp financial reporting structure

(see Chapter 11). Furthermore, international institutions are subject to the regulations by the Basle Committee of BIS and IOSCO.

The action by the Basle Committee and IOSCO is, in principle, benevolent. Both try to bring to life some universal standards and rules of conduct. But these do not supersede existing national rules of bank supervision, and so the dichotomies currently present not only remain but also tend to get deeper.

Unavoidably, there is another problem. Because rules and regulations evolve over time, in the absence of a single universal authority for financial institutions they continue to diverge. As an example, Table 6.2 presents in a nutshell the evolution which has taken place during the last 10 years in a transborder sense in terms of capital requirements.

Of course, in spite of their temporal and structural incompatibilities, all these rules and regulations have common objectives: for instance, to ensure that financial institutions provide sufficient capital against their credit risks and market risks, and achieve a cross-border regulatory treatment which is as consistent as possible; but global finance requires a single body of well thought-out global supervisory rules which is comprehensive, complete and presents no contradictions. The goal of all regulators should be to define such a common framework for measuring and monitoring risk exposures, whether these show up in the trading book or in the banking book.

As cannot be stated too often, the problem is that today's regulations are not co-ordinated through a single global authority, with the result that

Table 6.2 Milestones in the evolution of capital requirements

April 1988	Basle Capital Accord (Cooke Ratio)
December 1989	Solvency Ratio Directive by EU
March 1993	Capital Adequacy Directive (CAD), by EU
April 1993	Consultancy proposal on market risk (working paper) by Basle Committee
March 1995	Amsterdam Agreement by EU on Capital Adequacy
April 1995	Revised proposal by Basle Committee to include models in calculating Market Risk
January 1996	Market Risk Amendment by Basle Committee
September 1997	Modification to Market Risk Amendment, for Treatment of Specific Risk
1998	CAD II by EU, integrating all changes included in modified Market Risk Amendment
2000?	Expected new regulations redefining the computation of capital adequacy in terms of diversification and other criteria, based on 'A New Capital Adequacy Framework'

national rules and regulations are not compatible among themselves. As I have already pointed out, this does not even happen in Euroland because the ECB was given no bank supervisory duties.

The fact that in the EU responsibility for bank supervision and provision of liquidity in the event of a bank panic will officially remain with national regulators and national central banks is part of the problem, not part of the solution. Already, however, many experts admit that in the event of a serious crisis the ECB would have to step in, and also that bank supervision will eventually be handled at the regional level, rather than piecemeal nationally.

A similar argument is valid in connection with the regulation of global markets. Dr Henry Kaufman, a Wall Street financial consultant, would like to see a Board of Overseers of international financial markets which would develop global financial standards, as well as supervise and evaluate institutions under its authority. The British have also proposed a permanent Standing Committee for Global Financial Regulation to do this job.

What these initiatives help to demonstrate is that experts, governments and bank regulators are waking up to the wisdom of a clear and unambiguous convergence between the different sets of supervisory rules and methodologies, at least at four levels of reference:

- conceptual and theoretical supervisory infrastructure;
- requirements of audits and examinations including internal control;

- quantitative and qualitative risk measurement solutions; and
- the nature of supervisory follow-up for pro-active reasons.

While there might be, for some years, differences as to detail, there should be no differences concerning basic principles: for instance, the minimum internal control standards, the value of the parameters entering a risk calculation, the accuracy and sophistication of models being used, the level of technology being used for more advanced reporting practices, and so on. The goal should be to inform senior management both on business and on exposure the way Figure 6.2 suggests:

- from any part of the world;
- with any client;
- with any product; and
- at any time.

Tier-1 banks have already done this for their internal planning and control purposes, but the majority of institutions are still in the Dark Ages in terms of methodology and of technology. One of the better examples is that of the State Street Bank which makes available to its senior management virtual balance sheets which are fully updated every 30 minutes. The next goal is to have updates available every 5 minutes.

Real-time information technology and modelling are the cornerstone of such solutions. The expansion of the domains where models are used will, in the coming years, make a fairly significant difference in the sophistication of management, all the way through to capital adequacy and risk control. Through simulation approaches, tier-1 banks will be able to integrate credit risk and market risk adding up all potential losses by major client and deriving capital requirements which are future business oriented. Other factors will also come to the foreground: for instance, bringing into the picture settlement risk, and large exposures.

CAD already has a clause intended to prevent a bank from having a large exposure with a single counterparty. Also, while the previous regulation merely included commodity risk, CAD II stresses it, thereby permitting a more comprehensive approach to risk management. The next major step in regulation, ideally through the Basle Committee, will be the individual computation of capital requirements taking into account, on a factual and documented basis, the diversification of a bank's portfolio, and prevailing leveraging through derivatives and other instruments.

The way to bet is that banks who carefully diversify their commitments will see their capital requirements reduced. On the other hand, institutions with geared positions will have to put aside a higher level of capital for prudential reasons. This is not to be confused with what has become known

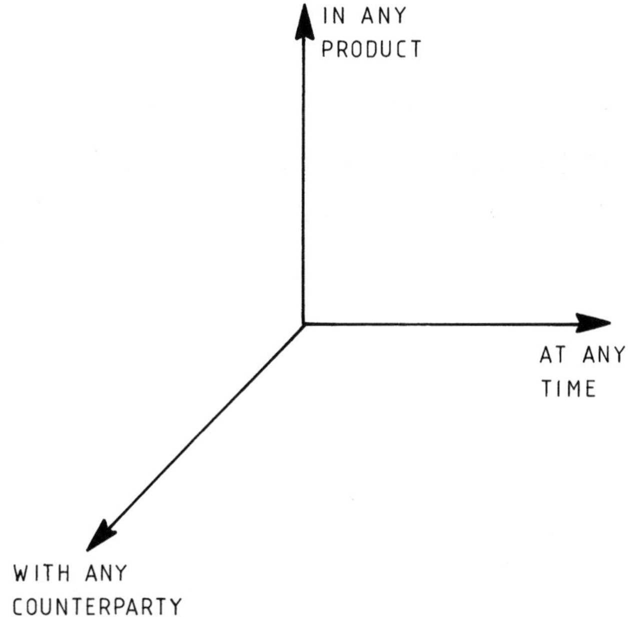

Figure 6.2 Technological support should be provided for deals in any currency, country, industry and industrial sector

as the 'precommitment' approach, which would have allowed the institution to precompute its capital adequacy needs.

Ideally, also, regulation will address the issue of intraday risk management, reflecting the fact that current approaches to the control of exposure are too coarse-grained in timescale. A three-dimensional structure for technological support is suggested in Figure 6.2. By using sophisticated models, intraday data feeds and database mining a bank can keep a steady watch over its exposure. Intraday solutions are necessary to provide senior management with an instantaneous visualisation of risks taken in connection with the bank's operations.

Such a level of detail, of focus, and of rapidity in visualisation and response can in no way be achieved with currently prevailing methods which were primarily designed for average banks, with average technology and with an average management. Please keep in mind that high-technology solutions do not come about as a matter of course. Banks able to move ahead of the bunch will evidently have a major competitive advantage, but they will have to work for it all the way, from cultural change to technological preeminence.

7

The Integration of Supervisory Duties by the Financial Services Authority: An Example from Britain

1 Introduction

Until the reorganisation which took place in the UK and the Financial Services and Markets (FSM) Bill, published in draft by the Treasury on 30 July 1998, supervisory duties in the UK were divided between different agencies: the Bank of England had authority for the prudential supervision of banks, acting as their lead regulator; the Securities and Futures Authority (old SFA) was responsible for their securities activities; the PIA for the banks' sales practices, also covering insurance; IMRO for fund management; and there were also five other authorities which, as shown in Figure 7.1, have now merged into one organisation.

With restructuring, all this comes under one new body, the Financial Services Authority (new SFA), which was set up in October 1997, with a mechanism permitting the co-ordination of all the regulatory activity concerning British financial institutions and their services which, as everywhere else in the G-10 countries, is becoming increasing complex. The new provisions also cover the UK operations of foreign institutions.

FSA is a private company limited by guarantee, with regulatory functions conferred on it by statute. In addition to the responsibilities and powers of a financial services regulator, the FSA will also take over the authorisation and supervision of financial services provided by those professions regulated by the recognised Professional Bodies and the statutory functions of mutual organisations.

The need for an integrated approach to regulation has been underlined in section 6, Chapter 6. To appreciate the evolution towards an integrated approach in the UK one has to remember that the financial regulatory system has attempted to keep up with the development of the banking industry, but this can hardly be done in an effective manner when the supervisory system itself is fragmented, and therefore costly and inefficient.

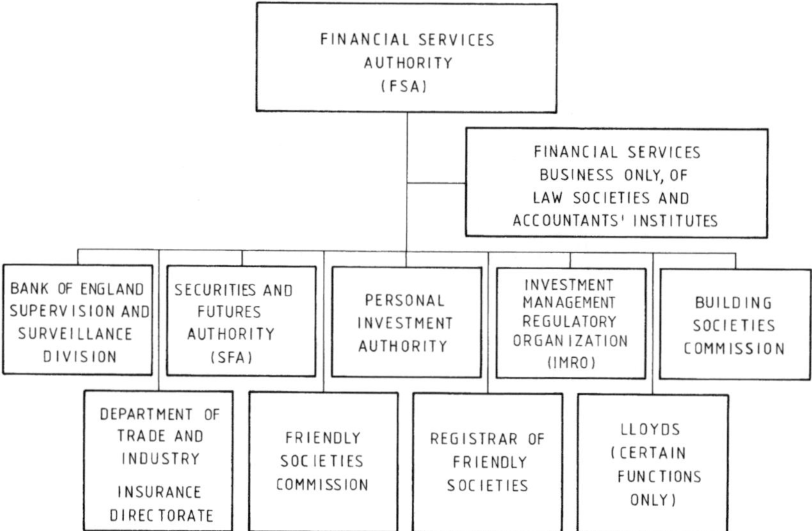

Figure 7.1 Formerly independent regulatory agencies, divisions and functions which merge into the new agency

Let me add a bit of historical perspective. Britain has seen four separate acts devoted to financial regulation during the 1980s: the Insurance Companies Act of 1982, the Financial Services Act of 1986, the Building Societies Act of 1986, and the Banking Act of 1987. In 1992 came the friendly Societies Act, the regulatory aspects of which have been included in the FSM Bill.

The government's aim is to harmonise the provisions of the previous acts and create a single integrated regulatory agency which can eliminate present unnecessary distinctions between different sectors of the financial industry. This will reduce duplication. Ideally, it will also allow for a relatively flexible, quick and systematic introduction of new regulation. However, the regulatory functions of the exchanges and clearing house and of the Occupational Pensions Regulatory Authority still remain separate.

2 Understanding the fact that regulation is in full evolution

Many people, including financial experts, are of the opinion that regulatory ways and means never really change. These have classically been: auditing the books of banks and other institutions, ensuring there is no fraud in financial statements, building market confidence, protecting the investor and the consumer, and other worthy and necessary tasks. Similarly, there is a widespread opinion that financial instruments never change. Both notions are awfully wrong.

'Clothes and automobiles change every year', said Paul M. Mazur of Lehman Brothers:

> But because the currency remains the same in appearance, though its value steadily declines, most people believe that finance does not change. Actually, debt financing changes like everything else. We have to find new models in financing, just as in clothes and automobiles, if we want to stay on top. We must remain inventive architects of the money business. (Joseph Wechsberg, *The Merchant Bankers*, Pocket Books/Simon & Schuster, New York, 1966)

The same is true of the ways and means of regulation and supervision.

A 1996 example from the regulatory activities of the Bank of England, and the regulatory changes associated with them, can serve to prove this point. At the end of July 1996, the Bank of England announced a major step forward in the way it regulated banks. This step followed on, to a large measure, from the recommendations made by Arthur Andersen.

Since Barings collapsed in February 1995 after amassing £860 million ($1.4 billion) of trading losses, there have been many outside assertions that poor supervision by the Bank of England was partly to blame for the Barings bankruptcy. Arthur Andersen was hired as an external auditor in the aftermath of Barings. The Bank of England agreed to the report's recommendations which constituted a programme of change. The British bank regulators also commented that weaknesses existed in the way central banks and other financial control authorities keep watch over their charges, themselves included. A major reason why the old regulatory regime has been outdated, and this is true all over the globe, is that money centre banks and global securities firms have developed and use far-flung networks (see Chapter 1) as well as employing lots of rocket scientists (see D.N. Chorafas, *Rocket Scientists in Banking*, Lafferty Publications, London and Dublin, 1995). National regulators simply do not keep up with the necessary technological resources that would allow them to control the funds traffic going through the networks of the commercial or investment banks, or to cope with the sophistication of their financial models. This is a 'minus' for regulation.

The trading risks that sank Barings occurred in Singapore and Osaka, not in London, and they were executed through networks. This underlines the need for closer co-ordination between regulators world-wide. In their Frankfurt meeting of 20 May 1996 the G-10 central bankers agreed to provide such co-ordination, but such initiatives should not stop at the G-10 level (see also Chapter 8).

The second major outcome of the 20 May 1996 meeting of the G-10 bank governors has been a co-operation accord between central bankers, regulators, and securities and exchange commissions. Barings, like many other modern financial conglomerates, owned both a bank (which took deposits) and a securities firm which assumed trading risks. However, most regulators are still divided along traditional industry lines (a condition which, in the UK, changes with the new FSA). At the same time, the different supervisory groups are struggling to understand the complex trading risks that banks run with derivatives and other instruments in full evolution. According to an official report into Barings' collapse published in July 1995, regulators admitted to Barings executives in February 1993 that they did not really understand Baring Securities. This is indeed something which needs to be corrected. Because the banking business changes so rapidly, it is absolutely necessary to have intensive life-long training programmes for regulators.

Training bankers and supervisors for the real world is a demanding business. A fast-evolving financial market wants professionals who not only understand fundamentals but are also familiar with new product development, risk control and high technology (see Chapter 10), making bankers capable of multi-disciplinary work.

While traditional education provides the basic theories bankers need, it has been less successful at teaching other skills which historically have not been learned in the classroom. The mastery of these requires training at every step of the financial process, from the conception of a new product idea, to its design, implementation, and operation, and to its measurement and control. All bankers, no matter what their specialisation, need to be given an understanding of complex market behaviour, the interactions involved in multiple disciplines, and the practice of working in a modern team-based financial environment where commitments are made in a split second. I see these requirements as part of the supervisory authority's responsibilities.

To educate bankers for the real world, it is not enough to change a list of topics to be covered from time to time, or to choose a new syllabus. The traditional education in banking and finance is based on the breakdown of knowledge into disconnected pieces. It only becomes more focused and specific in the longer term through practice. But the pressure of everyday practice does not permit the banker to appreciate that today's financial world is not only globalised and increasingly interactive but also *non-linear*.

The fact that, following the Andersen study on the weaknesses of current regulation, the Bank of England recruited more supervisors and technical experts is positive. Less well known is whether these new recruits were appropriately trained in non-linear thinking. The Bank also developed new ways of monitoring the risks that institutions take. Still, this is only part of the measures required.

While these comments are made in the aftermath of Barings as a prelude to the discussion on the FSM Bill, their context is much more general. So far central bankers and regulators have relied mainly on the simpler types of qualitative and quantitative analyses:

- measuring a bank's capital adequacy;
- looking into its biggest loan exposures;

- inspecting the liquidity in its treasury; and
- checking the volatility of its portfolio.

Regulation and supervision is bound to be weak and ineffectual without high-technology supports (see also section 5). Risk modelling is a new culture and therefore it has to be evaluated through a multiple perspective. Is the sophistication of the model used by the bank commensurate with the instrument? With the timing of the transactions? With the volume of the transactions? With the financial commitment these transactions represent?

Only recently have people started to appreciate that spotting weak management and poor internal controls is also a very important task for regulators (see section 6). This type of qualitative analysis is not yet part of all central banks' culture, and neither is rocket science an integral part of the supervisory armoury.

Judging the quality of a bank's internal controls and management skill requires much more than supervisors visiting their charges more often. There should also be regulatory procedures explaining how the central banks might better control the exposure undertaken by commercial and investment banks through their international operations. These comments are written in a constructive way. The new SFA, in my judgement, should go well beyond the integration of the activities of the regulatory bodies which have merged into it.

3 Fundamental changes in the Financial Services and Markets Bill

As we have already seen, the most significant change which took place in British banking in 1997/98 was the fact that a single statutory regulator, the FSA, replaced the former constellation of regulators. FSA has been endowed with a coherent set of regulatory powers, providing:

- a single regime for authorisation; and
- a single regime for supervision.

Risk-based audit will probably characterise its approach to regulation (see section 5): SFA will apply fines to those committing market abuse, as well as for breaches of listing rules and other misdemeanours. But there will be an appeals tribunal (see section 4).

The FSM Bill specifies that FSA should make arrangements for the independent investigation of complaints made against it. If a complaint is found to be justified, the independent investigator has the power to appoint his own team and make public recommendations as to the corrective action to be undertaken by FSA.

The new legislation in the UK pays particular attention to financial promotion activities. It distinguishes between firms and persons which are authorised and those which are not. Those authorised are able to engage in financial promotion, subject to FSA's rules. Failure to comply with these provisions will be a criminal offence punishable by a fine and/or by up to two years in prison. Contracts entered into as a result of prohibited promotions will be unenforceable, and investors and consumers who have unknowingly got into such contracts will be able to claim compensation.

The five main compensation schemes prevailing in Britain before the Bill are being replaced by a single Financial Services and Markets Compensation Scheme. Tax treatment of the contributions made to this scheme will be the same as has been the case in the past for contributions to the five main schemes.

FSA will be required to meet its regulatory objectives in a way which takes account of compensation, but which also preserves regulatory effectiveness. The Financial Services Act of 1986 included arrangements for competition scrutiny. The Financial Services and Markets Bill gives FSA similar power, extending it so that it applies to all sectors of industry. For its part, the Treasury has new powers which enable a wider range of authorised open-ended investment companies (OEICs) to be formed, and institute pooled unauthorised open-investment companies (PUNCs).

The LSE remains Britain's competent authority for listing, including the maintenance of an official list of securities which may be traded on investment exchanges as well as the monitoring of issuers' adherence to the listing rules. The Bill also introduces fines for breaches of listing rules, and addresses the issue of more effective regulation of those who acquire influence over investment firms. Furthermore, the FSM Bill establishes a common approach to winding up and insolvency across all branches of the financial services industry. It also addresses the crucial issue of protection of confidential information, with the previous set of rules being simplified and rationalised.

The new rules target a consistent use of external auditors and actuaries in helping banks and other institutions to ensure that their books are in order, their financial reporting is reliable, and they have adequate controls. External auditors are projected as a means of reducing the amount of direct supervision from FSA, which is a way of saying that for the time being the new regulatory authority will not have its own examiners. The tracking down and prosecution of insider trades will be taxing but also rewarding in terms of public confidence; for instance, in Britain insider trading was not a criminal offence in the 1980s, but now it is.

Considering what the SEC had to do to combat insider trading, in Britain this job would require an enormously rich database, intelligent artefacts, patterning programs and datamining software. SEC's database features not only the family members of all company directors including spouses, children, parents, sisters, brothers and cousins, but also their old college roommates and other friends.

A trading pattern which may superficially look legal may turn out to be illegal after due experimentation, so trading patterns must be analysed through computers and checked against a vast network of possible connections.

A key question often asked when a new regime is put in place is: what about the costs? So early in the implementation of the new rules it is difficult to assess the cost burden of the integrated regulatory system and its tools. The British government hopes that, in principle, the new structure will reduce duplication and therefore costs; on the other hand, a number of changes could have significant costs attached to them. An example is the requirement to detect money laundering. What is suggested as a solution is a much more rigorous approach than that of current requirements: to recognise it and report it. Quite likely there will be both administrative and technological costs attached to the execution of this directive (which, however, is welcome).

A similar statement is valid in regard to the projected integration of risk-based approaches to supervision into a coherent system. This particular application is projected to materialise in year 2000. In order to be executed in the proper manner, it will require a significant amount of high technology and rocket science.

Though the Bill does not specifically say so (and this is an omission), in the next couple of years SFA – like every other regulator, particularly of the G-10 countries – will have to address the supervisory challenges posed by IBC. This, too, will call for copious amounts of technology and brainpower (see also Chapter 1). It is a domain where being thrifty is the wrong kind of economy, because it will put the regulators at the bottom of the food chain.

4 The new powers of the Financial Services Authority

The FSA will become the single regulator for UK financial services upon the entry into force of the FSM Bill, which may be after 1 January 2000. Until then, the FSA is directly responsible for the authorisation and prudential supervision of banks, a responsibility transferred to it on 1 January 1998 from the Bank of England under the Bank of England Act 1998. FSA also has authority over the wholesale markets regime for money market institutions, listed under section 43 of the Financial Services Act 1986, and the integration of self-regulating organisations (SFA, IMRO and PIA).

In addition FSA is responsible for the recognition of investment exchanges and clearing houses; the listing and supervision of money market institutions providing settlement arrangements under section 171 of the Companies Act 1989; and the authorisation and supervision of certain investment firms which include nine service companies providing services to the financial sector as part of the infrastructure that supports markets (for instance, as information vendors or clearing entities). At present, only ECHO falls under section 171 of the Companies Act 1989; this is the foreign exchange clearing house providing a cross-border, multilateral netting facility for foreign exchange spot and forward contracts. FSA will authorise commercial and investment entities to carry on specific classes of financial services. Should a company wish to expand its business into a different field, it will have to apply to FSA for further authorisation, with the regulators retaining the power to decide whether or not to grant such authorisation based on the company's past record.

The governing body of FSA consists of a chairman and members appointed (and, if necessary, removed) by the Treasury. The Bill also instructs that FSA must set up a committee of non-executive members, to be drawn from the ranks of the governing body. Note that there is a significant difference in status between the old FSA and the new FSA. Under the Financial Services Act 1986, the powers given to the old FSA were resumable by the Treasury. By contrast, the FSM Bill gives functions directly to the new FSA.

The committee of non-executive members is essentially a supervisory body which will review FSA's internal control, monitor its performance against the requirement that it uses its resources efficiently and effectively, and set the pay of FSA's chairman and members of the governing body. This supervisory committee will report to the Treasury on an annual basis and its report will be laid before Parliament.

Such reports will no doubt be factual and documented since SFA deals with the different sorts of market abuse which may occur in the UK. The Bill directs that the FSA prepare and publish a Code, detailing the sort of behaviour that constitutes market abuse. The new regulators will be able to impose fines on companies and persons not only because of their actions but also because of their failure to act, which may lead to abuse of the market.

Though it may be only an indirect example of the point made in the preceding paragraph, it is appropriate to bring to the reader's attention a study by the FSA which hit the financial press on 15 February 1999. This study shows that investors in a typical unit trust (mutual fund) have to put in £1.55 ($2.36) to get the equivalent return to that on £1 ($1.66) invested directly. Much of the loss to investors, totalling several billion pounds a year, is caused by poor management and excessive charges. Among the excessive charges are those for sales and marketing, adding up to an exorbitant price for retail investing. These figures suggested by FSA are disputed by the UK fund management industry which is fighting for its survival. The Association of Unit Trusts and Investment Funds, the industry body, suggested: 'The interesting question is what they [the FSA] do with it because there is not much point in producing this if it is not acted on.'

Bankers and financial analysts in London were also to comment that the creation of an integrated FSA with the power to police its huge constituency is a complex and demanding task. It was stated that the experts who helped to draft the Financial Services Bill were well aware of the perils that they face, particularly:

- the risk of leaving loopholes which some people and companies might slip through; and
- the opposite risk of being too heavy handed in constricting financial markets.

In fact, some senior executives in the City are concerned that the new legislation gives the regulators too much power, while it does not insist on a proper separation of their role as investigators of market abuse, prosecutors of rule breakers, and disciplinary authorities. These concerns are answered, at least in part, through the constitution of the Financial Services and Markets Appeals (FSMA) Tribunal.

The regulated community has the right of appeal to the FSMA Tribunal against decisions by FSA. The tribunal is separate from the FSA and is run as part of the court service by the Lord Chancellor's Department, which selects appointees from amongst the legal profession and experts in the financial industry. On points of law, there will also be a right of appeal from the FSMA Tribunal to the courts.

A system of checks and balances is necessary to counterbalance the rule-making powers because the FSM Bill provides FSA with a wide authority to make any of the rules it considers essential to the protection of market confidence and of the investors subject to compliance with its regulatory objectives and notification to the Treasury. For example, FSA will be free to amend or revoke rules and make new ones in response to market developments and because of specific business conducted by financial institutions.

Finally, while until the Bill comes into force legal responsibility for the exercise of regulatory power remains with the regulatory bodies that will retain their independent responsibilities, the new FSA has created a management structure to cover all of its eventual line of authority. Most of the staff of the old FSA and some other entities immediately integrated into the new FSA and became its employees on 1 June 1998. Other staff (for instance, of the Insurance Directorate, Building Societies Commission, Friendly Societies Commission and Registry of Friendly Societies) became employees of FSA in January 1999.

5 The Financial Services Authority and the role of regulators in controlling risk

The concern the FSA expresses in regard to the exposure taken by institutions is highly relevant because of the Authority's own prime mission: ensuring that the financial fabric remains intact. As with other bank supervisors, prevention of systemic meltdown will be accomplished by means of:

- establishing rules and guidelines;
- proceeding through rigorous inspection; and
- looking after risk management through appropriate directives.

Supervisors, too, wish banks to be profitable, because profitability is a condition of survival; but taking extravagant risks in the name of greater profitability is a sign of trouble. Also, arrogance or cowardice by a chief executive or his assistants is a sign of past and future mistakes which endanger the survival of the institution.

In 1953 I had a professor of banking at UCLA who taught his students that when the boss of an institution becomes nervous, the chances are that he has something to hide: perhaps he knows his bank is in financial trouble. FSA acknowledges that firms can go bankrupt, but also appreciates that this probability increases with weak management. There is a paradox in financial regulation and supervision, because while business is an enterprise that makes no sense without taking credit risks and market risks, the control of risk should be a central objective of every firm (which is far from being the case).

The role of the regulator is that of looking at credit risk and market risk within the framework of each of the financial institutions which it supervises and the branch in which it belongs. This rests on two pillars:

- capital adequacy for financial staying power in times of trouble; and
- the evaluation of the exposure being assumed, both in absolute and in relative terms.

Up to a point the concepts expressed by these two bullets overlap, but only up to a point because capital is not a substitute for good risk management, just as an insurance company is not compensation for drunk driving. Few firms have the experience, and the wisdom, to understand this reference. In a similar manner, only top-tier senior management appreciates that control practices must be tuned to the size and complexity of the institution; without this, there is an uncontrolled amount of exposure, including reputational risk.

In the course of the First International Conference on Risk Management in the Banking Industry (London, 17–19 March 1997), Dr Andrew Street, head of the market risk management group of the then SFA (predecessor of the FSA) insisted on the fact that able management rests not only on understanding the trading mandate but also the risks involved at all levels of the firm. This requires:

- a clearly written policy regarding the magnitude of each type of risk;
- accurate and timely risk information, which reaches unaltered top management;
- liquidity adjustments effected through appropriate modelling; and

- the provision of adequate reserves to enhance the survivability of the institution.

The best route to follow after the satisfaction of requirements implied by these four points is through an independent risk management organisation which can ensure not only timely measurement of exposure but also price testing facilities, risk modelling and the quality of information technology.

As I never tire of repeating, among the factors underpinning high quality of information are real-time processing of transactions; real-time calculation of exposure; the existence of any-to-any intelligent networks; requirements connected to data accuracy and integrity; database mining facilities; and rigorous security measures and countermeasures.

In banking, security has many aspects: one of them is classical. Recently the story of Rabbi Prushenowski was published (*Time*, 7 December 1998). He was being investigated by Israeli authorities when Holland's ING Bank presented evidence of a $50 million scam. According to the Dutch institution's lawyer, Prushenowski deposited cheque and promissory notes convincing ING's management he was very rich. The bank let him cash cheques not yet cleared, including a $50 million cheque drawn on the Republic Bank of Granada; there was no such bank. Institutions which fall for such old tricks are not only highly imprudent but also willing to be raped.

Theoretically this is a matter to interest the bank's board of directors, not the regulators (in this case the Netherlands Bank). Practically a swindle involving that amount shows poor judgement and stupid management, which is a frontline concern of supervisory authorities.

There are also new ways to take people for a ride, including using the Internet. An example is given in Chapter 8 with *day trading,* in connection with IBC. The new communications media offer many ways – some subtle, others less so – to mishandle accounts. Supervisory authorities must have specialists with skills which can penetrate these. While cases like the $50 million at ING Bank will continue to occur innovations in swindling by using the networks may surpass them both in frequency and in the severity of losses.

6 The supervisory scrutiny of poor management practices

Well-managed banks appreciate that volatility and liquidity correlate (see D.N. Chorafas, *Understanding Volatility and Liquidity in Financial Markets,* Euromoney Books, London, 1998). Is the model we use addressing both of them individually and in conjunction with one another? Is the modelling process properly accounting for liquidity? Is it reflecting the fact that liquidity has the habit of hitting at the worst possible moment? These are queries regulators should ask when examining the technology of an institution under their authority, and the way it is used by senior management.

Questioning the 'obvious' is also the best strategy in regard to pricing sophisticated financial products. Price testing may be defective not only because the pricing model is inadequate but because the assumptions bankers make are incorrect, simply lenient, or designed to promote sales without accounting for risk. An example is the often used volatility simile, which is much more wishful thinking than a fact.

When they test the output of the models of commercial and investment banks, supervisors should ensure the institution's management realises that models are approximations to reality and contain assumptions which do not necessarily hold true when compared against facts. This brings about the need for stress testing, both of models and of the assumptions underpinning them.

These are crucial aspects of modern bank supervision which interest all regulators. They fit well with proposals which a few years ago were established by the FSA, that senior executives of banks and securities firms have to demonstrate that they will not fall down on the job if something goes catastrophically wrong. Integrating such concepts into the rule-book of supervisors requires a thorough review of their own responsibilities and those of the bank's top management and board of directors.

The old FSA's plan to reverse the burden of proof when something calamitous happens, such as the Barings collapse, and make top management more accountable for financial failures, can serve as a guide. Within this is embedded the principle that there can be more than one senior executive officer responsible for mistakes, or an outright collapse, and that the Chief Executive Officer is not immune to prosecution.

One of the objections advanced by the securities industry to that concept has been that the obligations imposed on senior executive officers, and most particularly the chief executive, were so heavy that they would have had to spend most of their time checking up on what was happening within their organisation. But as Nick Durlacher, then FSA chairman, was to say, 'When (we) get a catastrophic failure, the very least we should be able to do is get the very senior figures in front of a tribunal (*The London Financial News*, 17–20 March 1997).'

In fact, the old FSA had started imposing penalties on senior executives whose efforts were shown to be hollow. In mid-March 1997, a punishment was handed out to Ian Hopkins, the former Barings director; it was the most severe penalty imposed on any of those censured over the bank's collapse, and included:

- a ban of at least three years from acting as a director of a City firm; and
- having to pay £10 000 (a trivial sum) towards the FSA's costs.

City analysts said that this was no worse than that imposed on Peter Norris, the former chief executive of Barings. More damaging to Hopkins was the publication of the findings of the independent tribunal which heard the FSA's case. Far from being the 'whistle-blower' he purported to be, Hopkins turned out to have been party to vital information. As reported by the *Financial Times*, about six months before Barings collapsed he was told there was a problem reconciling about £100 million of margin paid to Baring (Futures) Singapore. This was meant to be money advanced to clients, but in fact it was going to support Nick Leeson's unauthorised trading.

It is interesting that despite challenging the FSA at every opportunity, Hopkins did not enter a formal defence against the charges. The irony of this case has been, however, that the two top executives in the organisation, Peter Barings and Andrew Tuckey, did not face any charges yet, in every failure, the final responsibility lies at the top.

Precisely for this reason the FSA was seeking to remedy the gap in its rulebook by imposing tougher responsibilities on senior directors, as well as proving personal accountability when something is wrong with the balance of risk and reward. How is it possible for someone, be they a chief executive or a trader, to collect huge bonuses when the business appears to be steaming ahead, but carry no blame when it suddenly implodes as a result of uncontrolled speculation in derivatives?

As an example of poor senior management practices, I was told in one of the London meetings about a bank audited by the regulators which presented a fully priced derivatives portfolio. Included in it, among other securities, were US Treasury bonds. 'If you need to raise money quickly, which asset do you sell?' asked the supervisor. 'The Treasuries,' answered the chief executive. This gave the supervisor the message, subsequently proved through careful auditing, that the financial institution in question was not well organised to face a time of stress. Its senior management seemed to live in a world where speeding through red lights was safer than stopping. The institution was not sure of its risk management practices, nor did it fully appreciate its positions, and there were securities in the portfolio which senior management knew were overpriced, but yet they did nothing towards damage control.

In this case, for instance, selling the Treasuries would have reduced the bank's liquidity and made it vulnerable to a fire sale if an urgent need arose. Also, as the audit found out, the institution under inspection had not put in place a real-time monitoring of its exposure position-by-position. Yet anyone in senior management who could read and write should have understood the practical issue raised by 'Black Monday' scenarios of a quick but temporary financial market meltdown. Many cases of bankruptcies and near-bankruptcies demonstrate that when crisis hits management can no longer be sure of survival because the assets are weak and liquidity is non-existent.

In conclusion, an integral part of the responsibilities of regulators is to ensure that the management of institutions is always alert and, through drills, to ensure that everybody else in the organisation is on his or her feet. Nobody knows when a sharp fall in market values will take place, but under no condition should management be taken by surprise. A sound policy would see to it that there is in place:

- critical analysis of what works and what does not work with loans, investments and trades;
- continuous review and monitoring by senior executives using feedback loops;
- levels of decision for Black Monday cases as well as thresholds which are continuously tested.

All regulators should appreciate that the worst possible symptom in a financial institution is complacent management. The best is the culture which tests and trains; which rewards but also penalises. Management must not only be on the alert but also be able to expect the unexpected, and be ready at all times for extreme events. Regulators should never fail to press this message on the entities which they supervise.

8
Cross-Border Supervision of Banks, Non-Banks and Internet Commerce

1 Introduction

Blandly, the question is whether it is possible to create a system of mutually independent bank regulators and supervisors in the absence of a global government. The answer to this question starts with a subquery: is it possible to develop a framework which permits supervisors from all countries, not just G-10 to:

- use the same standards for the examination of banks and non-banks;
- ensure there is reliable financial reporting and transparency on a cross-border basis;
- share their findings in an uninhibited manner, but also in real enough time; and
- act upon delinquent entities in unison no matter from where they come and where they operate?

Starting with the fundamentals, such a system would require common understandings and shared views on: what constitutes normal business behaviour; the standards to which the financial institutions are expected to adhere; and the criteria of deviations from norms and rules. Answers have to be given both for calm markets and for times of crisis, without necessarily involving the IMF as *deus ex machina*.

Also, because prodded by huge money flows the global capital market might become even more unpredictable, can regulators develop a framework to detect the amber lights and to stop them turning to red because of a systemic crisis? This query is not new, but it has so far been handled through a fire-brigade approach rather than by means of prognostication and shared values.

As time passes the solutions regulators seek become more complex not only because of globalisation, which has become embedded into the system, but also because technology is changing single-handed the rules of the game. So far we have had emerging markets, but in the coming years regulators will need to be concerned with:

- a rapid succession of emerging financial products (see Chapter 9 on risk management and Chapter 10 on the control of eigenmodels); and
- IBC, which makes the principle of sovereignty and nation-by-nation regulatory activities nearly irrelevant. In principle, it should not be that difficult to agree upon the crucial issues and develop a global control framework. But in practice, it is not that easy because there are many current developments affecting the different areas of responsibility to which regulators address themselves.

During the 1990s hedge funds have demonstrated how obsolete are most of the current prudential supervision rules, but many people have said, 'Forget about the hedge funds; they are beyond the financial landscape's frontiers.' This, however, cannot be said about IBC, and most particularly of day trades, because the challenges IBC poses are not merely passing problems, and therefore they need the undivided attention of regulation and governance.

2 Cross-border supervision, internet commerce and knowledge management

In practically all countries bank regulators are keen to promote prudent standards of behaviour in the industry but, at least so far, they do not use common norms, a common language or the same set of shared values. Algorithms and metrics, which can act as yardsticks regarding the prudent behaviour of financial institutions and other firms, as well as triggers for corrective actions, have yet to be streamlined in a cross-border sense. Even the way VAR is implemented varies within the same country, let alone among different countries (see also Chapter 10).

Since legal issues underpin most of the references connected to cross-border supervision of institutions, if regulators wish to establish and observe common norms then all countries must draw up fairly homogeneous legislation: essentially a blueprint permitting them to cope with malfunctions in their banking system and with the spread of events which might create systemic risk. This requires:

- the normalisation of the legal code, from default and bankruptcy acts to the rules of bank supervision; and
- pragmatic solutions embedded in a new regulatory culture which filters all the way to senior bank management.

In October 1996, BIS released a new international directive on Supervision of Cross-Border Banking, prepared by the Basle Committee on Banking Supervision of the G-10 central bankers. According to my records, this is the first time central banks have drawn in the administrative authorities of the world's major offshore havens, including the Cayman Islands, Gibraltar, Guernsey, Hong Kong, and Netherlands Antilles.

The cross-border BIS rules are designed to close regulatory loopholes under which banks are able to go offshore and carry out banking activities prohibited in their country, as well as operate unchecked through their complex networks of affiliates. The objective of the Cross-Border Banking rules was to introduce at least a minimum of regulatory controls affecting banks which are active in more than one country.

It is absolutely reasonable that central banks want to prevent any future BCCI-type risk and therefore that they address systemic dangers to the global financial fabric. Central bankers collaborating through BIS are perfectly aware of the growing number of *de facto* bankrupt banks across OECD countries as well as the emerging market economies, including Russia, Brazil, Mexico, Thailand, Indonesia, South Korea and numerous other countries in Asia and Latin America; in short, the 'emerging countries'.

Less evident is the existing degree of awareness that emerging products, not just emerging markets, may constitute a danger to the international financial fabric if they are not taken into full account in the process of regulating both banks and non-banks. The first steps in this direction should be:

- the understanding of risk factors embedded in new products;
- the institution of consistent reporting requirements in their regard; and
- the analysis of processes made possible through global networking.

As the Internet operates 24 hours per day, 7 days a week, it is necessary to account for IBC in novel ways, not just by accepted routes. Because Internet commerce is the first to take off and much of its success depends on emerging products, let me start this discussion with how well-known companies use high technology to re-invent their business. From General Electric (GE) to Federal Express (FedEx), the foremost companies are looking at ways to channel the Internet's vast resources to:

- spot market trends early;
- switch to information-intense solutions;
- speed new products to market;
- cut costs and build a new profit base.

For many firms this is no less than a sweeping change in corporate culture. The pivotal point of the new trend, which is amplified through networks, is *knowledge management*. Adapting to it means tearing down walls between departments and individuals, inside and outside the company, while implementing real-time communications with business partners.

Is this point pertinent in a book on bank supervision? It certainly is. About 50 per cent of GE's yearly business and a good deal more than half its profits come from GE Capital, a major non-bank bank. Even 50 per cent of GE's capitalisation is more than double the capitalisation of (taken individually) the new Citigroup, Chase Manhattan, BankAmerica, NatWest, Barclays, Tokyo-Mitsubishi, UBS, Credit Suisse, Deutsche Bank or any other bank.

What interests me most in this reference to GE and the Internet is the latter's impact on what makes a company tick. Often, a change in management culture starts with conducting *in-house audits* to pinpoint who knows what inside the company, and immediately posting the findings on the private intranet. But clear-eyed managements think that the change now taking place is much deeper, and eventually leads to:

- reinventing the company;
- restructuring its business; and
- revamping its products.

For instance, Federal Express is on its way to being transformed into an Internet company. Its Web site is one of the most heavily used on the Internet, and the firm claims its army of 1500 in-house programmers write more software than almost any other non-software company. Regulators, particularly those with global ambitions, could use the transformation of FedEx as a model.

FedEx management believes that today, and in the years to come, leadership in information technology commands a higher premium than the trucks and planes which have so far been the firm's main assets, but these can be outsourced. This is a major shift in strategic planning: in the past the added value of FedEx was built on big planes and the trucking routes, but now management is working towards the day when the competitive advantage is built on databases, networks and know-how.

Reinventing FedEx has been based on two pillars: forward-looking strategic planning and astute use of technology. Financial trading on the Internet is another example of a major change. In 1997, LIFFE, London's futures exchange, boasted a 70 per cent market share in the German government bond future, Europe's most heavily traded contract. A year down the line, in 1998, Germany's DTB had succeeded in capturing most of that market. LIFFE operates with a trading floor, whereas DTB is all networked.

Is it conceivable that the ultimate trading network is the Internet? A late 1998 survey by Credit Suisse First Boston (CSFB) counted at least 70 on-line brokers, including some of the fastest growing companies in the business, such as Datek, SureTrade (owned by Quick & Reilly, a large discount broker) and AmeriTrade.

Another on-line broker is E*Trade; and still another, Investtrade, has announced a way to allow trading through wireless gadgets such as smart cell phones. While Investtrade is offering more than just cut-throat pricing, its value added approach includes research and other novel banking services. With this, it starts to compete directly with the full-service brokerages.

Experts think that the world of IBC will be greatly affected by the Next Generation Internet. This is projected to encompass much more than just the US government-funded academic and research initiatives. With the broadband Internet, every significant Internet service provider, product vendor, and sector of the economy may have to reinvent itself. How far ahead may that date be? A recent study shows that:

- by the end of 1999, 2.2 million US households will have broadband Internet connections (*Communications of the ACM*, January 1999, Vol. 42, No. 1);
- by 2002, one in four on-line homes will have broadband access, which means more than 10 million households in the USA alone.

This access will be providing an *always-on* capability at speeds at least 100 times faster than today's dial-up modems. The competitive advantages of these solutions are so considerable that it is not surprising that practically every major country has its own Next Generation Internet under development. All of these cover a large horizon of developments, collectively involving billions of dollars a year in investments which will eventually unfold into waves of financial services; it is surprising the regulators have not joined this effort, in spite of the perspectives it offers in cross-border trading.

Regulators should appreciate that as the Next Generation Internet evolves, commercial banks, investment banks, hedge funds and other players will join it with a stream of emerging products with which the supervisors themselves will have little or no experience. Administered through networks, rapid fire financial solutions will book economic activity but also presents new and major challenges to the control of risk. Day trading, discussed in section 3, is one of the most interesting examples.

3 Day trading, technology and the global market place

With the momentum currently building in the financial industry against a background of the merger of technology and the global market place, some of the recent policies at government level seems mischievous and ill-considered at best. This leads to a number of fundamental long-term implications for countries which fall behind and supervisory authorities which still have not come to grips with the new landscape.

The core issue with the Internet is *political*, not technological. It revolves around the notion of whether national governments – and by extension national regulators – have sovereignty over the various possible Internet-based products and services connected with financial transactions. This reference is far-reaching and includes the creation of money as well as just about anything else that can exist in the virtual world of cyberspace.

Starting with the fundamentals, the concept of the nation-state, and therefore of sovereignty, is that of supreme and absolute power. For nearly three centuries, in the post-medieval society, the nation-state has seen itself as having God-given authority to do practically everything within its domain, without accountability. Sovereignty works within definitive geographical borders on real people and real objects. By contrast, the Internet is a global and growing shared virtual space where notions of state sovereignty do not exist.

Sovereigns could take heart from the fact that when they master high technology they can gain a lot in employment terms. As high-tech speeds ahead it takes up the slack in jobs created by the shrinkage of manufacturing industry, the economy's real goods sector. Figure 8.1 presents American statistics from the share of job growth coming from information-related service industries.

In the world of the Internet, it is the users themselves who collectively constitute a sort of sovereign, a very unsettling experience for nation-states indeed. What is more these are formative times, with the Internet's growth

Figure 8.1 US growth in employment from information-based service industries

and development coming up against older established institutions and models of thought with full force. The seemingly crazy pricing of Internet stocks is an example (see section 4).

Section 2 spoke of brokers who strive for Internet leadership and of exchanges which capitalise on networks to achieve market clout. Both get results in the virtual world. Other Internet-based financial firms turn themselves into consultants. Financial Engines, a company established in late 1998, helps investors to:

- plan their desired retirement income;
- specify how much risk they want to take; and
- calculate the odds of reaching their target.

The services of Financial Engines seem to be sponsored by a number of big 401-k providers (the US government-instituted retirement plan) who wish to alleviate some of the fears caused by the global shift of retirement pensions to individually managed savings accounts.

Day trading is another example of IBC. A day trader is one who trades stocks intraday and liquidates all positions by market-close back to cash, rather than holding positions overnight. Though exact statistics are not available, it is generally thought there are about 5 million day traders in the market. Most of them hold positions for minutes, not hours, let alone days.

The supervisory authorities are not so happy with day trading. '[Day-trading firms] have taken the art of losing money and turned it into a science', says Philip A. Feigin of the North American Securities Administrators Association (NASAA) which represents state securities regulators (*Business Week*, 18 January 1999). In the USA, dozens of day-trading firms are being targeted in a crackdown which may result in significant industry reforms. But other people say that day traders are not so different from currency traders who grease the wheels of foreign exchanges, since they drive up share prices rapidly, and drive them down again by short-selling.

Day trading started in 1988, when US federal regulators changed stock-trading rules to allow individual investors to execute deals more easily on NASDAQ. This business, however, really took off just a few years ago with a proliferation of firms using new software designed for executing split-second deals. Day traders monitor small price movements in active stocks, and profit from changes of as little as a quarter or an eighth of a percentage point. They hope to make money from the commissions, usually 2–3 cents a share, but through their deals they play a major role in the 100 most actively traded NASDAQ stocks. While these firms are promoting electronic day trading as a way to make profits, regulators are keeping a close watch on their marketing claims, which sometimes hide the risks.

The positive aspect of day trading is that it provides liquidity for all companies on whose volatility it capitalises. The negative reference is that when stocks start to crash, the small retail investors can get hurt more than ever before. The true day traders just shorten the stocks and ride the crash down during the day, liquidating by the day's end.

Internet commerce is also in its way displacing business communications solutions and protocols, such as the UN-sponsored Electronic Data Interchange (EDI). In 1998, in America, EDI served to exchange some $250 billion worth of products, usually over expensive private networks. However, EDI is notoriously pricey and complex to set up, effectively shutting out of its system millions of smaller businesses; it is also inflexible, because it only transmits rigidly formatted electronic documents such as purchase orders and invoices.

By contrast, Internet commerce allows businesses to swap all kinds of data cheaply, from sales contacts and product brochures to engineering drawings. In 1998, Boeing booked $100 million in spare parts orders from airlines through its Web site; and Cisco Systems books $11 million in orders each day, or around $4 billion a year, on its Web site.

It is no less true, however, that not everything is handy and dandy with the Internet. Two-gun Dillinger was once asked why he specialised in bank hold-ups. His answer was: 'Because that's where the money is.' If the Internet has money, banking services and commerce opportunities, then there will be also crooks, or at least players, processes and products which should attract the attention of regulators.

On 25 January 1999, a scam on Ebay, the auction outfit on the Internet, was announced. Ebay said that it had no responsibility because it could not control what is posted by its clients on its Web site. Some years ago in the UK, IBM put forward a similar argument regarding some scam on its network but the court was not convinced. Somebody has to exercise control. Therefore, not only should there be rules but also supervisors checking closely on compliance through technology who are able to separate the black from the white sheep.

The challenge is that if only current notions and old tools are employed, it will not be possible to regulate Internet financial transactions without impeding the dynamics of the virtual economy. This is all the more true as the nature of IBC is rapidly changing and this happens in conjunction with a dramatic squeeze on costs because one of the drivers of the consumer market is cost swamping. Other growing requirements are a higher quality of services as well as diversification and personalisation without cost increases.

Most likely, there will be in banking a repetition of what happened in merchandising in the 1970s. Once committed to discounting, Sam Walton began a crusade that lasted the rest of his life, driving costs out of the merchandising system wherever they lay: in the stores, the manufacturers' profit margins, the middlemen. That is exactly what the financial system needs today, but where does this streamlining leave the regulators?

4 An example using emerging products: the valuation of Internet stocks

No regulator would find it difficult to appreciate that there is a genuine currency crisis in emerging countries. Post-mortem the world finds out that stable exchange rates were a tremendous factor in the globalisation of the economy. By contrast, today many currencies are in trouble and this does not result in a good market because it is not possible to sell financial products without a currency, while currencies which are too volatile are no good for IBC.

Yet, as we have already seen in Part One, today flexible exchange rates are the only solution in a world where cross-border capital flows are tremendous and have the power to flatten any barrier. At the same time, investors feel more comfortable with dollar-valued products (eventually, perhaps, also with euro-valued products) which they know how to analyse, or at least they understand better their swings between volatility and stability.

During the 1990s volatility and its effect on the pricing of financial products has significantly increased (see D.N. Chorafas, *Understanding Volatility and Liquidity in Financial Markets*, Euromoney Books, London, 1998). Few people truly appreciate that instantaneous communications magnify volatility's aftermath. At the same time, 'emerging products' are now replacing emerging markets as focal points of investors' attention. This is one of the reasons which made the end of 1998 and most of 1999 an exceptional time for technology stocks, especially for Internet outfits.

Technology plays a triple game: it underpins fast innovation and new product development in the banking industry; provides the networks for any-to-any globalisation in finance; and brings to the foreground of investment opportunities fast-growth companies whose leveraged stocks are emerging products. With Microsoft by now an institutionalised growth firm, emerging companies are America Online, Amazon.com, @Home, Yahoo and others. Experts project:

- big changes in the financial markets, particularly in intraday trades, because of the Internet (see section 3); and
- a greater volatility because of the convergence of Internet services and emerging products.

Regulators find themselves at a loss in this environment. As long as emerging products, emerging companies and emerging markets abide by the old rule book, they cannot intervene; yet they see that all three of them are highly leveraged, and thus greatly increasing the likelihood of a crash and its severity.

It used to be that professional investors and institutions made the market. Now the market is increasingly made seven days a week, 24 hours a day by the Internet fellows. Globalisation is driven by technology but there is always a learning curve with any type of stock or other products. Wall Street analysts believe that:

- most of the Internet companies that will lead the technology wave have not yet been conceived; and
- given that today there are relatively few companies characterised as Internet stocks, these companies are overvalued.

In the opinion of a growing number of analysts, all current attempts to value Internet stocks using old concepts are ineffectual, and some are plainly ridiculous. For some, the mania of over-gearing Internet stocks has spread and, while the price of these stocks continues to increase, eventually it will cave in. It did so mid-January 1999, but then these stocks recovered as if an invisible hand pulled them out of their valley.

Shortly after the Internet stocks started recovering, *The Economist* published an editorial and an article which predicted that Internet shares will fall again, and pointed out the surge of trading among people unskilled in the art of valuation and unburned by past losses (30 January 1999). It also quoted Dr William Sharpe, who said: 'We are pretty much flying blind'; and Jeff Bezos who commented about Amazon.com's sky-high share price: 'Really we don't think about it that much.'

However, on Wall Street financial analysts do think about it, and a growing number of other cognisant people now believe that Internet stocks should not be looked at as classical options on the company's assets (which are very few) but as enablers of a steady cash flow without heavy capital investments. Therefore, discounted future cash flow rather than price/earnings should be used as the criterion for their valuation. The models these analysts use are:

- a discounted, aggregated free cash flow over a 5-year period;
- a segmented and focused discounted cash flow;
- a discounted subscriber approach; and
- a price-to-sales marked to a universe of comparable Internet companies.

This list of criteria shows why some of the experts do not agree with Sharpe on the likelihood that the price of Internet stocks will return to the basement, even if today the pessimists outpace the optimists by nearly 10 to 1. The outcome of a vote taken at Comdex '98 (Las Vegas, Nevada, 16–18 November 1998) involving some 300 people with experience in valuing Internet stocks suggests that, in the opinion of the experts:

- 69 per cent say they are too expensive;
- 24 per cent say they are conectly valued; and
- 7 per cent say they are too cheap.

The majority of the participants in this *ad hoc* Internet stock valuation stated that the company able to win in the Internet market will become very big; but which one will win in a market which is still at the very early stage of its evolution? At the same time there was a widespread opinion that a lot of the current Internet firms will go bankrupt, as happened with Videotex firms 20 years ago.

Always according to the experts, the big question is: 'What's the franchise value being created?' Telephone companies which have been able to reinvent themselves seem to answer the franchise value criterion because telephone penetration in the world is low, below 20 per cent; and in the coming years it may reach 40 per cent, with cellular and broadband in the lead. Bandwidth is subject to Moore's law, which states that microprocessor capacity doubles every 18 months at practically stable prices. However, the new *law of the photon* says that bandwidth effectively doubles every 9 months while the price stays put.

This doubling of bandwidth at stable cost every nine months will see to it that there are rewarding results in Internet commerce. For instance, as a proxy for e-commerce, Amazon.com reflects the dislocation in the economy which pushes away from legacy systems, while through its access to a broadband environment @Home changes the rules of access to the market.

According to cognisant analysts, both broadband and e-commerce may be emulating the PC market. Let us remember that the PC industry started 29 years into the commercial and industrial computer life cycle, which began in 1953. A similar phenomenon may now be taking place with the Internet and broadband stocks, some 18 years down the line from the PC's push in the computer market.

Some of the participants at my seminars ask: 'Is the PC a spent product?' 'No!', is the answer, but it does go through a process of morphing. The PC may not be an emerging product, but there is still life in it. Even with 300 million computers in the world, utilisation stands below 5 per cent of the global population. Nobody really knows where the saturation level is. Investment experts, however, caution that the 'important sectors' and the 'high growth sectors' of the economy are not the same thing. One issue on which expert opinions converge is that the age of vertical integration is over. Modern industry is reorganising along horizontal layers with a golden horde of products which are not institutionalised. Amazon.com, @Home and other Internet players are instrumental in horizontalising and de-institutionalising the vertical industry. This is true all the way from manufacturing to banking, and regulators are caught in the middle of this transformation. While some countries are integrating and streamlining their regulatory activities (see Chapter 7), decisions have not yet been taken on which strategy regulators should pursue because of the Internet's impact.

Should the laws and the rules favour financial supermarkets, such as Citigroup, which are a sort of vertical integration, or should they promote the concept and practice of horizontalisation of financial services through small and focused Internet financial institutions, along the lines we examined in section 3? Should regulatory guidelines promote the coolly analytical and self-controlled entities or give way to the cocky (and rather undisciplined) visionaries who try to climb to the top of the financial ladder?

5 A horde of issues: from financial engineering to fees rewarding inefficiency

Cross-border supervision becomes even more complex than might otherwise have been the case, because in many companies today treasury operations are not limited to finding the best sources of financing. They operate for profit and engage in extensive financial engineering practices, which blur the distinguishing signs between a treasury and a bank.

Producers are keen to exploit new financial instruments. Gold producers, for instance, sell through futures and forwards their minerals for years ahead. Because the price of precious metals is so depressed and, short of a global financial crisis, the prospects for recovery are rather bleak, through derivatives they are able to capitalise when prices rise to lock in future profits. Gold companies are by no means the only firms to use financial engineering methods.

Intel, Microsoft and Dell Computer, among others, sell put warrants on their own stock to investors. The warrants give buyers, for a limited period, the right but not the obligation to sell shares of stock back to the company at a set strike price below the market at the time they get into the transaction.

Carried out by professionals with a sense of the most likely market direction, this game has become quite profitable. In the quarter ending 30 September 1998, and only for this time period, Microsoft took in $225 million from the sale of puts. This was equal to 13.4 per cent of its net income in the aforementioned timeframe. Financial analysts think that these transactions are ingenious, because the tax law makes any dealings that a company has in its own shares tax-free. Such transactions help the capital-intensive technology firms, because operating costs are often so close to operating income that it is difficult to generate positive cash flows.

Companies that sell puts are betting that their shares will not fall to the options' strike price during the transaction's timeframe. If they are lucky, the put expires and the company keeps the money it has received for it. By contrast, the buyers of the warrants are betting that the stock could fall.

Regulations have not caught up with the practice, however, and the money received in these deals is not detailed on the income statement as financial engineering income. Therefore, it is unclear whether investors understand how much the sale of puts can contribute to a company's financial position, even if the proceeds show up on statements of cash flows which investors read and are supposed to appreciate.

There are also other fallouts from financial engineering that should be of interest to prudential supervisors. For instance, when companies are forced to buy back shares, they often have to use hard-earned money that could otherwise be reinvested in their business. Given that the company is obliged to buy back its shares from the outside investors, if its stocks drop below the strike price the warrants are a potential liability.

This is not the only challenge from modern financial practices connected with the protection of investors and the proper functioning of financial markets. Loads (sales fees), yearly management charges, and advisory fees of mutual funds (unit trusts) and other funds are another example. In the USA, the SEC has pushed the mutual funds industry to list expenses and fees clearly on proxy statements sent to investors, but progress has been slow. More needs to be done as novice investors pour billions of hard-earned money into the nearly 7000 US funds every month.

Getting rid of jargon would be a good first step. In May 1998, SEC Chairman Arthur Levitt asked the securities industry: 'Do you really expect investors to understand the alphabet soup of A,B,C,D,I,Y and Z shares – to figure out what combination of front-end loads, contingent deferred sales loads, charges, commissions and who knows what else they're paying?' Firms break up a fund into a variety of classes, from A to Z, each with different charges and benefits.

Surveys show that investors are almost completely in the dark about mutual-fund fees and the way they affect the bottom line. One survey showed that only 12 per cent of investors know the difference between a 'load' and 'no-load' fund, and very few realise that they have paid a 2 per cent or 3 per cent sales commission to brokers prior to making any profits. Funds take in about $6 billion a year in marketing costs billed to individual investors, and even small differences in load add up to big money.

The same goes for different management fees. Mutual funds have many ways to charge investors, and jargon makes understanding these fees so much more difficult. Reducing the number of fees and simplifying their computation as well as their jargon would help. The rules of prudential supervision should see to it that each fund:

- shows its charges clearly;
- demonstrates how charges have changed over the years; and
- gives investors personal information about the expenses they have paid.

Funds and other asset managers should also explain the sense of compounding gains. Even a seemingly small 1 per cent annual fee for an investment adds up over time. On a $10000 investment, for instance, a 1 per cent annual fee cuts the investors' return by a whopping 30 per cent ($197000) after 40 years. (See above in Chapter 7 the reference to a study in the UK by SFA, which adds up to similar results.)

While regulation in front loads, management fees and advisory charges to mutual funds is not around the corner, market forces may be doing the job of regulators. As investors who have had substantial stakes in funds or money management formats that struggle to make a profit look at the performance figures, they start to reason that they can surely do as badly on their own, and not have to pay a fee for the privilege.

Therefore we might well see investors shift more of their money to a self-management practice. They would actually select the individual stocks and use Internet brokers for the transaction. Self-management is an important issue impacting on money flows, and one which could cause some amazing differences within the stock market, reinforcing some of the existing trends which concern growth investing. Experts think that self-management could be particularly favourable for equities in technology and especially for Internet stocks.

6 Hedge funds, junk funds and big losses

Hedge funds have been one of the sectors of the financial industry which have persistently avoided the regulators' hand, yet the years of easy money and fat profits seem to be approaching an end. Today the hedge funds market is overcrowded and some are so badly bleeding that they have become *junk funds*. Practically all hedge funds take enormous risks as their mandarins scramble for a different version to old solutions which no longer work.

The blood bath of 1994 when the Fed successively raised interest rates is too well known to be retold. A recent case is the Russian meltdown in August 1998 followed by the fall in the Western stock markets which produced hefty losses for highly leveraged hedge funds. The Soros outfits were said to have lost $4 billion out of $21.5 billion under management. Half the money went down the drain in Russia, as a result of a crisis George Soros himself helped to produce; the other half was lost on the worst day of 1998, 31 August, when the Dow Jones Index fell by 512 points. But altogether, 1998 was not as disastrous as 1994 with its bond market meltdown. In spite of the loss of nearly 20 per cent of its capital, Soros Fund Management showed a gain of about 7.5 per cent for 1998. This, however, is far from being a stellar performance. In 1998 Soros Fund Management has underperformed the Dow Index by quite a margin.

Among hedge funds, other big losers in 1998 have been Leon Cooperman, Marty Zweig, Jo DiMenna and Julian Robertson. Julian Robertson lost a rumoured $800 million. The biggest of all losers was John Meriwether, of the now famed LTCM and its Nobel Prize winners. At the end of August 1998, Meriwether's hedge fund had lost $2.1 billion, or 50 per cent of its assets. A month later it came to the brink of bankruptcy.

Being beaten by the market on repeated occasions, hedge funds seem to be losing some of their will to fight on all fronts. In a letter to shareholders dated 23 October 1999, George Soros announced a restructuring of his $20 billion Soros Fund Management, following the $2 billion in losses on Russian investments as well as other red ink. He also announced that he was closing his Quantum Emerging Growth Fund, which lost about one-third of its net worth in 1998 alone, dropping to $1.5 billion in assets. Its remaining assets are to be merged into another Soros fund, the $2 billion Quantum Industrial Holdings.

This fairly extensive restructuring became necessary because Soros Fund Management also lost heavily on its other investments. For instance, its US stock portfolio was worth $3.9 billion on 30 September 1998, a 50 per cent decline from the $8 billion value reported the previous quarter. During the third quarter of 1998, among the big funds, Soros's Quota fund declined 24 per cent, which was followed by drops of 21 per cent at Quasar International fund, 20 per cent at Quantum Industrial fund, 13 per cent at Quantum Emerging Growth fund; 10 per cent at Asian Infrastructure Development, and 5 per cent at Realty Trust fund.

Julian Robertson's Tiger Management also suffered heavily in the wake of the Russian debt crisis. Tiger's funds lost $2.1 billion in September 1998 and $3.4 billion in October. The two-month drop left the fund's assets at $17 billion. Tiger lost nearly 10 per cent of its value on one day alone, 7 October, when the dollar fell sharply against the yen.

Since misfortunes rarely occur singly Robertson's Jaguar fund lost 6 per cent of its value, leading to the need for rationalisation. Tiger said it had liquidated between $25 billion and $30 billion in assets, reducing its leverage from 5.5 to 1 to about 4 to 1, which is still high, but it is a trifle compared to the 50 to 1 leverage of LTCM which has earned the honour of being the junk fund of the year.

Leon Cooperman's Omega Overseas Partners lost 21 per cent of its value. Even harder hit were the Infinity Investors fund, down 28 per cent; Latinvest Fund and Apam High Performance Capital fund, each down 33 per cent; Everest Capital International fund, down 42 per cent; Appaloosa Investment I and Palomino funds, each down 43 per cent; Oscar Investment fund, down 54 per cent; Everest Capital Frontier LP and Everest Capital Frontier funds which lost 61 per cent of their assets in the third quarter of 1998.

Still worse off were three hedge funds run by McGinnis Advisors. They filed for bankruptcy protection because they could not meet margin calls from their brokers and bankers. This is an abuse of the protection provided by Chapter 11. Other funds were forced to liquidate significant portions of their holdings to meet margin calls, which is a splendid example of *the costs of leveraging*.

These are the people who thought they not only knew the market but they could also master it. They simply could not do anything wrong and nobody could stand up to their expertise in making double-digit profits, or in repeating that feat year-after-year. But in real life they were devastated twice within four years: first in 1994 with the bond market meltdown, as the Fed kept on increasing the interest rate, and then again in 1998 with the credit market crash, and the beating administered by the stock market.

The truth is many 'experts' do not like to hear that nobody really knows the financial market in all its breadth, depth and ramifications. Junk funds are not the only ones who suffered huge losses. With stocks taking a severe beating in September/October 1998, during the third quarter of 1998 the market capitalisation of the top 100 US bank holding companies dropped $242 billion, or 23 per cent, while the market cap of the world's top 100 financial services institutions sank by $635 billion, or 22 per cent.

Some analysts are now saying that the label 'hedge funds' is no longer representative of what these institutions are doing. They suggest that 'junk funds' is much more appropriate for those who think they 'know the market', while in reality they have become the most incompetent investors of the 1990s. After all there are junk bonds; why shouldn't there be junk funds, provided they are regulated?

7 Should the hedge funds industry be regulated?

Along with the 23 September 1998 bailout of, or more precisely foreclosure on, LTCM through the 12th hour injection of $3.6 billion engineered by the New York Fed, the high losses in the financial industry dramatise the need for regulation of the:

- global derivatives market at large; and
- the wheeler-dealing of the hedge funds.

In response to a growing demand for increased regulation of the hedge funds, BIS is now considering, indirectly supervising them through closer control of their counterparties. What is suggested is looking closer into the banking book of credit institutions to identify the loans they give to hedge funds. This is definitely too little, and it is coming too late. But regulation usually proceeds step-by-step.

After the $3.6 billion bailout of LTCM, Alan Greenspan testified to Congress that it is questionable whether global hedge funds should be regulated by the USA alone. Instead, he said, regulators should impose controls on bank lending to the funds.

Following this testimony several central bankers and regulators of the G-10 have endorsed Greenspan's recommendation. The Fed itself is issuing new rules for hedge-fund lending, while a panel of the Basle Committee on Banking Supervision warned on 28 January 1999 that some hedge fund activities may threaten the world financial system.

The world's foremost reserve institutions want banks to monitor loans to hedge funds closely and become harder-nosed about the collateral hedge funds offer. Collateral can plunge in value when markets fear that huge portfolio liquidations are imminent.

Even with bigger haircuts, however, while a global and more focused supervision of securities firms, banks, insurance companies and generally financial institutions is necessary, strict rules are also needed regarding investment which financial history proves is speculative and poses systemic risk. It would be wise to look closer at the books of the parties providing the hedge funds with the large liquidity which they can move around the globe at a moment's notice, but it is wrong to keep the hedge funds themselves out of the realm of rigorous cross-border supervision, as if they were the sacred cows of the global economy.

The idea of limiting supervision of hedge funds to the inspection of the loans book of banks is a regulatory Trojan horse. While any bank talking about hedge funds will say they are risky, banks do trade with them and tend to implement less than would be prudent in order to control their exposure.

The regulators are also concerned about systemic risk because of the impact not of one event, but a whole series of events following each other in quick succession. This can lead to a deteriorating financial situation in different countries and in many institutions. Up to LTCM, very few banks knew the answer to the question of how creditworthy their hedge fund counterparties were, and there was no one centre in the credit institution which knew about hedge fund exposure.

Opinions are, however, divided on how far hedge funds supervision should go, or even what sort of extra reserves the banks should keep. Cognisant financial analysts believe that outside the USA there is less need for major provisions for hedge funds. They say that with few exceptions there is sufficient collateral deposited at the banks, or alternatively the banks tell the regulators plain lies.

'Regulating the hedge fund industry is not the real issue', said the executive of a rating agency in London. 'Hedge funds do not sell to the general public. But banks should know what they do with hedge fund exposure. The same is true of regulators.' For instance:

- what's the exposure of bank ABC to hedge fund XYZ;
- how much has this position deteriorated since XYZ's big losses; and
- how much volatility has increased because of hedge funds trading?

The same rating agency executive suggested that approaches which simply add up exposure numbers in a linear way miss the point. The big question is derivatives trades and there risks are non-linear while gearing is high and, as the LTCM case has shown, equity investment in hedge funds magnifies the risks.

Another one of the problems the G-10 regulators face is that many hedge funds are domiciled in loosely-controlled offshore financial centres. Tighter regulation could face big political obstacles as the offshores fight to retain the lucrative business of the junk funds.

Neither do the political problems end with the offshores. As I mentioned in Chapter 1, because solutions to these problems are so complex, Bill Clinton has instituted the President's Working Group on Financial Markets which includes, among other members, the Secretary of Treasury, the chairman of the Federal Reserve and the chairman of the SEC.

* * *

The themes treated in this chapter have become much more important after the US House of representatives passed, in July 1999, long-awaited reforms to Depression-era financial industry laws. These are essentially amounting to the abandonment of the Glass–Steagall Act of 1933. The overall aim of the House and Senate bill is similar: modernise America's banking laws by knocking down the barriers between:

- Banking
- Insurance, and
- Securities firms.

9 Rigorous Approaches to the Management of Financial Risk Factors

1 Introduction

In an interview she gave in October 1997, Federal Reserve vice-chair Alice Rivlin pointed out that the Fed is 'paid to worry' (*Strategy Weekly*, 15 October 1997). She also implied that it was an open question, not a settled matter, as to whether the economy was on an unsustainable track. While those remarks were made with monetary policy in the background, they fit hand in glove with the way central bankers and regulators look at the management of financial risk factors. Risk factors are usually calculated using historical volatilities at a 90 per cent, 95 per cent or 99 per cent confidence level; increasingly, however, the definition and computation of risk factors is affected by extreme events which do not fit a normal distribution.

The blurring of classical divisional lines adds to risk factor uncertainty. There is, for example, a discussion on whether the traditional distinction between banking and commerce is sustainable, particularly in the context of Internet banking and Internet commerce. Even those experts who think that such distinction should be made, and that dividing lines could still be drawn with some accuracy, believe that during the 1990s the distinction has definitely become less clear, and the risks more pervasive.

A problem which has often been presented, and is still in search of a solution, is that of an international framework to serve as a guide to both the regulators and the management of commercial and investment banks in regard to the identification of risk factors and their control, especially those which have been amplified because of deregulation, globalisation and technology.

While the explosive growth of derivative financial instruments, and the credit risk and market risk factors they brought along (D.N. Chorafas, *Derivative Financial Instruments. Strategies for Managing Risk and Return in Banking*, Lafferty Publications, London and Dublin, 1995), is often cited as an example, there are others which also have the potential of upsetting the markets. During the research I did in Germany in 1998, Commerzbank said that its chairman targeted three key issues for 1999: 'Derivatives risk, the euro, and the Year 2000 problem' (for Y2K, see section 5).

There are many risk factors of fundamental importance in the regulation and stability of the financial system, and not all of them can be covered in one chapter. Ironically modelling, which developed as an aid to the management of exposure, has also become a risk factor (see Chapter 10). Others will be surveyed in Part Three, which addresses the fact the global operations of financial institutions have outgrown the national accounting, legal and supervisory systems on which their safety depends.

A key message this chapter conveys is that core institutions in the financial system should take the lead in developing a framework for risk measurement and management, which is neither near-sighted nor one-way. Counterparties, and supervisors charged with the oversight of the financial system, need to adopt a global and polyvalent view of risk factors because in the end everybody is exposed to the ups and downs of the financial system, both in the sense of business opportunity and of risk.

2 The strategic importance of risk management with derivative financial instruments

Risk management is a life-long exercise. Because of the deregulation and globalisation of capital markets, a great deal of risk comes from gearing as well as from the fact that turnover in derivatives is much higher than in the underlying market. This is not a flat statement against derivatives. Modern banking would be inconceivable without new and flexible financial instruments which can be easily customised. It is the high and fast-growing size of exposure which preoccupies regulators. Not only is the notional principal amount of derivatives transactions at or above the trillion dollars level for each of the top 30 banks in the G-10 world, but in the case of some institutions derivatives is a multiple of all other business, and their associated exposure is a high multiple of their capital.

Due to pricing by models (which has been made possible through a vastly improved technological infrastructure), the booking market for derivatives expands at the rate of 25 per cent to 35 per cent per year. Most banks and non-banks now use eigenmodels to develop even more complex instruments (see Chapter 10). For their part, the regulators have evidence that the capital requirements established in 1998 are not sufficient to provide a risk cushion for worst case scenarios: the 1998 Capital Accord (see Chapter 11) must be supplemented by a rigorous risk measurement and control system, and it must be sustained through a clear-cut structure of organisational responsibility and top management accountability.

In every financial institution the board and senior management must have at their fingertips reliable data on exposure, understand the risks being involved, and try steadily to improve market transparency. This can be done by ensuring that internal controls, accounting practices and technological support keep up with real-time financial reporting needs. To a large extent, the inordinate amount of risk taken with derivatives exposure comes from the fact that business is concentrated in a small number of players. This number continues to shrink because of mergers (see Chapter 14) posing the problem of major systemic risk if one dominant player falters.

The good news is that Barings, LTCM, and other important failures serve as distress cases to motivate action, while they also show that the market can absorb the shock, if it is contained and if regulators act. The bad news is that a snowball effect can never be excluded. Therefore, banking supervisors seek ways and means to measure the exposure taken by the financial system and prevent excessive risk-taking. Central bankers, and most particularly the Basle Committee for Banking Supervision, are moving in this direction in successive steps. Examples include:

- the 1988 Capital Adequacy Accord;
- the 1996 Market Risk Amendment; and
- the 1999 discussion paper on 'A New Capital Adequacy Framework' (see Chapter 11).

The fact that market participants not only have to be active but also remain active in a process of increasingly more rigorous risk management, suggests that changes in organisation and structure are inevitable. This is particularly true as the measurement and control of exposure has become a factor in competitive edge.

Many issues regarding top management policy result from this simple observation of risk management's strategic and tactical importance. But at the same time, this upgrading raises a number of policy questions. Among the many queries that need factual and documented answers three are outstanding: first of all, should there be a rigorous audit of internal controls by the authorities? The answer is definitely yes! In Britain, in Germany, in Switzerland and in other countries laws and regulations now require auditors to audit formal and informal internal controls. The quality of auditing and its acceptance by the supervisory authorities greatly depends on this reporting.

Second, how detailed should the risk modelling procedures be ? In a nutshell, both pricing models and risk management models should be accurate. They should also be specialised according to the subject to which they address themselves. General models do not help, and indeed are often counterproductive. Algorithms and heuristics have to be customised to the problem under study.

Third, should non-bank banks be subject to the same risk controls and supervision as investment and commercial banks? In my view non-banks should come under the scrutiny of supervisors. This is particularly true as their derivatives portfolio is increasing in size and is geared through loans they take from banks (see Chapter 8); and non-banks usually have as counterparties in derivatives trades the same banks that give the loans. There should be total transparency in off-balance-sheet exposure by all players in the market (see Chapter 13).

This is an issue which has not yet been settled, and neither has it been studied in its fundamentals. In America and in England, the principle of voluntary disclosure existed already prior to the recent rigorous regulation by the Financial Accounting Standards Board (FASB) and the British Accounting Standards Board (ASB) respectively. In Germany, some companies, such as Siemens, have adopted disclosure of their derivatives book but others are not transparent in their exposure.

An equally important step in terms of controlling systemic risk is rating non-banks by an independent agency such as Moody's, Standard & Poor's or Fitch IBCA. This gives a better appreciation of exposure by making it part of rating procedures. Therefore it provides a more focused risk control strategy. Banks and bonds are rated; why not the hedge funds and pension funds?

Along this line of reference, BIS is working on a semi-annual report on 70 major institutions who are active in derivatives. Their exposure is to be monitored world-wide. A similar policy should be followed with hedge funds, mutual funds, pension funds, insurance companies and the treasuries of major industrial corporations.

3 The monitoring and reporting of derivatives risk

The disclosure of the notional or contract amounts of derivative financial instruments is indicative of the extent of involvement in a particular class of financial transaction, though it is not necessarily a rigorous indication of overall market risk. The demodulation of notional principal to an exposure level equivalent to classical loans, and therefore credit risk, serves in stress testing. For risk management purposes, derivative positions should be measured and valued daily, through:

- quoted market prices; and
- the use of pricing models.

Values are affected by changes in interest rates, currency exchange rates, and credit spreads as well as by market volatility and liquidity. Because the market is dynamic, clear-eyed management focuses on intraday changes, which can be obtained at a reasonable cost through the right technology.

Every bank should monitor its exposures by means of analytical techniques. Market risk is mitigated by the establishment of trading limits (D.N. Chorafas, *Setting Limits for Market Risk*, Euromoney, London, 1999), hedging transactions and the review of trading activities. This review should be carried out by both management of the trading areas and the corporate chief risk management structure – and it should be steady.

In the G-10 countries, supervisory authorities try to ensure that banks are adopting appropriate procedures for measuring and control reasons. They also issue directives which guide the hand of institutions in applying risk measurement at an increasing level of efficiency. But at the same time innovation in financial instruments moves fast and makes obsolete even the best of yesterday's risk management tools.

Since supervisors appreciate that some of the commercial and investment banks are ahead of them in the manipulation of derivative products and in technology, they try to keep abreast of new developments by engaging in dialogue with these institutions and other parties active in innovation. They also review reporting systems, either directly or through external auditors, to ensure that all major on-balance-sheet and off-balance-sheet activities are adequately captured and reported.

How well are commercial and investment banks organised for risk management, and how big is their derivatives exposure? I will start with the second part of this query, taking as an example the ALFA money centre bank. The name of the institution is fictitious, but the statistics I present are real. In 1998, ALFA posted a significant increase in off-balance-sheet contract volume. Derivative financial instruments, both exchange traded and OTC, expanded by 37.5 per cent to $3.1 trillion in notional principal amount. The aggregate volume of OTC contracts registered a 45 per cent yearly increase to $2.9 trillion, compared with a 1997 level of $2.0 trillion. The gross positive replacement values at the end of 1998 amounted to $63.5 billion, a very large sum indeed. This amount represented 2.2 per cent of the total OTC contract volume, up from 2.1 per cent in 1997. Taking account of legally enforceable netting agreements and following the deduction of deposits pledged as security, AFLA's credit risk at the end of 1998 stood at $31.1 billion as against $23.1 billion in 1997. This, too, was a hefty one-year increase.

About 52 per cent of the volume of all derivative contracts open at the end of 1998 had a maturity of no longer than one year. This was not an improvement because in 1997 this per centage was 54 per cent. At the same time, 1998 saw interest rate swaps grow by $363 billion to $1.2 trillion, a rise of 47.2 per cent.

The volume of forward rate agreements and other interest rate futures increased by 41.0 per cent during 1998, to $161 billion. The total volume of interest rate instruments expanded by $484 billion (or 36.5 per cent) to $1.8 trillion, as a result of demand by customers for hedging transactions and the bank's own proprietary trading.

The contract volume of currency derivatives grew by $340 billion to $1.2 trillion. About half of this increase was the aftermath of a larger trade in forward contracts, swaps and option purchases/sales (see section 4). ALFA said that this statistic reflected burgeoning demand for customer-specific solutions which hedge against market risks associated with foreign exchange volatility.

The data presented in the preceding paragraphs poses a question: are the board and senior management of the ALFA Bank really in charge of risk resulting from derivatives trades and associated positions in its portfolio? Asked about this, a cognisant senior banker said: 'There are about 10 banks in the world who know what they do with derivatives. The others are also-runners.' He did not specifically comment on the ALFA Bank.

This leads to another critical query: what can be done to improve an institution's risk management systems and procedures? One solution currently being tried by some banks is to use dual risk measures for both market risk and credit risk. With this, the focus is placed on the common intersection of the two risk lines over a one-year period. For instance, for market risk, the bank determines its risk assumption level by allocating capital at risk. This is subsequently reallocated into 10-day and one-day VAR limits, and is carefully controlled.

In a similar manner, for credit risk some banks track and control their exposure in two timeframes: first, VAR over the remaining life of the credit portfolio, and most particularly over the longest remaining maturity; second, VAR over the next one-year time horizon (and, in some cases, beyond one year).

Credit VAR limits for both timeframes are set during annual budgeting and they are re-evaluated in the course of budgetary revision as well as in connection to plan/actual comparisons. This helps in developing a culture that is risk-sensitive and driven by profitability. The latter should be risk-adjusted to account for the cost of risk.

A key feature of a system able to control credit exposure is that it takes the risks on individual deals and local counterparties and rolls them up through: global counterparties; branches and affiliates; specific instruments; and portfolios. This should be done in real-time and be associated with the intraday production of virtual balance sheets.

A solution worth its salt will be able to consolidate the exposures according to the way, or ways, in which the bank wants to monitor its credit risk and market risk. An integral part of such strategy is the existence and use of a *limits system* which puts tolerances on to dealing and provides the metrics for measurement (D.N. Chorafas, *Setting Limits for Market Risk*, Euromoney, London, 1998).

Credit exposure analysis should embody the bank's strategic approach to risk, going beyond calculating the exposures being taken or already embedded by monitoring the limits and flushing out deviations as well as trends which may unbalance the system. As we have seen in section 2, a most efficient solution would operate at the strategic level and be adapted to meet the goal of managing risk in an integrated way across the bank. There is also a need for qualitative analysis, as explained in section 4 with an example on options.

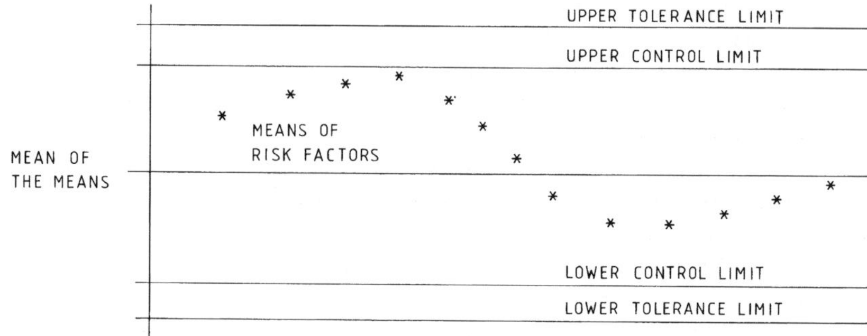

Figure 9.1 Statistical quality charts are powerful tools with significant opportunities in banking

Prior to this let me briefly bring to the reader's attention the service provided in risk management through time-sensitive *quality control* charts. Figure 9.1 shows a statistical quality control (SQC) chart by variables with tolerance limits and quality control limits which helps to measure statistical variation in a basic characteristic *x*: it permits the disclosure of the tolerances of a process, such as giving loans or trading, and it shows the quality trend, during operations, as well as whether it is in control.

Think of the tolerances as counterparty limits, currency exposure limits or other quantitative targets established by senior management, and of the variables plot in the chart as risk factors. SQC charts should be viewed as tools which influence decisions related to specifications, operations and supervision. They provide better quality assurance at lower inspection cost. They have been very successfully used in manufacturing for 60 years, and they are currently being tested by tier-1 banks and certain supervisory authorities for financial industry applications.

4 Critical questions in analysing the options book

In a spot transaction the agreed price is paid immediately and the buyer takes possession of the asset. In futures and forwards, the price is agreed when the transaction is concluded, but the payment occurs some time down the line, and so does delivery. Futures are traded in exchanges; forwards are bilateral OTC agreements. Options are like forwards except that the buyer has the right but not the obligation to execute the deal. This is a privilege for which he pays a premium to the writer (seller) of the option.

The option may be a call, giving the buyer the right to buy a certain asset; or a put. A put option offers the buyer the right to sell an asset (see Chapter 8 on computer companies writing options on their own stock). European options have to be exercised at maturity. American options can also be exercised prior to maturity. Bermuda options combine American and European characteristics.

Futures, forwards and options are derivative instruments because, through the appropriate algorithm, their value is derived from that of the underlier. Equity indices and different debt schemes are also derivatives. Many analysts consider equities traded in exchanges to be derivatives. Theoretically at least, the market determines the value of a firm's equity by reference to:

- the underlying fair value of the firm's assets;
- the earnings' stream the firm derives from its operations; and/or
- the discounted cash flow of the firm's business.

If the equity of a company is a call option on its assets, then by buying stock the investor gets an option on the future value of its products and facilities: for instance, buying the stock of a gold producer is equivalent to buying an option on gold.

Several factors enter into options pricing, the underlier, the leveraging algorithm and market conditions being the prime points of reference. The value of options is significantly affected by movements in rates, whether they concern interest rates, currency rates, indexes, commodities or synthetics. Therefore, the exposure connected to all derivative financial instruments (whether included in the portfolio, or connected to a given transaction) has to be adjusted to obtain a realistic estimate of gains and losses confronting the bank or individual investor. There are two approaches in reaching this goal:

- an *instrument specific*, detailed approach, customised to in-the-money or out-of-the money options; and
- a more *generic* solution, which is less precise but more widely applicable, also differentiating between in-the-money or out-of-the-money conditions.

We will look at the second solution as it can help in elaborating the more detailed approaches. In so doing, we will follow two paths, the one based on the notional principal (NP), the other on a specific number of contracts (NC), as is so often done in the options industry. Before doing so, however, it is important to know the degree of mastering our bank has over its options trades, by finding the answers to some analytical queries.

1. Are we net buyers or net sellers of options?
2. Do we have a preference in maturities?
3. What type of option do we buy or write?

We also need to know what the senior management policy is in connection to options underwriting and are there well-established limits? Other crucial questions requiring a factual and documented answer include: how does our net premium compare to what we lost with options last week, last month or last year? Do we know if there is a concentration of strikes in our options book?

The analyst who looks after risk factors should also care to know how well pricing executives and traders control the volatility smiles and how sound are their volatility calculations. Have they detected cases of mispricing? If yes, what action has been taken? If no, has senior management examined *if* there is option mispricing in *our* bank's portfolio?

While these queries are vital to senior management for control reasons, they are also of importance to supervisors. When examining how well a bank is managed and what is the reliability of its risk control system, supervisors typically use the same battery of queries in order to form an opinion and apply the necessary controls.

Algorithmic solutions, like the example presented in the following paragraphs, can provide an important insight, but the qualitative aspect of a rigorous analysis should never be downplayed. When it precedes the modelling effort, as should be done in the general case, a rigorous qualitative analysis offers a good basis on which to build valid assumptions.

For the modelling part of this exercise we will look at the buyer rather than the underwriter. The principle which will we use is that the buyer of the option is exposed to market risk as long as his asset is out-of-the-money or at-the-money; that is, at the edge between profit and loss. But at the moment the option is in-the-money, the buyer faces credit risk rather than market risk, though market risk is always present throughout the life of the option.

The switch from primarily market risk to primarily credit risk means that the holder of the option faces delivery risk. With the exception of currency options, this risk exposure is one-sided, primarily affecting the winning party.

The buyer's exposure is essentially dual: loss of the premium he has paid to the writer, and loss of the financial gain he is entitled to in case he decides to exercise an in-the-money option. By contrast, once the writer of the option receives his premium, he is no longer dependent on the buyer for future performance as a counterparty.

In other terms, the seller has no credit risk but he continues being exposed to market risk until the buyer exercises his legal rights or the option expires. Based on these premises and looking at the risk from the buyer's viewpoint, we can express in an algorithmic form the market risk equivalent exposure resulting from the option:

$$MR = RF \cdot \frac{NP}{SP} \cdot (MP - SP) \tag{9.1}$$

where

MR = market risk
RF = risk factor

NP = notional principal
SP = strike price
MP = market price

The ratio NP/SP is an estimate of NC, the number of contracts when commitment is made. Equation (9.1) is valid in the case of calls. For put options, it will be:

$$MR = RF \cdot \frac{NP}{SP} \cdot (SP - MP) \tag{9.2}$$

Some analysts prefer to use instead the equation:

$$MR = \frac{NP}{SP} \cdot ((RF \cdot MP) + (MP - SP)) \tag{9.3}$$

This algorithm, however, does not make much sense because the product (RF . MP) does not fit well in terms of equivalent market risk. On the contrary, it is correct to state that at any given time MP is subject to the effects of the risk factor RF. The pattern of these risk factors could be plotted in a statistical quality control chart, like the one shown in Figure 9.1.

While this example has used algorithms, it is also a good demonstration of how subjective the modelling choices being made can be. Whether the algorithms are developed by the rocket scientists, commercial and investment bankers or by regulators, they involve a number of hypotheses and choices which make them dissimilar to one another, therefore producing results which are not necessarily comparable. Let us keep this in mind when in Chapter 10 we talk about the control of eigenmodels by regulators.

5 Regulatory action and the Year 2000 problem

Exposure can hit the banking industry from many sides, not only from loans, interest rates, currency exchange rates and derivatives. Technology which provides the infrastructure of modern banking also involves risks. When in the early 1990s the central computer systems of the Bank of New York went down for about 24 hours, to avoid bankruptcy the institution had to take a line of credit from the New York Fed. For this it paid $50 million in interest, which is a benchmark to remember in terms of technology risk.

By the mid-1990s it finally started being appreciated that a more widespread and potentially much more costly technology failure may hit the banking industry because of the Y2K problem (see D.N. Chorafas, *Cost-Effective IT Solutions for Financial Services*, Lafferty Publications, London and Dublin, 1998). American and British supervisors were the first to realise the importance of this issue, and its impact on the banking industry. This obliged them to consider how institutions approach Y2K solutions, analysing how effective were their approaches, and examining their implementation timetables.

This and the next section outline some of the more difficult supervisory and public policy issues regulators have been handling in connection with Y2K. They also look into supervisory contingency planning and public communications strategies which have been developed to face the Y2K challenge but bear a much larger impact. Last but not least, this text looks into the litigation aftermath which still looms on the horizon.

Those central banks and other supervisory authorities which took a lead in attacking the Y2K problem and in guiding the institutions under their authority towards its solution believe that this problem has been the major safety issue facing financial companies as the twentieth century drew to a close.

To start with, Y2K originated because in the 1950s when computers were first used in the banking industry they worked side-by-side with accounting machines and input/output was done through punched cards. Punched cards had 80 columns with IBM, but 90 columns with Remington and Power Samas. There was therefore every reason to economise with digits. Punching '56' rather than '1956' looked reasonable.

What was unreasonable is that this practice continued for 40 years, even if by the mid-1960s punched cards were phased out and magnetic tape input/output no longer required being digit thrifty. Also the internal storage of computers had expanded and the cost of storage shrank, making the failure to revise programming policies that much more irrational.

Time of course does not stand still, and while many threats are posed by the Y2K problem the worst of all is the failure to wake up in time. Data processors should have appreciated long ago that in a high-tech society, as the end of the century approaches, the two-digit identification of the year has the potential of a nuclear explosion. Therefore, they should have taken corrective action way ahead of the millennium deadline. Many companies did so, and Figure 9.2 presents statistics on the allocation of time, money and manpower between the five most critical tasks.

Institutions have been especially vulnerable to Y2K because so many of their services and products use date-dependent calculations. Therefore, supervisors took on themselves the responsibility for examining and assessing Y2K readiness, not just once but on a continuous basis till the problems were fixed.

Let me first address the systemic risk issue of Y2K. According to most regulators, the safety and soundness of financial institutions rests on cooperation able to avoid the contagion effect: in the global economy, troubles in one bank can easily spread to others, and from there they spread to the markets.

In examining how tier-1 supervisors attacked the Y2K problem, and in evaluating what was done (particularly in connection with mission-critical

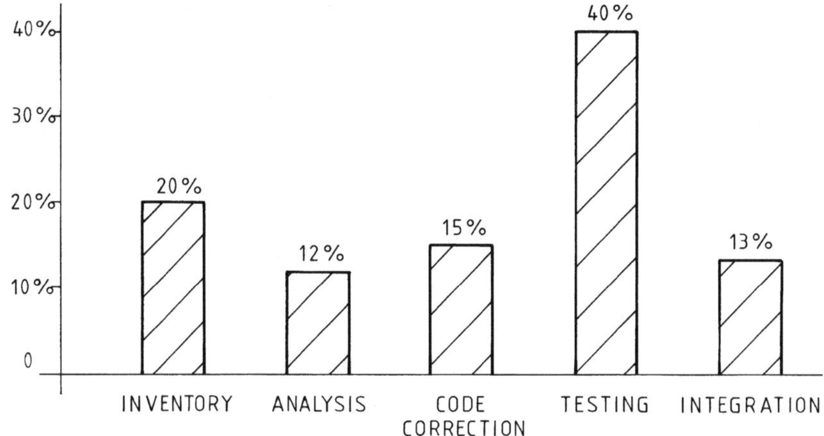

Figure 9.2 Percentage of time typically allocated by companies to each phase of year 2000 problem

issues), we should pay attention to supervisory policies and communications strategies beyond the financial institutions as such, to include the information technology service sector. The action by American supervisors offers a good example.

The Federal Reserve Board, FDIC, OCC and OTS have examined 350 data processing bureaux and software providers regarding their preparedness for Y2K and their ability to solve the associated problems. Ten per cent of these companies, the 36 which are large multi-regionals, have been examined by joint teams of supervisors.

The premise underpinning this scrutiny is that today IT is a core activity in banking. Failures in IT translate into failures in the financial system. Therefore it comes as no surprise that US supervisors kicked out of the network of banking services one of the IT companies whose services were found to be wanting. This firm was handled *as if* it were a financial institution.

Another lesson which can be learned from the action of US supervisors is the need for openness and for communication of the findings. 'Media coverage intensifies', said a senior executive of FDIC. 'If we don't tell the story the media will cover the blanks. There will be problems and we need to condition the public to them.' American examiners found a number of challenges connected with Y2K compliance, including:

- electronic funds transfer (EFT) issues;
- the lack of seamless database solutions; and
- a lack of readiness in infrastructure.

The ability to look in detail at so broad a range of issues was helped by the fact that US bank examiners have included Y2K in their on-site reviews. Up to the end of August 1998, the time for which I have statistics, 300 actions were taken on Y2K preparedness by FDIC alone. Here are the overall results on a per centage basis at that point in time, roughly 16 months prior to the final deadline for Y2K compliance:

- 92 per cent of the US banks had made satisfactory progress;
- 7 per cent needed improvements in senior management oversight; and
- 1 per cent did not provide satisfactory answers in resources and timetables.

Design reviews by the US regulators have documented that both supervisory action and business incentives are needed to beef up Y2K examination procedures, upgrade the level of project management, improve the quality of testing, and provide for contingency planning. Incidentally, these same factors apply to IT preparedness at large, not only to Y2K compliance.

Part and parcel of the extensive outreach efforts by US regulators have been one-day seminars for financial institutions, service providers and software vendors. For instance, more than 125 seminars offered across the US by FDIC were attended by over 10000 bank executives, IT managers and other people.

This activity helped the individual banks to decide who is going to be in charge of Y2K compliance and who should to be responsible for the results the regulators requested. Through it, the supervisors made it clear that senior management could not afford to become complacent, even if it felt encouraged by progress in meeting Y2K deadlines.

Aside from other important considerations, looming on the horizon were – and still are – major legal costs associated with Y2K. While the programmers' and computers' costs of Y2K are estimated to be at the level of $500 billion to $600 billion, according to expert opinion, the lawyers' fees for Y2K could exceed $1 trillion. Throughout 1998 and 1999 lawyers have been attending seminars on how to *bring* and *defend* Y2K cases. According to estimates made in America, there will be more *lawyer-driven* cases on Y2K problems than *customer-driven* ones. Andrew Grove, Intel's chairman, has predicted that:

- the US will be bogged down in a sea of litigation; and
- Y2K problems will put the asbestos litigation to shame.

Some experts think that over the years court cases concerning the Y2K bug will hit both banks and technology companies. Because of the risk of extended litigation, since 1998 some big integrators in America have refused new Y2K projects for fear they will be held liable for unresolved problems.

Credit institutions cannot take this approach. Therefore, the board and top management must be well aware of major risks created by Y2K, such as:

- *risks to capital*: credit risk, settlement risk;
- *risks of market exposure*: market risks, operational risks;
- *liquidity risks*, including risks to income stream in the longer term.

These Y2K risks are over and above the *legal and regulatory risks* to which all institutions are subject because of failure of their mission-critical systems. Regulators have also been seriously concerned about systemic risk, including failure of the banking infrastructure to perform its assigned duties. Curiously enough, some banks considered reducing their Y2K exposure by entering into derivatives contracts that postpone loans payments and cash flow swaps from December 1999 to March 2000; but superimposing two complex issues has never been a good solution.

6 Supervisory authorities which have been alert regarding Year 2000 exposure

For its own Y2K compliance needs FDIC established an Oversight Committee on Y2K, which reports to the board. Members of the Oversight Committee went out with the examiners to see first-hand the problem at the controlled financial institutions. Some 1800 FDIC examiners received Y2K training, and the inspection teams also included systems examiners to beef up the know-how and provide advice.

The overriding policy of US regulators has been to identify institutions which will probably not achieve complete Y2K readiness, and press the point that they need to be ready in time. Given the magnitude of the problem, it was important to identify such situations as soon as possible so that an orderly resolution could be effected for damage control.

Institutions were asked by the supervisors to test all interfaces between systems they own as well as their interfaces with external parties. Senior management was required to use internal auditors, external auditors, or other qualified individuals to evaluate the tests and audit the results presented by the IT people.

To help the banks with know-how on software companies, the federal examiners shared with financial institutions the results of service provider and software vendor reviews. They also encouraged banks to join user groups to increase the leverage of their internal know-how through sharing solutions to common problems and avoiding duplication of efforts.

The frequency of Y2K inspection by supervisors was individualised by credit institution and it depended on results. Banks, service providers and software vendors rated satisfactory received quarterly reviews. Companies rated less than satisfactory underwent a more intense regulatory scrutiny, and were subject to corrective action.

This rigorous policy has given the regulators a good indication as to where each bank stands on Y2K compliance. If the supervisory authority's view was that the bank will not be ready, then they tried to find a buyer or effect a merger. FDIC has been particularly sensitive to this issue because, as deposit insurer, it serves as receiver for failed banks. To preserve public confidence in dealing with failing institutions, it makes a concerted effort to identify a timely, orderly and least cost solution, through:

- exploring cost-effective ways to sell institutions with Y2K problems;
- developing methods to handle customers of institutions with major Y2K problems; and
- establishing logistics strategies for staff and equipment to support closures.

Valuable information on Y2K compliance was provided through testing, with priority given to critical systems. The examiners ascertained the reason for slippage(s), and evaluated integration testing. Integration testing proved to be more complex where there was more than one IT service company helping in Y2K compliance. At times, the regulators used external auditors to ascertain tests and results from the tests.

All this identifies a rigorous Y2K policy on behalf of the regulators. All four major regulatory agencies in the USA made good use of their supervisory mandate to establish and maintain critical information elements affecting the financial sector. These included, among other things, balances, accruals, customer information, and historical data, so that the banking system and its files could be reconstructed if necessary.

FDIC identified 56 critical elements which were needed for reconstruction purposes, in a complete information system sense. The efficient and timely identification of critical information elements proved to be key to the bank supervisors' contingency planning. Contingency planning for banks has been a priority. No central bank or other supervisory authority can afford to lose sight of its responsibilities in this area. Regulatory authorities:

- must be prepared to deal with the probability of individual or widespread disruptions in the banking industry due to critical problems; and
- must account for the fact that some countries are not making progress compatible with systemic risk requirements, as happened in ensuring Y2K readiness.

Section 5 has made reference to the US supervisors' awareness of risks posed by relationships with third parties, such as software and service providers. Other companies examined by American bank supervisors for Y2K dependability have been energy producers and distributors, telecommunications firms and stock exchanges, and also, obviously, payment systems. These references help to identify external risks. Financial services firms can only then successfully address problems that they will face if they do not find themselves side-tracked by major failures among their suppliers.

American regulators also reviewed the legal powers available to them to deal with disruptions in supply chains. Taking care of possible failures because of Y2K led to resolution strategies which are similar to handling bad banks. Worst-case scenarios were developed, including plenty of 'what if's.

1. What will happen if we have 20 bank failures, 50 failures, 100 failures?
2. What type of command centre is necessary for intelligent decisions and for damage control?
3. If the worst comes to the worst, how can we fix the situation as fast as possible to reduce spillover?

Answers to these questions necessarily included communications strategies, fraud that might occur, the sharing of resources among regulatory agencies, and international connections because catastrophic risks could be imported.

Part of the strategy has been to encourage public disclosure, and this led to legal initiatives. A new US law promoted disclosure by providing some relief from liability. The bottom line is that disclosures are an effective method for commercial banks and investment banks to inform customers of their readiness. Open disclosure is also the best method by which supervisors can gain and maintain public confidence in the financial system.

10
Model Risk and the Control of Eigenmodels by the Supervisors

1 Introduction

Following the 1996 Market Risk Amendment by the Basle Committee on Banking Supervision, and the adoption of VAR as a measurement of market exposure, the examination, control and approval of financial reporting based on internal bank models (eigenmodels) has become a core activity of supervisors. This task is increasingly demanding owing to the evolving complexity of financial models, and the need to judge the assumptions employed in eigenmodels and the way these are used.

Different central banks and regulators follow different policies in carrying out this task. In Germany, for instance, the first examinations of internal models took place in August 1997; these aimed to give the so-called 'Basle banks' the possibility of calculating VAR and associated capital requirements as of 31 December 1997, although official reporting through VAR was scheduled to start a year later.

Fifteen German institutions had plans to use VAR models at the time of the first 1997 examination. The term 'Basle banks' identifies the institutions which complied with the 1988 Capital Adequacy accord. However, during the experimental phase at the end of 1997, only six of these banks passed the VAR test.

Supervisors appreciate the fact that trading activities, market parameters and organisational issues concerning a bank under their authority are constantly in flux, and this has a direct impact on the use of internal risk measurement and management methods, models being no exception. Neither are the models static. Therefore, the tests and conditions for approving eigenmodels must be appropriately adapted whenever material changes occur.

Figure 10.1 presents in a nutshell the information processes and computational procedures for VAR. The system described is fairly similar to other modelling efforts. As the reader can appreciate, the algorithm of the model is only one component of the system. No engine can function without each one of its parts playing its intended role.

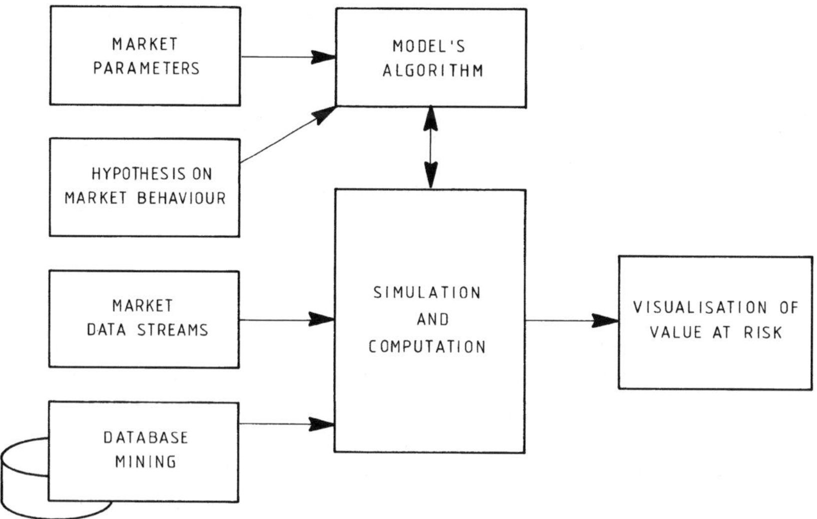

Figure 10.1 Information processes and computation procedures for VAR

The test of eigenmodels by regulators should not be limited to the mathematics, but extend all the way to the basic assumptions and hypotheses. Theoreticians, for instance, say that hedging models create a risk-free portfolio. What this fails to bring into perspective is that even the most perfect hedge can be invalidated because of market changes which were not foreseen or have been poorly judged.

The best test of a model is to compare its results with the actual market position. Based on observation and reasoning, many tests can be carried out post-mortem to assist in deciding whether the modelling solution has an acceptable accuracy. A good example in applying this principle is the classification of model results into green, yellow and red zones specified by the Basle Committee (see D.N. Chorafas, *The 1996 Market Risk Amendment. Understanding the Marking-to-Model and Value-at-Risk,* McGraw-Hill/Irwin Professional Publishing, Burr Ridge, IL, 1998).

2 The challenge modelling solutions pose to regulators and to the bank's own board

Since financial markets are not only globalised but they are also very dynamic, central banks and other regulatory bodies have no alternative to carrying out longer-term research on ways and means to steadily improve bank supervision. Models are part of this drive for better control over risk and, for many years, there has been a great deal of work on what these algorithms can deliver in terms of insight.

The emphasis on research in connection with interest rate risk, currency exchange risk, equities risk, derivatives risk and other exposures is a direct reflection of the fact that credit risk and market risk are in continuous motion, with the one being morphed into the other. To a substantial extent this happens as a result of derivatives. Hence the need to have good models for:

- the pricing of financial instruments; and
- the steady measurement of exposure.

The family of metrics which we develop and use must operate across the bank's portfolio. The measurements resulting from simulation and other modelling approaches are to a large extent based on analytical thinking. There is always a subjectivity coming into modelling. To keep it in check, solutions must be guided by a structure which is cumulative, permitting both the calculation of details and discovery of the compound figure of exposure.

Models are no one-off business made once and serving forever. As suggested in the Introduction, they have to be constantly re-evaluated based on their results, and the way these compare to real life. Other factors, too, lead to model revisions: for instance, changes in data streams and structural issues.

The need for steady evaluation accompanied by changes is by no means a new issue in banking. As the price of a hedged commodity changes over time, the institution must alter the composition of its portfolio in order to hit a given target of risk and return. Only steady vigilance can ensure that a watchful eye over holdings has risk under control. This will not be so easy with models, but it is nearly impossible through manual methods.

No undocumented adjustments should be made to models. Therefore follow-up checks are absolutely necessary to ensure that the hypotheses are still valid and the algorithms are appreciated and are being applied correctly. This leads to an ongoing process of examinations and a continuous dialogue between supervisors and bank management, whereby the specific situation of the bank is always taken into consideration.

Such dialogue between modelling and real life can see to it that the institution has developed for itself the platform needed for proper identification of weaknesses in risk controlling, and it does so on a dynamic basis. This entails decisions on important issues involving methodology and organisation as well as the quality of management. Whether carried out by supervisors or through internal inspection, the control of eigenmodels is not just a question of mathematics.

Both model accuracy and flexibility are, so to speak, on the block. Greater flexibility is made possible through well-chosen simulation methods, and this helps to explain a major difference between the 1996 Market Risk Amendment by the Basle Committee and the EU's CAD (see Part Three).

VAR models give results which are rather flexible and cumulative, leading management towards an understanding of exposures. The 1988 Capital Accord, and CAD itself, are cut along lines which are cast in stone, they do not adapt well to prevailing conditions.

Readers with experience in simulation will appreciate that the real impact of models comes from two facts: their ability to set the stage for experimentation, and their ability to evolve over time. For this purpose several central banks of the G-10 countries are currently doing research on VAR. The Bank of England for example, has used four real-life trading books from financial institutions for experimental reasons. These are addressing:

- five government bond markets (UK, USA, Japan, Germany and France);
- fourteen maturity buckets for each of these markets;
- currency exchange risk in five markets; and
- equity position risk, also in five markets.

In this particular experiment, the returns data covered the timeframe from July 1987 to April 1995, and included zero coupon yield curves, equity indices and foreign exchange rates. As this and similar research projects have documented, there are certain conditions necessary for obtaining reliable results, very good *data quality* being at the top of the list.

The fact that reliable information is the cornerstone of successful modelling solutions is known from engineering, but it poses problems in finance. For some markets, particularly for emerging countries, data is poor or even non-existent. However, in G-10 markets where many data sources are generally good, data collection by some individual banks is poor, and sometimes their datamining culture and tools are not state of the art.

Database mining is crucial, but many banks do not have the necessary experience and their data handling procedures are altogether wanting. Neither has the majority of institutions the organisation necessary for real-time information and the production of virtual financial statements which offer one of the best applications domains of advanced IT.

The lack of first-class data collection and data running leads to inaccuracies. Models using incomplete or inaccurate information provide forecasts which are prone to be wrong. As an old hand at modelling and simulation, I am appalled by the way some institutions use VAR and other algorithmic solutions.

Also unwise is the widespread employment of normal distributions when handling financial data. One of the characteristics of globalisation of banking is the existence of outliers; yet only recently have some credit institutions come to appreciate the effect of extreme events, such as severe stock market corrections. In the bull market of the five years 1994–99 there have been significant pullbacks every so often which drop from the modelling screen if spikes are not given the attention they deserve.

Data is not the only weakness faced by institutions which tool up for modelling, and by supervisors whose mission is to control the results of these models. Many banks are behind in algorithms and heuristics for real-time calculations and/or find it difficult to understand the sense of confidence intervals and their service to the evaluation of exposure. The 1996 Market Risk Amendment specifies a confidence level of 99 per cent. As with the 90 per cent and 95 per cent levels of confidence, this is a measure enabling management to appreciate both what is the level of the bank's exposure today, and the probability by which this level will be exceeded.

The higher is the level of confidence (for instance, 99 per cent is higher than 95 per cent), the higher will be the estimated level of exposure, but the lower is the probability this level will be exceeded in actual life (1 per cent and 5 per cent, in this example). Banks which lack the culture to understand this difference chose for internal management accounting reasons 90 per cent or 95 per cent levels of confidence, instead of 99 per cent as specified by the Market Risk Amendment. By so doing, they were kidding themselves.

In conclusion, failure to satisfy the basic prerequisites of model literacy on behalf of the senior management of financial institutions raises a number of issues because banks cannot position themselves in terms of effectively controlling risk. The members of the board of directors, the chief executive and the members of the executive committee must be able to realise what is meant by model parameters such as 99 per cent confidence and 10-day holding period.

They must also appreciate what is meant by the green, yellow and red zones and the overall multiplier: 3 × 60 day average of VAR. This is a prerequisite to appreciating that in a control environment such a multiplier holds under normal conditions, but it is quite likely it will not be enough when spikes are produced (for example, by runs on the market or mini panics). Even a multiplier of 5 would not cover big outliers, a fact which has a major incidence on required reserves.

3 Basic notions to keep in perspective when modelling the real world

From cultural challenges to algorithmic deficiencies and the problems connected with data collection and mining, the examples shown in section 2 identify the daunting task faced by regulators when they audit the results of the bank's eigenmodels, or look at management policies and procedures surrounding their implementation. It is not the objective of this book to explain what financial models are and are not, or to outline a step-by-step procedure for their application.

However, some basic notions contained in this section may help in appreciating what underpins the development and use of models by financial institutions, whether for pricing, forecasting market trends or risk management. I will keep this discussion as close as possible to the fundamentals, and as comprehensive as it can be in a few pages.

Modelling is a thought experiment which aims to represent the real world in a fairly accurate manner. This representation, or mapping, needs a theory and this is exactly where the first major challenge is presented. A complete theory, Albert Einstein once suggested, would have to satisfy a number of conditions: for example, each element of model (or virtual reality) must have a corresponding physical existence. Physical reality is defined by a fairly pragmatic criterion which is valid in physics, engineering and finance: '*If*, without disturbing the system in any way, we can predict the value of physical phenomena with certainty, *then* an element of physical reality exists that corresponds to that (represented)physical magnitude.' From this perspective simulation becomes a working analogy, where the physical existence is mapped into, or represented by, an algorithmic expression.

When analogous systems are found to exist, experimentation on one of them can lead to tentative conclusions on the behaviour of the other. Notice, however, that the physical magnitude remains in the background. As Albert Einstein explained to mathematicians, their abstract concepts were pure speculation unless they paid due regard to facts (Albrecht Fölsing, *Albert Einstein*, Penguin Putnam, New York, 1997), and hence to reality. This is as true of physics, to which Einstein made reference, as it is of banking.

A very interesting distinction made by Einstein in terms of modelling was between *wholesale* and *retail procedures*. Retail, he explained, was the customary way of theoretical physicists and it consisted of solving one equation after another. But Albert Einstein demonstrated that one can handle equations wholesale by counting:

- the number of unknown quantities; and
- the number of marginal conditions.

Having done this, the rocket scientist can follow another lead from the great physicist: that of comparing the results to the number of degrees of freedom (see D.N. Chorafas, *How to Understand and Use Mathematics for Derivatives*, Volume 2, Euromoney Books, London, 1995). Furthermore, rather than focusing on the solution of equations as a primary objective, Einstein's method addressed, first and foremost, whether the problem had a solution and, if yes, whether that solution was the only one possible. Among other benefits, this approach allows us to look at a theory on the strength of the facts, rather than try to interpret the facts on the strength of the theory prevailing at a certain time, eventually finding out that that theory has been superseded by a new one, and that the old postulates mapped into the model have been abandoned.

The great tragedy of science, as T.H. Huxley famously put it, is the slaying of a beautiful hypothesis by an ugly fact: for instance, in finance, the slaying of VAR by extreme events which were considered to be most unlikely outliers (see section 4). The regulators who control the eigenmodels of financial institutions should keep in perspective the wise remarks of both Einstein and Huxley. *If* they do not, *then* they are not executing appropriately the mission with which they have been entrusted.

Furthermore, there are organisational prerequisites to successful financial modelling, some of which have been identified by the Federal Reserve. One of these is that rigorous risk management should be conducted by a well-specified control area of the bank as well as for the whole institution. In addition, the models to be developed must be sophisticated, leading to an increased use of Monte Carlo simulation for complex products. Besides that, models must be tested and backtested. The people assigned to control the modelling process and its implementation should:

- evaluate the bank's internal controls;
- analyse the model and its variables;
- evaluate the simulation and pricing consistency;
- ensure that Profit and Loss manipulation is avoided; and
- guarantee there is an overall risk management system solution.

All this is an integral part of model literacy on senior management's part. Another characteristic is the ability to realise that the bank cannot take a model off the shelf and use it. A basic prerequisite is to understand what the model delivers and to administer stress tests. There is also a critical list of other issues regarding modelling: for instance: the effort to capture specific risk.

Specific risk is the risk that the price of an instrument will move out of line with similar instruments, due principally to factors relating to its issuer. The 1996 Market Risk Amendment does not exactly cover specific risk, but many central banks are now focusing on this issue and we can expect an extension of current models towards specific risk.

Another issue concerns studying market volatility by instrument. This is becoming important in fine-tuning management controls: for instance, bond options have different volatilities from swaptions, and these are also different from caps and floors. Swaptions can be seen as a collar at the same strike price. Because institutions have a different product mix, price volatility by instrument is important.

Yet another issue is that of combining volatility with market liquidity to study compound effects. This is an analytical domain still in its infancy. Volatility and liquidity correlate (see D.N. Chorafas, *Understanding Volatility and Liquidity in Financial Markets*, Euromoney Books, London, 1998). The assessment of profit and loss cannot be done without accounting for liquidity, because we cannot close any positions if there is no liquidity. Figure 10.2

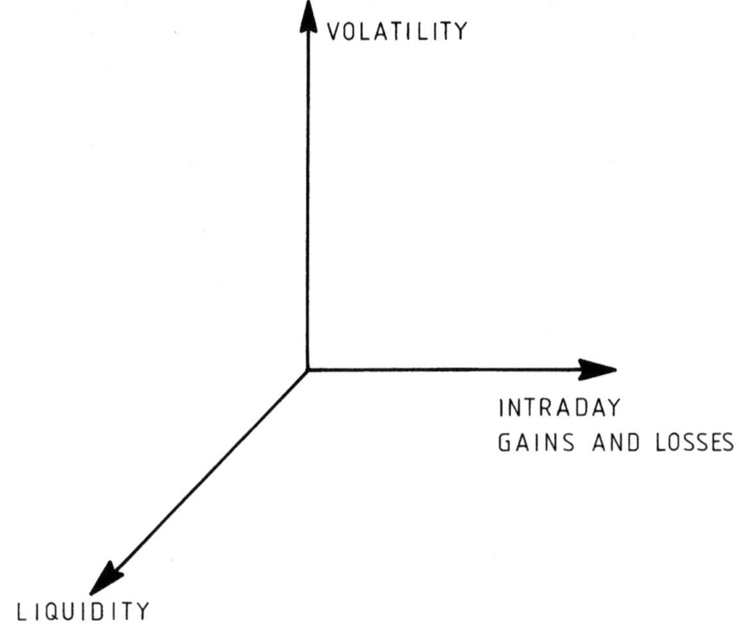

Figure 10.2 An intraday computation of gains and losses in function of volatility and liquidity can be vital to risk control

shows a three-dimensional frame of reference with intraday computing of gains and losses. There is enough evidence pointing to the relevance of this type of study because of what can be revealed in terms of intrinsic market risk.

A fourth issue concerns the ability to integrate counterparty risk and market risk. A prerequisite to integration is the use of credit risk models. The 1988 Capital Accord by the Basle Committee provided a blanket coverage of credit risk through the 8 per cent capital requirement, but it did not model counterparty risk in the way market risk was modelled some years down the line. Credit risk modelling has only now started to be done among tier-1 banks for internal management accounting reasons, and also in the expectation that the capital adequacy regulations may change.

Finally, there is the issue of collecting and exploiting intraday time series for fine-tuning risk and return. Since 1994, the more technologically advanced money centre banks have been focusing on the capture and exploitation of high frequency financial data (HFFD: D.N. Chorafas, *How to Understand and Use Mathematics for Derivatives,* Volume 1, Euromoney, London, 1995). The current state of the art is a 5-minute interval, though available technology will soon make it possible to work subminute. Precisely because few financial institutions have the knowledge to work effectively with HFFD, cognisant analysts foresee a new industry of intraday data providers. They also project a parallel industry of financial instruments pricing and of publicly available pricing databases.

4 Errors in financial modelling and model risk

Model risk is a term which describes how different models, whether developed by the institution or bought from third parties, can produce very different prices for a given financial product: for instance, in pricing an option. The problem with differences in pricing is that they create opportunities for gains and losses in the market which are not well known in advance and may not show up until more than a year later in the form of hefty losses. In the general case the model's complexity can lead to erroneous valuation of a given instrument, but a greater enemy is inaccurate assumptions underlying volatility.

A different way of putting this is to say that errors enter into calculations based on models for a number of reasons. The most potent is that something is wrong or inaccurate with the hypotheses being formed: for instance, regarding volatilities. But, as we have seen in section 3, the data being used may also be inappropriate or incomplete, or the algorithms may lack focus.

Other errors in modelling are present on account of some common practices which are out of tune with rigorous modelling methods and procedures: for example, relying heavily on long historical averages and on guestimates from experience in evaluating the risks currently associated with specific categories of assets and market events. In many cases, banks are:

- deriving asset risk premiums from tenuously related estimates of aggregate debt and equity costs, which typically have non-compensating errors;
- using heterogeneous database elements, or too much interpolation between sparse values to cover the gaps in time series; and
- relying too much on linear relationships between crucial factors, while market behaviour is non-linear and the underlying distribution is not normal.

One of the major error sources is the frequently used assumption that events are normally distributed. In fact, they are not, yet the use of the normal distribution is today so generalised that for many bankers it has become a second nature. Even some rocket scientists do not readily appreciate this fact.

If, for instance, loan values across the portfolio were uncorrelated, the central limit theorem might be invoked and portfolio VAR distributions could be approximated through a bell-shaped distribution. But in practice, because of systematic risk induced by prevailing correlations, the portfolio value distribution generally takes on a non-Gaussian character, being skewed or kyrtotic (D.N. Chorafas, *How to Understand and Use Mathematics for Derivatives*, Volume 2, Euromoney, London, 1995).

The error introduced with the normal distribution hypothesis leads to the fact that the value distribution for, say, individual loans assigns high probability to relatively small gains or losses and a low probability to relatively large gains or losses. Similarly, correlation between borrowers causes the portfolio value distribution to become leptokyrtotic in the lower tail. In a way this is welcome because it helps in prognostication, but also it invalidates the hypothesis of a normal distribution.

A further defect is that because they are built in an inflexible way and/or are based on too narrow assumptions, many models do not cope well with sudden alterations in the relation among market variables. Examples include changes in normal trading range between the dollar and the pound, or the effect of illiquidity in the market (see section 3).

There is also a silver lining, however. An opportunity which comes with model risk is that astute traders with better models can capitalise on mispricings in another trader's model to sell, for instance, an overvalued instrument or commodity. This practice has become known as *model arbitrage.* The irony with losses due to model risk is that it constitutes one of the rare cases which can be taken as a financial zero sum game.

More often than not, however, model risk translates into losses. The estimates made of how much money is gained and lost vary widely and none of them is documented well enough to be taken seriously. One estimate is that model risk losses amounted to 20 per cent of the money lost in 1997 with derivatives, but this is an assertion which does not hold water because:

- so many reasons lie behind model risk, from hypotheses to algorithms and data, that sorting by source of error is pure fantasy; and
- what one trader lost because of coarse grain models another trader gained, supported by fine grain models and high technology (this is the sense of 'zero sum').

This does not mean that models can match, let alone overtake, an expert trader's skill and gut intuition about the market. On the other hand, even the best trader needs assistance to cope with the dynamics of the market, and this is what correctly designed models should provide, beyond the ability to keep exposure under lock and key.

5 The control of eigenmodels by the Swiss Federal Banking Commission

In its mid-1998 report on the investigation of serious losses sustained by UBS in 1997, the Swiss Federal Banking Commission identified *model risk* as one of the reasons for such losses. According to this investigation, the errors were connected to a pricing model known as Worst and Dual Asset Call Spread Options (WOCS), then used by UBS.

In the background of this investigation has been the risk of mispricing, already brought to the reader's attention. A loss of SF120 million ($90 million) was suffered because of mispricing structured instruments traded OTC. Options models are not the only ones which can err. Default models might also give the wrong signal by predicting default when it did not occur, or failing to predict default when it did.

When this happens, the model risk has its origins in the hypotheses entered into the algorithms, the data used for evaluation and for deriving model values, and/or the rating factor used which has influenced the construct's predictive power. The reason for deviations with options pricing are fairly similar and there is also a volatility factor. Furthermore, in many transactions and instruments model performance depends on the development of two indices: the use of models is necessary for these complex trades because the products they involve have no clearly observable market price. If the hypotheses built into the models are incomplete or unrealistic, the final outcome is mispricing.

However, not everything should be ascribed to models. As in the case of £200 million ($328 million) in losses suffered by NatWest Markets in March 1997, commissions have played a key role in option mispricing. The assumptions being made were skewed because the traders assumed a volatility smile which did not materialise.

In the case of the investigation by the Swiss Federal Banking Commission the examiners aptly noted that trading income should be ascertained by a unit which operates independently from the trading department itself. Because operating results determine the level of commissions payable to traders, such commissions tend to lead in choosing pricing assumption, and as a result they tend to be exceptionally high. High commissions bias the assumptions being made.

The completeness or incompleteness of information in developing and testing the model also plays a crucial role, as noted in section 4. To evaluate whether or not a model used by a bank is appropriate, the Swiss Federal Banking Commission requires 1 year of data. With this information, model tests are conducted prior to their approval. The required timeframe may be reduced to 6 months only if the tests concern a modification rather than a new model.

Data requirements concerning tests are part of the approval process. The Federal Banking Commission also asks that the commercial bank present qualitative information: for instance, certain specified organisational criteria, and also how and how often the model will be used for the control of exposure, and what kind of management decisions will be made based on its results.

The strategy followed by the Federal Banking Commission in regard to models is worth studying because, while it is favourable to the use of simulation, it wants to see adherence to prudential rules. For instance, the Commission looks rather positively on the development and use of credit risk models, but it does not accept them for the determination of capital requirements. Instead, according to the Swiss Federal Banking Commission, credit risk models should be developed for a better management of the financial institution, enabling a quantitative appreciation of credit risk both at board level and by senior management. This is a sound policy.

In the general case, central banks and other regulatory authorities of the G-10 look favourably on the development and use of models by commercial and investment banks. They see them as part of modern finance, but they are also trying to use mathematical analysis themselves, in order to understand the risks and benefits which it brings to the banking industry.

The majority of the regulators I talked to in the USA, the UK, Germany, France, Switzerland and Austria expressed the opinion that the design, development and use of eigenmodels fits well with the evolving supervisory control policies. Regulators appreciate that management control procedures must continue to evolve. If they become stagnant, then there will be crevasses in the risk control structures of commercial banks, investment banks and even central banks, with loopholes being created through which major risks can escape prudential supervision and grow into financial crises.

Special mathematical units have been created by regulatory authorities to control the output of models of commercial and investment banks (particularly the VAR output) but, because in the majority of cases the institutions which they control are just starting to use simulation, the current trend is to offer advice and assistance rather than carry out an audit. Regulators duly appreciate what many commercial banks have not yet fully understood: that the real challenge with eigenmodels is not in the mathematics and the algorithms, but in:

- the definition of market parameters;
- choice of critical risk factors;
- hypotheses concerning market behaviour;
- limits of variation of crucial variables; and
- the databases and input data feeds.

Another tough job concerns the compromises necessary between detail and the avoidance of solutions where the trees hide the forest. This comes with experience and it must be admitted that while the development and use of models is becoming fairly popular among institutions, experience with modelling is not being built fast enough or in a way commensurate with outstanding objectives.

A major job concerning the specification of market risk and credit risk factors regards a selection of variables able to capture the exposure associated with on-balance-sheet and off-balance-sheet trading positions. Examples include spread risk, yield curve volatility, the covariance between liquidity and equity prices, the impact of political news on the prices of equity and debt, and so on.

Other challenges are connected with regulatory specifications and the bank's own qualitative standards for eigenmodels. These include the model's integration in the day-to-day risk management; the independence characterising risk control agents; and, most importantly, the active involvement of the board and senior management in the control of exposure. Quite often, the bottleneck is at the top of the bottle!

6 Regulation of eigenmodels by the Austrian supervisors

The Austrian rules and regulations regarding the banking industry stipulate that credit institutions shall establish such administrative, accounting and control procedures as are necessary for the purpose of recording and evaluating the risks of banking transactions. This directive also includes operations risks. As everywhere else, Austrian institutions must record and evaluate potential exposure resulting from their daily business; but the Austrian regulators also provide the banks under their authority with a certain freedom to design their own tailor-made system, including eigenmodels.

There are constraints as well. Credit institutions which use models for calculating their own funds need the approval of the Federal Ministry of Finance to use a model for that purpose. The Austrian supervisory authorities have established qualitative standards applicable to modelling. For instance, institutions must not only set up and maintain a separate risk control unit, independent of the trading units, but they should also endow it with sufficient resources for risk management. The regulators further stipulate that the risk control unit has to analyse the output of the model, produce daily reports on exposure, and inform the executive board directly. Furthermore, the reliability of assumptions on which the model is based, data sources, and methods of measurement have to be checked constantly; and at least once every quarter the risk control unit has to conduct a systematic and comprehensive programme of stress testing. This is an excellent initiative.

Results of this stress testing exercise have to be submitted to the board. They must also be taken into account when setting risk policies and defining trading limits. When stress tests reveal vulnerability to certain circumstances, the regulators expect prompt action to be taken to ensure that those risks are managed appropriately.

An interesting part of the Austrian regulatory armoury is the requirement that, every business day, the risk control unit must run a backtesting programme for the preceding business day. This permits rapid feedback, and lays the groundwork for immediate corrective action to eliminate model risk. This, too, is a first-class initiative.

Another part of the Austrian regulations addresses senior management responsibilities. As an integral part of the risk control units of commercial banks the supervisory authorities want to see specific criteria of *management accountability*: for instance, the clear definition of the decision-making powers and responsibilities of individual organisational areas, as well as:

- a strategic study by the executive board based on the daily reports from the risk control unit;
- the consistency of formal organisational structures with actual work in process; and
- in-depth risk analysis carried by the bank prior to the introduction of new products.

Austrian regulators insist that trading limits are well understood by the executive board, the dealers and the other relevant officers, whether they work in general management, the front desk, back office, risk control or internal auditing. Limits and models correlate, the regulators suggest, as the algorithms have to be integrated into the day-to-day risk management. Model output must be an integral part of the process of planning, monitoring and controlling credit risk and market risk.

The credit institution's internal audit has been given responsibility by the supervisors for regularly reviewing the risk control process and the model(s) being used. This comes over and above the auditing of the activities of the trading units, administrative offices, and the risk control unit. Such a review must address the:

- adequacy of the documentation of the risk management systems and procedures;
- organisation and functioning of the risk management process itself; and
- integration of values at risk into the daily senior management reports.

Internal auditing needs its own skills in rocket science because Austrian regulations endow it with the approval for risk control models and pricing models used by front-desk and back-office staff; the examination of any changes made to the model; the scope of market risks captured by the model, and generally the quality of management information.

Part of the quality-of-information requirements defined by Austrian supervisors is the accuracy and completeness of position data; verification of the consistency, timeliness, reliability and independence of the data sources, including those used in models; accuracy and appropriateness of volatility estimates and correlation assumptions; accuracy of valuation and risk transformation calculations of the model; and the appropriate use of backtesting. In all, this makes a set of very sound regulatory measures which should be a model to other regulators.

Part Three

The Capital Base of Financial Institutions

11

Rethinking and Revamping the 1998 Capital Accord : A New Capital Adequacy Framework

1 Introduction

During the last three or four years international bankers have been calling on the Basle Committee on Banking Supervision to change its formula for calculating how much capital institutions need to hold as a cushion against credit risk. According to the 1998 Capital Accord banks are required to hold capital equivalent to 8 per cent of their assets, with some less risky assets such as mortgages and sovereign loans (see Chapter 15) carrying a reduced risk-weighting.

Published on 3 June 1999, *A New Capital Adequacy Framework* is a consultative paper issued by the Basle Committee on Banking Supervision for public discussion. Though this document is due for comment by 31 March 2000, and by all likelihood there will be some changes, the subjects that it includes will, in one form or another, become regulatory directives of the Group of Ten. Therefore, they deserve the reader's attention (see sections 3 and 4).

As they gain confidence in their modelling procedures, commercial bankers also want supervisors to begin a process of recognising the credit risk models they use internally, a statement which is valid only in regard to the most technologically advanced financial institutions. The G-10 central banks more or less admit that the 1998 Capital Accord may need to be revised, but they are resisting calls to use models for precommitment on capital requirements, while accepting that some formula needs to be developed which accounts for the diversification of risk.

The term *precommitment* stands for regulatory provisions allowing credit institutions to calculate their own fund requirements for both general and specific risk in debt instruments, as well as their exposure in interest rates, foreign exchange, equities, commodities and derivatives. Admittedly, this is a very complex task which so far has not been solved in such a way that supervisors can feel confident that precommitment really works. Capital requirements are an even more complex issue now that institutions hold assets for sale on trading books, and with them longer-term derivatives.

There is also a case for optimisation of capital levels because regulators tend to assign different, generally less onerous, capital requirements on the banks' trading book compared with their banking book. Collateralised loan obligations (CLOs) also contribute to the ongoing change of credit institutions' exposure figures. Like collateralised bond obligations (CBOs), CLOs are structured financing instruments. Backed by the bank's corporate loans, CLOs are an attempt to turn below investment grade assets into investment grade securities, upsetting the basis on which the 1988 Capital Accord rested.

What institutions want is to be allowed to compute the risk they take in these positions by means of models, and to do so regularly, as a sort of extension of the 1996 Market Risk Amendment by the Basle Committee. But both within and outside the G-10, central bankers are not keen on this idea because they perceive the dangers embedded in it. In a recent meeting in London a senior executive of FSA was saying that one of the British money centre banks came up with a model which computed its capital requirements at 5 per cent instead of the regulatory 8 per cent: a 37.5 per cent reduction.

2 The flat 8 per cent capital adequacy by the Basle Committee and its challengers

One of the arguments heard in banking meetings and conferences is that an 8 per cent charge might be about right for an institution with a concentrated portfolio, but not for one with carefully diversified risk positions. Another opinion is that the rating of lenders and borrowers by independent agencies should also be taken into consideration in establishing capital requirements. Still other bankers suggest that not only the borrowers should be considered but also the bank's own financial staying power.

Let us examine, one by one, the different issues involved in these arguments: first, loans diversification. There is no question that a concentration in loans means greater exposure. The institution assumes more important risks if it enters into contracts with a smaller number of counterparties but bigger amounts per transaction. However, *if* the bank's information system cannot take account of concentration and diversification throughout the range of instruments, partners and subsidiaries, *then* senior management cannot get the right answers in terms of concentration or diversification, let alone sustain diversification in the longer term. For this reason, concentration and diversification in loans is often an issue devoid of substance. If we do not know in a timely and accurate manner our exposure, the notion of diversification by itself does not help. Also, knock-on effects such as those involved with LTCM see to it that the whole market moves the same way, turning a hypothetical diversification into a concentration.

Therefore, while there is fairly general agreement that if diversification characterises a bank's portfolio this factor should be incorporated in the revision of the 1988 Capital Accord, opinions among central bankers tend to differ about calculations of exposure. Much of the difficulty has to do with the degree to which diversification of the loans portfolio is real or imaginary.

International bankers who press for lower capital requirements say that both higher rating and diversification from geographical or industrial concentrations tend to reduce risk. Not only credit institutions suggest this, but also Dr Alan Greenspan, who is a supporter of quantitative risk management. Greenspan has criticised the increasingly evident weaknesses of a fixed capital ratio and its inability to adjust for:

- highly rated counterparties; and
- factually documented effective management controls.

Rating systems by independent agencies help in getting a better picture of risk associated with counterparties. This is of great assistance to banks who, because of globalisation, no longer possess the same feel they used to have for the other party's dependability. Some credit institutions now suggest the 8 per cent ratio might be right considering the chances of, say, A-rated companies defaulting and the amount the bank might expect to recover post-liquidation, but it is too high for AA and AAA supranationals.

Not everybody, however, agrees with this concept. Many experts argue that there is a long list of issues connected with diversification, not least among them being that its targets are difficult to define and maintain. Limits set to concentration are easily breached when a given transaction looks really attractive, or has evident advantages over other, alternative transactions.

Diversification as opposed to concentration lines also become blurred because of imprecise definitions. Sometimes they become amplified due to human factors. It is a natural tendency for loans officers to follow names that are highly correlated with one another, either because of ownership or through some other criterion such as industry, product or friendship.

Concentrations inadvertently result when an institution or an investor has a level of exposure to a single name, be it a company or a sovereign. Over time, developments because of this exposure not only hit the bottom line but also hamper the institution's ability to function properly in terms of risk control: for instance, concentrations of credit risk may be generally characterised by inordinately high levels either in absolute numbers or relative to capital.

The Bank of England wants to know if a credit institution has 10 per cent of its capital put at the same name. Other central banks think that new capital requirements should also reflect the fact that the credit risk embedded into the banking book has grown almost exponentially in the 1990s because of economic changes and for political reasons. The aftermath is felt by both banks and borrowers who, to capitalise on greater liquidity promoted by globalisation, have to manage a variety of financial sources rather than depend solely on the classic type of banking loans.

Not only loans but also securities with some characteristics correlating with affected entities or groups of entities also constitute a concentration. A different way of looking at this is that the amount of credit risk diversification achievable in a portfolio depends on the correlation between default risks within this portfolio. The securitisation of loans has made it possible for banks to shed unwanted credit risk concentrations, but this does not mean that those weeded out are not replaced by others equally unwanted as a matter of course. In fact, asset concentration refers to:

- an unacceptably high exposure; or
- an exposure which steadily underperforms.

Mergers in the banking industry have also had a concentration effect on correspondent banks, and something similar can be stated about other industries. But the most pronounced and dangerous effects of concentration are due to derivative financial instruments often traded with a small, select number of counterparties.

A growing number of supervisors believe that even if there were no other issue involved in çoncentration other than derivatives exposure, that would have been enough to make void much of the talk about diversification of risk. This is all the more true as, in practically all financial institutions anywhere, derivatives exposure and its aftermath on credit risk and market risk rises significantly from one year to the next.

For money centre banks as a group, year-on-year the growth in volume of swaps, options and forwards is significant (see also Part Two), currently standing at the 25 to 30 per cent annual level. But there are also sharp differences between banks in terms of the instruments in which each has been most active. For one of the money centre banks I have in mind, the interest rate swap portfolio jumped far more in 1998 than in 1997, while options were the fastest-growing interest rate product of another well-known institution.

In a third, the growth of equity and commodity derivative positions was confirmed by the disclosure of outstanding notional amounts in these markets; while in a fourth, its involvement in interest rate futures and forward contracts soared. In keeping with its strong position in foreign exchange, in a fifth money centre bank the outstanding forward contracts in exchange markets leapt forward a great deal, while other derivatives increased by less than 20 per cent.

In all five institutions, the net result of huge derivatives trades was to swell the balance sheet, hitting the ratio of equity to total assets. But the credit and market exposure did not necessarily grow the same way. Many regulators think that the relative weight and riskiness of different instruments will have to be reflected in the revamping of the 1998 Capital Accord. Event risk, such as the near bankruptcy of LTCM (see Chapter 1) – an extreme event – adds to the exposure of the bank which lends money to the hedge fund.

3 A New Capital Adequacy Framework by Basle Committee on banking supervision

One of the significant differences between the 1988 Capital Accord and the New Capital Adequacy Framework is that the former addresses only credit risk. It makes reference neither to market risk in the banking book, nor to other risks like operational, reputational and legal. Market risk has been regulated through the 1996 Market Risk Amendment, but only in regard to trading book exposure. By contrast, the new framework addresses interest rate risk in the banking book.

The New Capital Adequacy Framework by the Basle Committee, nicknamed by the banking industry 2000+, pays a great deal of attention in encouraging high disclosure standards by credit institutions and other market players. It also enhances the role of market participants by inciting banks to hold adequate capital. The framework's core issues can be expressed in three top rules and five essential guidelines:

Top Three Rules

1. Minimum capital requirements will be computed under either the 'standard' and or an 'advanced' solution;
2. There will be steady review of capital adequacy by national supervisory authorities;
3. Market discipline is necessary to encourage reliable financial disclosures.

Next Five Guidelines

4. There is need to analyse operational risk and provide capital for it;
5. External ratings by reputable independent agencies: S&P, Moody's, Fitch IBCA can be effectively used;
6. Loans made by banks to high leverage institutions should be the subject of special treatment;
7. Credit derivatives are recognised as means of managing credit risk volatility;
8. Internal ratings by technologically advanced institutions may be acceptable and will probably leading to precommitment.

As the careful reader will notice, the New Capital Adequacy Framework provides an option between the standard 8 per cent capital requirement (see section 2) and an advanced solution which promotes both the employment of *credit ratings* by independent agencies (D.N. Chorafas *'Credit Risk Management'*, Volume 1 *Analyzing, Rating and Pricing the probability of Default*, Euromoney, London, 2000.) and an *internal ratings-based* (IRB) approach (see section 4). The discussion document by the Basle Committee suggests that sophisticated financial institutions might use IRB for estimating capital charges pertinent to their exposure.

In connection to computations addressing minimum prudential levels and the steady review of capital adequacy by national supervisors, risk weights will be applied to different types of exposure. For instance, in regard to sovereigns, the Basle Committee proposes replacing the existing approach by a system that would use external credit assessments for determining risk weights. A similar concept will apply to varying degrees to the risk weighting of exposures to correspondent banks, securities firms, high leverage institutions (HLI, read hedge funds) and corporate clients.

The background notion is that with appropriate diversification and choice of business partners, it might be possible to reduce risk weights for high quality credits while introducing a *higher-than-100 per cent* risk weight for low quality exposures. A risk weighting scheme is also projected to address asset securitization. The discussion paper advances the notion of a 20 per cent credit conversion factor for certain types of short-term commitment.

The third of the top three rules addresses *market discipline* – a sort of self-regulation. This is seen as the means to encourage high disclosure standards, as well as a way of promoting the role of market players in inducing credit institutions to hold adequate capital, commensurate with the risks they take. The Basle Committee intends to issue further guidance on public disclosure, but also looks at market discipline as having the potential to reinforce capital regulation and other supervisory procedures.

- The goal of international regulators is to put in place strong incentives on institutions to conduct their business in a safe and efficient manner;
- this includes the establishment of appropriate cushions against potential future losses arising from trading, investments, loans and other exposures.

Bank supervisors have a strong interest in facilitating effective market discipline as a lever to strengthen the banking system and its safety nets. Issued in September 1998, the Basle Committee's *Enhancing Bank Transparency* explains how a credit institution that is perceived as safe and well-managed in the marketplace is likely to obtain more favourable terms and conditions in its relations with depositors, creditors, investors, correspondent banks and other counterparties.

The global capital market requires higher risk premiums and additional collateral or other safety measures, if the credit institution with which it deals presents more risk. An example is *Japan premium* instituted by the financial market in the late 1990s as soon as counterparties detected specific risk associated with overexposure which characterised Japanese institutions.

The Basle Committee acknowledges that market discipline may in a way be affected because of differences in legal systems in various countries with the result being difficulties in implementation of this third pillar of the new Framework. It also recognises that differences in a credit institution's reliance on financial markets can see to it that the potential of market discipline varies across countries or regions.

An example cited in a New Capital Adequacy Framework is that a bank may not be subject to market discipline from fully insured depositors who have nothing at risk, hence no motive to impose discipline. While it is true that public opinion may exercise pressure, by all likelihood this will be felt in an indirect way via legislators. By contrast, a proposal made by the faculty of Columbia University in the direction of market discipline is that institutions buy equity in each other, thereby having a say through management control.

The Basle Committee also wants to see that credit institutions adopt a consistent approach in using a particular assessment approach and do not try to capitalise on differences existing among assessments – the so-called cherry picking. The guidelines being provided divide between different categories of claims on: sovereigns, non-central government public sector entities, banks and securities firms.

A 'first' in regulatory guidelines is the formal reference made to *operational risk* and associated reserve requirements. This is followed by the statement that the Basle Committee is soliciting comments on a range of approaches which will enable an objective evaluation and measurement of operational risks. The New Capital Adequacy Framework:

- acknowledges the importance for institutions of risks other than credit and market risk; and
- suggests that a rigorous control environment is essential to prudent management of operational and other risks.

The goal is that of limiting exposure to risks, leading to the notion that additional steps to those taken with credit risk and market risk are necessary to assure the sound management of banks. The growing importance of risk categories such as operational, reputational and legal has led the Basle Committee to conclude that such exposures are too important not to be treated within the capital adequacy framework.

Analytical solutions aimed at managing the broad class of operational risks are currently under development, but still at an early stage. Even tier-1 banks have only recently begun to develop systems and procedures for explicitly measuring and monitoring operational risk, in recognition of its importance to banks. The good news is that they start devoting resources to quantify the level of operational risk and incorporate it in an assessment of overall capital adequacy.

4 Enriching the supervisory review of Capital Adequacy through external and internal rating

The definition of a framework regarding supervisory review of capital adequacy is important because, as with the 1995 Market Risk Amendment, national regulators retain significant freedom of action. The Basle Committee seeks to assure that a credit institution's capital position is consistent with its overall risk profile and management strategy. This approach is intended to encourage early supervisory intervention.

The basic thinking is that within a framework of global rules and guidelines national supervisors should have the ability to require banks to hold capital in excess of minimum regulatory capital ratios. Concomitant to this is the drive to convince the senior management of commercial banks about the need for:

- developing a rigorous internal capital assessment process; and
- setting targets for capital commensurate with the bank's particular risk profile and internal environment.

The expectation is that this internal control process would be subject to supervisory review and intervention, where and when such action proves to be appropriate. In a way emulating COSO guidelines, the Group of Ten central bankers want to see that a bank publicly discloses qualitative and quantitative information about its risks.

- transparency regarding the risk profile inherent in on-balance sheet and off-balance sheet activities allows to judge about the stability of an institution's financial position;
- in association with the disclosure of a bank's capital position, information on exposure helps in illustrating whether an institution will be able to remain solvent under stress.

The New Capital Adequacy Framework emphasises the need for information on the sensitivity of a bank's earnings to market changes. Therefore, it specifies that a credit institution should present sufficient qualitative and quantitative information to help regulators in understanding the nature and magnitude of exposures. *Position data* are an example of quantitative information while *management intent* and *corporate strategies* constitute qualitative information.

The discussion paper also asks for comparative data of previous years able to provide regulators and other users of financial statements with a perspective on trends in the institution's underlying exposure. A bank is asked to disclose its risk-based capital ratios calculated in accordance with the methodology prescribed in the 1998 Capital Accord and any other regulatory capital standards that it must meet. The goal is to provide enough information for assessment of whether available capital is sufficient to meet credit risk, market risk and other types of risk.

Confirming the policy that has been developed by many central banks regarding the examination of internal controls, the New Capital Adequacy Framework specifies that a bank should make qualitative disclosures about the internal processes it uses for evaluating its risks and its own capital adequacy. The underlying concept is that these disclosures will assist market participants in judging:

- If an institution manages its capital adequacy in a manner commensurate to its other risk management processes; and
- How well will the credit institution be able to withstand future volatility and liquidity stress in financial markets.

This leads to the issue of *capital structure*. The new regulations specify that a bank should disclose information about its capital structure, including the components of capital and terms, as well as key features of capital instruments. This is particularly required in connection to innovative, complex and hybrid capital instruments (read: derivatives).

A credit institution should also disclose information about its reserves for credit losses and other exposures leading to potential losses. Such information must provide a clear picture of the bank's capacity to absorb losses including any conditions that may merit special attention in an analysis of the strength of financial staying power including:

- maturity;
- level of seniority;
- step-up provisions;
- interest or dividend deferrals; and
- terms of derivatives embedded in hybrid capital instruments.

For the first time, to my knowledge, has been included in regulatory rules and directives specific reference to disclosure requirements regarding Special Purpose Vehicles (SPVs) – which are set up and capitalised by several institutions as a way of improving their rating. SPVs are important to counterparties whose policy is to deal only with high-rated business partners.

Also more or less for the first time, the Basle Committee emphasises outsourcing credit risk evaluations to independent rating agencies. The two biggest rating agencies are: Standard & Poor's (S&P), an independent business unit of McGraw-Hill; and Moody's Investors Service, an independent business unit of Dun and Bradstreet. Both are New York-based. Third, at a certain distance, comes the Anglo-American Fitch IBCA. There is also US-based A.M. Best which specialises in ratings in the banking industry.

While smaller rating agencies do exist in other countries, for instance Japan, they tend to be local and therefore do not enter into a discussion about global rating. The Basle Committee has used S&P's rating scales as an example, but (correctly) the discussion document explains this is only an example. One could equally use the rating structure of Moody's or Fitch IBCA, or some other agency's.

What the reader should retain from this outsourcing on credit risk rating is that the use of credit evaluation by reputable independent agencies helps in quantifying the exposure taken with counterparties and instruments. This is becoming an integral part of market discipline. It is advisable to take notice that an effective market discipline requires reliable and timely information enabling counterparties to make well-founded risk assessments.

This is the first time regulators specifically mention the evaluation by third parties as a means for fine-tuning capital requirements connected to credit risk. Just as critical is the attention paid by the regulators to credit risk models. In a way emulating the 1996 Market Risk Amendment, the New Capital Adequacy Framework introduces eigenmodels in connection to an internal rating-based approach to the computation of capital requirements.

The Basle Committee believes that for sophisticated banks an internal ratings-based solution could form the basis for estimating capital charges. Therefore, in consultation with the banking industry, the Committee would examine basic issues related to eigenmodels for setting capital requirements, seeking to develop a normalised approach.

The Committee realises that there exist both advantages and drawbacks connected to the use of internal ratings for capital adequacy. Greater detail on individual credit exposure is one of the modelling advantages. Among technologically advanced institutions, such detail is increasingly incorporated into various functions, including:

- operational applications, like determining loan approval requirements; and
- risk management, from analysis of pricing to internal control and the adequacy of limits.

Mathematically speaking, it is feasible that eigenmodels for internal ratings will incorporate supplementary customer information through detailed monitoring of customer accounts, as well as specific knowledge of all guarantees and value of collateral. An internal ratings-based method may also cover a broader range of borrowers, providing assessments of the credit quality of individuals and different sized companies through credit scoring and detailed analysis of individual firms.

Indeed the Basle Committee hopes that banks will be encouraged to further develop and enhance internal credit risk measurement and management techniques than they have presently available. An IRB solution shares certain similarities with credit risk models in terms of reliance on the institution's internal credit assessments and the use of conceptual measures of risk. It may as well provide incentives for banks to further refine their credit risk management methodology.

5 Diversification is good, other things being equal

Chapters 9 and 10 addressed the issue of models, their strengths and their weaknesses. This subject comes again under perspective in this chapter as commercial and investment bankers promote the use of models in connection to the calculation of capital requirements. The argument is that since with the 1996 Market Risk Amendment the Basle Committee has accepted that internal models can play a role in determining capital adequacy for market risk, credit risk models should be used to quantify the degree of diversification of exposure in regard to counterparties.

In the course of our meeting, the senior executive of one of the major rating agencies answered this argument in the following way: 'Model's benefits lie in their ability to rapidly and cheaply update credit opinions based on summary data. We have conducted research indicating that they are not more accurate than our analysts' opinions. This is not surprising since standard models for predicting credit quality contain typically less than 5 explanatory variables. Analysts consider thousands of data points.'

This does not diminish the contribution of models but it positions the issue. Not only quantification may have its limits but also certain qualification factors have to be studied in a more rigorous manner than it has been the case so far. The problem is that: some of these factors, such as 'better management' and 'better internal control' are subjective, and because standards defining what is meant by 'better' or 'worse' are missing, such factors do not lend themselves to modelling.

Besides this, the concept of diversification and higher rating which is advocated in order to reduce unsystematic risk is sometimes in conflict with strategic goals. For instance, many banks tend to specialise in certain industrial sectors, or other types of business activity. This results in risk concentrations in both:

- individual credits; and
- specific fields of activity.

A similar case exists with industrial companies. The reliance upon certain customers, as well as suppliers (through supply chain solutions), can lead to highly concentrated credit and economic exposures to a number of counterparties whose creditworthiness might become subject to a herd syndrome. For instance, the semiconductor industry tends to go up or down as a whole even if significant differences between companies exist. In other terms, diversification is good, other things being equal; but 'other things' are not equal, as so many factors enter into doing business.

If the flat rate for capital adequacy is substituted by a flexible and dynamic model, then it should definitely include market parameters. For example, the fact that the global economic and financial crisis worsened during the third quarter of 1998 led some eggheads at senior government level, particularly in Third World countries such as Malaysia, to the idea of capital and market controls.

Capital controls are a sovereign event risk (see Chapter 15), and therefore a repayment exposure. They make the capital that emerging markets need in order to grow more scarce, and they bring a correlation among risk factors, upsetting diversification plans.

Bankers advocating model-based capital adequacy (and I am inclined towards this solution) must realise that in a number of cases they may have to increase rather than shrink the 8 per cent; and this would happen at the worst possible moment as, for instance, after the Russian default of August 1998. A rigorous capital adequacy model must also account for the fact that unilaterally applied capital controls have the potential to tip the world into deflation, because:

- they quickly evolve into different forms of protectionism; and
- protectionism requires larger rather than smaller capital reserves.

In fact, protectionism based on capital controls rests on concepts which will return the world to 1931, when Austria experienced a major run on its banking system. Austria in 1931 resorted to capital controls to stem capital flight, just as Malaysia did in 1998. Soon after, the market's concern over default and convertibility risk in Austria led to capital flight out of neighbouring countries such as Germany and Hungary.

The flight of capital from Germany forced the government to impose capital controls in June 1931, but with global liquidity being squeezed the crisis moved to Britain. In September 1931 Britain was forced to sever the link of sterling to gold. While the value of the British pound sank, other Western countries devalued in an effort to undercut their neighbours by taking away from them advantages they had obtained through devaluation. Today, as this text is written, a similar risk exists with China; a capital adequacy model must fully account for such scenarios. Similarly, a capital adequacy model which prides itself on being accurate cannot leave out of its equation the effects of a stock market downturn on its assets. For any practical purpose, early in 1999 the majority of the bigger Japanese banks have gone

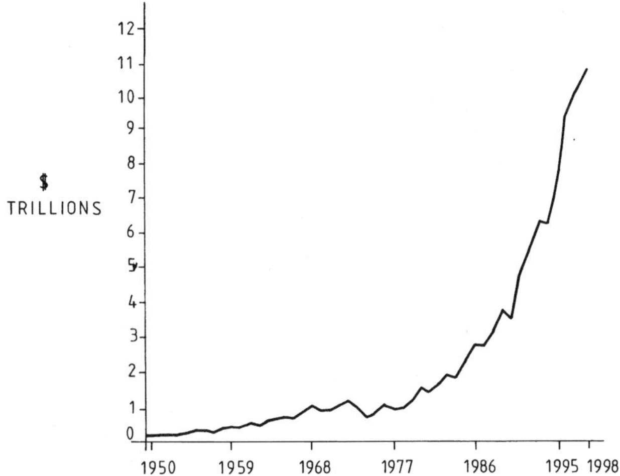

Figure 11.1 1950–98: capitalisation value of all stocks traded on American stock markets

bankrupt because the equities in their portfolio as well as the real estate have lost so much of their value.

When the stock market rises, like the pattern in Figure 11.1 from the USA, bankers and investors feel very comfortable, and all the more so as new capital adequacy rules might permit them to reduce their capital requirements. But the value of their equity can also go down in money terms or as a percentage of gross domestic product (GDP), along with the ups and downs of the stock market and the real estate market.

Figure 11.2 presses this point by comparing market capitalisation as a percentage of GDP in Year 1 and in Year 2 in the go-go late 1990s. Notice that in this example Japan is the only major country where market capitalisation significantly shrank, but the careful reader will appreciate that this case is by no means unique. It has happened to other countries in different times.

Both the bank's own portfolio and the collateral it takes for loans suffer in stock market downturns. The modelling of credit risk cannot be immune to this reality. Neither should it be forgotten that, as more emerging markets open up, the addition of country risk compounds the problems for companies operating internationally. A similar case can be made for currency risk.

In conclusion, credit risk models should be welcome as a substitute for a fixed capital adequacy rate, but they should be realistic, and not leave out any factor affecting exposure and associated capital needs. They should benefit from rich databases, be tested and be updated fairly frequently. And, if adopted, it should be clear to the management of financial institutions that their capital requirement may well increase above 8 per cent, depending on market conditions and the bank's own policies.

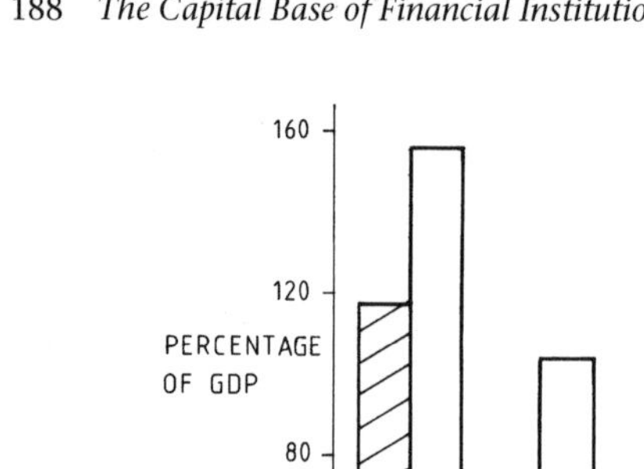
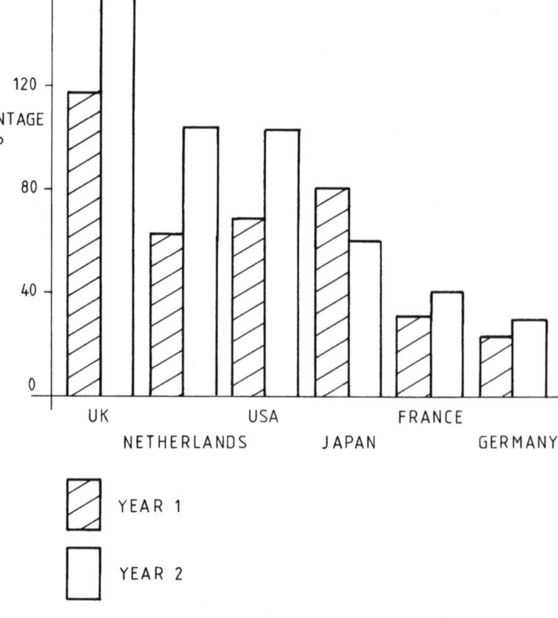

Figure 11.2 Market capitalisation as a percentage of GNP in the late 1990s

6 Why capital reserves, risk profiles and prudent management correlate

Since Chapter 1 it has been explained that rules regulating the financial markets are motivated by three key considerations: the need to protect investors and preserve the integrity of the market; the drive to sustain business confidence by weeding out fraudulent activities; and the containment or outright avoidance of systemic risk. Seen from this perspective, the role of regulatory capital is to:

- reduce the probability of an institution's insolvency to an acceptable level; and
- provide for an orderly wind-down in case this becomes unavoidable, without creating systemic risk.

Classically, supervisory authorities establish capital requirements in an industry-wide sense. They do not get involved in assessing each institution's day-to-day decisions. What sections 2 and 3 have suggested is that a more accurate approach would ensure that the level of capital is proportional to the risks being run by the bank. With this, the current 8 per cent will be just as likely to be reduced as increased.

The point has been made that short of including in the model *all* factors possibly requiring capital reserves, or affecting the level of such reserves, supervisors may give institutions the wrong incentive as capital charges shape the way institutions go after their business. One of the problems which I can see with the approach discussed in section 2 is that very few banks have either the skills or the technology to effectively handle, let alone develop, complex credit models. In a way regulators are caught between the demands of tier-1 banks who are the market leaders and who have available sophisticated modelling solutions to manage their credit risk and market risk, and smaller, less experienced institutions who simply cannot follow. The challenge is to find a balance that allows the bigger players to deal under controlled risk conditions, closely supervised by the regulators, but also protects firms who may be acting as counterparties yet who do not have the same advanced infrastructure and in-house skills.

Generally speaking, large commercial banks with significant lending, fixed income trading and high technology are best positioned to take advantage of the market-making opportunities in credit risk and market risk as well as the integration of the two metrics. They also have a reasonably rich internal database which can be mined, and from which they can derive quantitative credit risk factors.

Rich databases, algorithms, heuristics, trading skills and infrastructure are prerequisites. The same is true of the ability to move quickly because, all told, the debate focusing on issues of regulatory capital is essentially one of global risk management. The goal of a quantitative approach to credit risk is to find worst case loss if the counterparty forfeits, such computation being based at the 99 per cent, or better still the 99.9 per cent level of confidence, evaluating through simulation the whole loans portfolio over many runs (typically 5000 or more).

Contrary to creditworthiness which provides a single number, the simulation's result is repeated for different scenarios, permitting 'what if' experimentation: for instance, how are our credits distributed with the counterparty? With a group of counterparties? Within a given industry sector? By type of commitment? By currency? By maturity? Other questions to ask include the following.

1. What is the pattern of our credits by credit officer?
2. By branch? By foreign subsidiary?
3. Is there any abnormal number of 'weak credits'?
4. Is the same credit officer always dealing with the same counterparty?

A British bank, for instance, had a dealer who mostly dealt with the same company, a hotel chain. Nobody questioned this relationship until the hotel company went bust and the bank lost £30 million ($50 million). There exist many other critical questions for 'what if' analysis: are our credits diversified, or concentrated in a few names? What is the projected 'next exposure' of each of our favoured counterparties?

Scenario analysis must keep in perspective the fact that the calculation of prudential capital requirements became more complex the day regulators allowed banks to hold assets for sale on trading books. Part of the reason is that, generally, regulators assign different, less onerous capital requirements to these short-term instruments, though they also want to see them marked to market. The responses to the New Capital Adequacy Framework:

- will be an important indicator of where reform is heading in the new millennium.
- they will show how far regulators are prepared to rely on market incentives for supervision, and how far they want rigorous rules.

Now the Basle standards are being updated through a project expected to bear fruit right after the year 2000, and therefore known as 2000+. Under the chairmanship of William McDonough, president of the New York Federal Reserve, the Basle Committee aims to have concrete proposals, in the form of a discussion paper, ready before too long. As shown in section 5, which is based on information currently available, these proposals will be an important indicator of where reform is heading in the new millennium. They will show how far regulators are prepared to rely on market incentives for supervision, and how far they want rigorous rules.

Many regulators suggest that loans to emerging markets with poor financial systems carry a higher risk, and therefore the need for a greater capital cushion. Others would like to see a better definition of the creditworthiness of countries, not just of companies, possibly through a rating system by independent agencies.

This new emphasis on country risk springs from the fact that some of the current standards are, to say the least, questionable: for instance, the way to measure a country's financial health and, consequently, the riskiness of a loan. A sort of curious rule says that if the loan is made to a country outside the Paris-based Organisation for Economic Co-operation and Development (OECD), it carries greater risk. Commercial lending to governments of OECD countries has a zero risk-weighting, while that to non-OECD countries carries a 100 per cent weighting, a difference which is, to say the least, absurd. Thus, when Mexico joined the OECD in 1994 shortly before it crashed, a Mexican loan became an apparently non-risky asset. Why the former Marshall Plan, which was great in its time and essentially helped European countries in financial need, should become a sort of divine OECD bureaucracy is one of history's mysteries.

Exactly because there are so many mysteries around, banks need to put into their mainstream a deep-rooted questioning attitude which challenges old notions and stereotypes such as the OECD connection, which has proved to be a poisonous gift of assurance. This questioning attitude should not be seen as only applicable with credit models. It is a matter of good internal control to analyse credits from a polyvalent risk management viewpoint. The same sort of questioning should be carried out in regard to strategies followed with trading.

1. Is the same dealer following a similar pattern in trades with the same counterparty?
2. Why is *this* counterparty dealing in billions of dollars in swaps?
3. Is the counterparty a steady user of OTC or does it balance this with exchange traded products?

In short, 'What's the pattern *our* counterparty uses?' is as valid a question as the one addressing the net and gross exposure with this counterparty. Is the account executive aware of such pattern? Of the level of exposure being taken? What is he or she doing about it? Where is the evidence? Let me repeat in a nutshell the sense of these references.

1. The target of an individualised exposure analysis is to find worst-case loss if the counterparty defaults.
2. The goal of a global analytical exposure study is to compute the general worst case for *our* institution.

Both accuracy and precision are important in computing exposure over time, though the former is more important than the latter. There should be no averaging-out and no netting. All counterparties have a nasty habit of going bankrupt. 'What if' must be done fairly frequently, addressing exposure due to exchange rate volatility, the volatility of interest rates, stock market crashes, real estate slumps and other reasons.

For experimentation purposes, models should be used to simulate the whole portfolio, the counterparty relationship, and each individual contract. But we should be careful not to fall into the trap of estimating customer relationships independently from one another, unless we are perfectly sure they do not correlate.

7 The Capital Adequacy Directive of the EU

During 1996, practically all European banks implemented a risk system to support financial reporting in accordance with the EU's CAD, which became effective on 1 January 1996. CAD brought a new focus to the standard capital environment for financial institutions through the classification of asset-associated hedges. It also left an impact on the banking industry by emphasising once more the need for better risk control. The good news is that the regulatory infrastructure has been somewhat strengthened as more stringent requirements were introduced; the bad news is that the lack of emphasis on high technology does not push institutions in making substantial investments to ensure rigorous risk monitoring.

It is no secret that the CAD has had a rather a slow start. To understand CAD's course and impact one has to appreciate that the Commission is the rule-making authority at EU level, but it is not involved in operational supervision of the banking industry. Because of this, dialogue with the national supervisory authorities is the only way to get feedback on new directives and on how they are received. This is particularly true in connection with:

- capital adequacy issues; and
- the broader context of risk management.

The comment I heard from several bankers and analysts is that CAD was largely written by theoreticians lacking hands-on banking practice. What its authors did in the early 1990s was to take the 1988 Capital Accord by the Basle Committee and rewrite it. This saw to it that the first version of CAD was some seven years behind its time. However, other European bankers think that the CAD has several merits, wider coverage of exposure issues being one of them.

It is not easy to reconcile these two opinions. The key demerit which I see in CAD is the lack of co-ordination with the Basle Committee to avoid discrepancies. Though several initial differences between rules which came out of Basle and out of Brussels were later partly ironed out by the Amsterdam accord, which led to CAD II, others remain, as demonstrated in section 7.

A snapshot of what is covered by CAD II, in connection with international institutions, is given in Figure 11.3. Notice the distinction made between trading book and banking book exposure, as well the connecting lines of internal interest rate and currency swaps. CAD says the total capital requirements are reflected in this diagram. I am not happy with this view for two reasons:

- typically the trading book has short-term positions, but derivatives (which are part of the trading book) may also involve longer-term commitments;
- this should have been reflected in the graph at the trading book side, with specific mention of the level of leverage (also, forex forwards and futures are in the trading book).

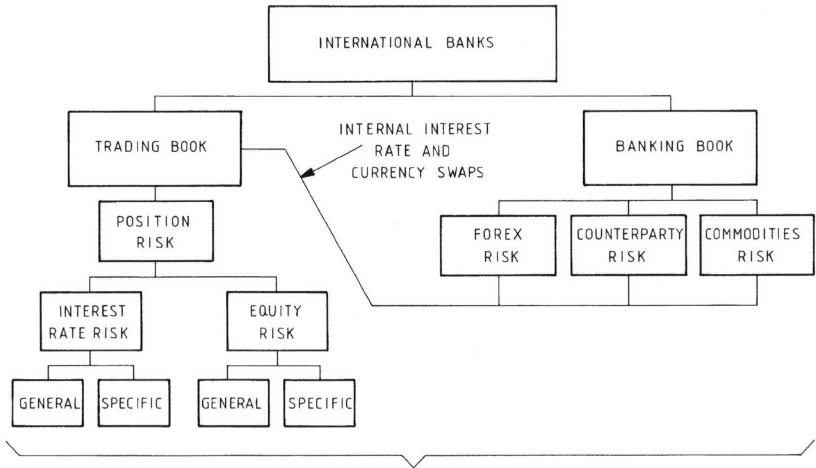

Figure 11.3 An amended CAD II definition of capital requirements for international banks

While one of the reason for discrepancies between the approach taken by CAD and that of the Basle Committee might have been the 'not invented here' syndrome, a more important origin is the fact that by the time CAD was off the drafting board, the Basle Committee was already well launched into what became the 1996 Market Risk Amendment, which promoted the use of eigenmodels. The difference in approach between CAD and the Amendment has been important because it splits a country's banking industry into two parts: for instance, in France the 1996 Market Risk Amendment applies to only 15 financial groups, which are basically international banks, whereas CAD applies to all French banks, which means that those who follow the Amendment were faced with contradictory rules.

Many banks were clever and exploited the weaknesses of CAD. Because they are powerful lobbies, they have been able to work round the EU's CAD. It would be pushing an already open door for me explain that rules which are incompatible or contradictory render a very poor service to the banking industry.

The regulators themselves were not sure whether they should concentrate on CAD's writings or on VAR. One of the supervisors said: 'You can use the models *if* you have excellent internal controls.' But most banks do not have first class internal controls, and besides, the requirement for rigorous internal controls should apply to all banks; it is not a prerequisite of only those who use eigenmodels.

Internal controls at the level of the board's and the chief executive's accountability is not necessarily one of the strengths of CAD which concentrates on the definitions of initial capital, provisions against risks, transitional and final provisions, monitoring and control of large expenditures, valuation of positions for reporting purposes, supervision on a consolidated basis, competent authorities and reporting requirements. As the directive specifies, each regulatory authority has to ensure that institutions falling within its scope (banks, brokers and also firms which only receive and transmit orders from investors without holding money or securities belonging to clients) have their own funds which are always equal to or greater than the sum total of the capital requirements for their trading business. These must be calculated according to the annexes relating to:

- position risk;
- settlement risk;
- counterparty risk; and
- large exposures.

Capital on hand should reflect all of an institution's business activities. Capital requirements are also imposed by the Bank Solvency Ratio Directive for business activities, excluding trading book business and certain illiquid assets, if these are deducted from their own funds in accordance with the CAD's annex on own funds.

The way the EC Directive defines it, a large exposure means an exposure to a client or group of connected clients which equals 10 per cent of the bank's own funds. This figure and the limit on large exposures were not easily agreed in the EC Council of Ministers. Consequently, the member states may increase (transitionally) the 10 per cent figure to 15 per cent under certain conditions.

To its credit, CAD did not fail to notice that capital adequacy and risk management converge towards the notion of minimum prudential standards on which the single European market in financial services must be founded. As a result, the underlying concepts and controls relate not only to the quantitative capital requirements but also to qualitative risk management perspectives.

The principle is that all banks and investment firms should be subject to the same regulatory conditions for the same business and the same risks. While regulators do not want to interfere with the professional market, they also need to be sure that there are no excesses involving systemic risk. Hence the need for minimum prudential requirements, imposed on all authorised institutions, and able to provide a level playing field throughout the EU.

It does not hurt to do some brainstorming concerning capital adequacy for Euroland's banks, and for the EU's super-region. Even if only modest practical results come at the end of this exercise, it is better to let fresh air into the room than do everything in a closed-door environment which characterises every bureaucracy. A good example of what I mean by a brainstorming reference is what has become known as the Group of Twenty-Two

(G-22, whose membership leads in the meantime increased to notably thirty, but still is known as G-22).

The G-22 is an informal group of representatives of 22 emerged and emerging economies, set up by Bill Clinton in April 1998. During that same year, it prepared three working papers, on transparency, on strengthening financial sectors and on dealing with crises. So far, this report-writing includes relatively modest suggestions. However, the aforementioned G-22 working papers have become a sort of unofficial agenda for reform. The IMF is said to be developing its own ideas for reform along the lines of the G-22 reports. But nobody is really sure if G-22 or G-XX will meet again, when, and on which agenda.

8 The brewing regulation of commodity trades and the association with the Investment Services Directive

The best way to appreciate CAD is to examine the purpose which it serves in the context of the EU, as well as its state of implementation by EU member states. Then, we should look into CAD II (the revision which incorporates eigenmodels and commodities); and some other aspects of the CAD which may need to be reviewed in the future. According to at least one of its authors, CAD is primarily intended to:

- fill the existing gap in capital requirements for market risk; and
- provide needed vital elements of a single market for financial services.

In June 1998 the European Parliament and Council issued three directives amending the EC *Solvency Ratio Directive* and the EC *Banking Coordination Directive*. The EU member states must translate these directives into national law by July 2000, at the latest. These amended directives essentially resulted in a broader adjustment of European solvency rules to the corresponding standards of the current Basle Accord.

Internal risk management models are now permitted for calculating overall capital requirements for market price risk, including specific risk. The *Expanded Matrix Directive* is an amendment of the EC Solvency Ratio Directive and it extends the obligation to apply the marking to market method. It also introduces differentiated weightings for protential future increases in exposure when determining counterparty risk for over the counter derivatives trades.

The *Mortgage Credit Directive* is the third amendment. This extended the exemption ruling which applies more favorable weightings to commercial and industrial mortgages, with a creditworthiness rating of 50 per cent by 10 years until the end of 2006. Institutions may now apply a reduced weight of 50 per cent to mortgage-backed securities. Under the amended version of the EC Capital Adequacy Directive (CAD II), commodity price risk has to be backed by own funds.

As DG XV of the European Commission suggests, there was a need for a 'European passport' for the banking industry through common prudential standards, which could be extended from banks to investment firms and commodities dealers. However, the principle of equal treatment made it difficult to reach an agreement on commodities. The argument has been that commodities are associated with different types of risk in different countries; yet the merchant and investment bankers make commodities trades. Originally CAD did not focus on this issue because commodities are no longer major business for international banks. And, as DG XV found out, the attitude of commodities firms towards the normalisation of risk is negative. There is also an uneven distribution of commodities firms among EU countries.

About 90 per cent of commodities specialists are in London with the majority of the rest in Amsterdam and Paris. These are professional traders dealing with producers/endusers, and they do not want to be subject to capital requirements, which would happen for the first time in their existence. Instead, commodities traders and merchant banks are calling for a system of differentiated charges based on observed volatilities of particular groups of commodities. This is a sophisticated approach, and it may well be that a single set of capital charges may not answer capital adequacy requirements.

At the same time, it has not escaped the attention of the European Commission that commodity derivatives are not only highly volatile but also inherently risky deals. With derivatives on commodities on the increase, there is a need to provide adequate coverage. The methodologies being considered are:

- a simplified method of capital requirements for incidental investments;
- a maturities ladder approach, resulting in lower capital requirements; and
- internal models for risk control, similar to the approach taken by the banking industry.

In all likelihood, there will still be a considerable amount of discussion since the issues of risk management in commodities, even the subject of commodities supervision, are novel. At the same time, as the Sumitomo Corporation's $2.8 billion to $5.1 billion losses in copper futures show, derivative financial instruments with commodities represent a significant exposure because commodities, and most particularly commodity derivatives, are volatile activities.

To the extent that investment firms and credit institutions undertake commodities trades, it is necessary to put up adequate capital. Financial staying power is needed to protect depositors and investors in these institutions as well as to avoid systemic risk. DG XV's capital requirements are not intended for *pure* commodities dealers and traders because their business is not included in the lists of activities covered by the Investment Services

Directive (ISD) or the Second Banking Directive, but credit institutions taking commodities risk must be supervised.

Let me add one more point. If CAD is to become a vital element of the single market in financial services, then in association with the ISD it should ensure equivalent prudential requirements for both banks and investment firms. In 1993, the EU's Second Banking Directive established a structural framework for the single market in banking, based on the principles of *a single licence,* which means that licences granted in one member state should be recognised in other member states (that is, a sort of European passport), and *home country control,* which means that the competent authority which grants a licence to a financial institution in its country of incorporation is responsible for its supervision.

In the opinion of DG XV a process based on these two pillars will create awareness not only of capital allocation but also of risk management. The Commission is monitoring CAD applications rather carefully through its working group on the interpretation and implementation of directives, and by means of special working groups of experts from member states convened to examine specific issues.

9 Six basic reasons for the revision of CAD

Current discussions in the EU go beyond the scope of internal models whose mission is to calculate capital requirements for market risk, even if this is a polyvalent issue which can lead to the modelling of credit risk. The new policy is that incentives would encourage institutions not only to use more sophisticated techniques for measuring risk, but also to establish rigorous internal controls in the context of an improved overall approach to risk management.

A fundamental argument regarding CAD's revision is the need to amend the standing directive in connection with eigenmodels and internal controls. Article 14 of the first CAD release talks of the need to re-evaluate and, if necessary, revise the directive in the light of developments in international markets or by regulatory authorities. This provision was intended to ensure that further work on market risk being undertaken in the Basle Committee on Banking Supervision, at the time the directive was adopted, would be taken into account in EU legislation.

Furthermore, Article 13 of CAD requires that 'the Commission shall as soon as possible submit to the Council proposals for capital requirements in respect of commodities trading [and] commodities derivatives'. As we saw in section 5, this task had been delayed to permit this subject to be extensively discussed with the relevant parties in an effort to reach a consensus.

It is to the credit of DG XV that, following the publication of the 1996 Market Risk Amendment, it worked (with the help of a group of experts from the member states) on the revision of CAD. Flexibility in updating rules and regulations is always welcome. The underlying principles which have been accepted by all participants can serve as precedents. A close alignment with the Basle Committee text is needed to:

- ensure compatibility between bank directives affecting the same financial institutions; and
- avoid possible competitive discrepancies between two different pieces of regulation.

Also, given the continuing study of modelling techniques at BIS, the Commission seems inclined to feel that the EU text should reflect general principles, in order to allow room for adaptation to possible future changes in Basle Committee rules.

There are six basic areas where flexibility in approach is welcome because of future developments in modelling techniques. First, the quality of specific risk modelling is still in question, particularly in regard to its ability to capture event risk (for instance, defaults). While neither DG XV nor the Basle Committee said so, I would suggest that extreme events are added to this frame of reference.

Second, there are differences in disallowance factors in regard to maturity brackets: CAD has three brackets while the 1996 Market Risk Amendment has 15. Other connected differences include: high-yield debt instruments, where the Basle Committee has special treatment while CAD has not; the duration method for debt instruments, leading to some inconsistencies between disallowance factors and number of maturity brackets; and the pre-processing of derivatives, where the use of sensitivity models is limited to swaps by the Basle Committee but not by CAD. There are also some issues regarding options, where Basle describes various alternative approaches while CAD is not specific.

A third area of concern, as regards current lack of convergence in regulatory norms, is the process of backtesting. Here some important queries about the most appropriate solution exist, including testing procedures leading to the rejection of models either when the results land too often in the red zone, or when they can be too easily manipulated to mislead senior management and the regulators.

Neither the Basle Committee nor CAD have addressed the issue raised by this second problem area in a fundamental manner. Yet this matter is pressing because, in the aftermath of the LTCM débâcle, it was found that some banks had greatly misused VAR, thereby hiding the level of their true exposure to LTCM superleverages.

Fourth, it is necessary to decide on the best strategy to be followed in terms of facilitating future model adjustments, and therefore the evolution of simulation as a valid approach to risk management. More sophisticated modelling brings with it a closer look at fundamental concepts and definitions.

These are not quite ironed out yet. Between the Basle Committee and DG XV there is, for instance, a difference in the handling of derivatives activities, particularly swaps.

Fifth, few people would argue about the need to pay more attention to international money flows connected with banking activities. This need goes beyond establishing coherent regulatory arrangements which reflect the globalisation of markets. CAD should match the work being currently done by the Basle Committee regarding both institutions in emerging markets, and financial conglomerates. Cross-border financial services are an urgent issue, but not one on which all regulators agree that explicit notification requirements are necessary. Different member states of the EU have different opinions on this issue. CAD cannot afford to leave this matter open. It has to establish consensus and firm rules.

A sixth crucial subject is the relationship to be worked out between DG XV and the Basle Committee. Since the 1988 Capital Accord the European Commission has sat on the Basle Committee and taken part in its work. Generally, however, Brussels takes a different view on several critical issues: for instance, DG XV suggests that its target is integrating financial services in a comprehensive sense, while the Basle Committee looks specifically at banks; hence its horizon is more limited.

It does not seem to me that the Basle Committee agrees with this. There are also issues on which DG XV does not get involved, such as settlement risk, which at BIS is handled by the Payments and Settlements Committee. The European Commission is not working in this domain which constitutes the very origins of the BIS but, if CAD intends to become the rule-book for all EU banks, it simply cannot turn its back on Payments and Settlements.

12
Central Banks, Commercial Banks and Repurchase Agreements

1 Introduction

The management of the monetary base and of the velocity of circulation of money is a major function of central banks (see D.N. Chorafas, *The Money Magnet. Regulating International Finance and Analyzing Money Flows*, Euromoney Books, London, 1997), sometimes assisted through repurchase agreements (repos). An example of the use of repos for monetary policy reasons is provided by the Bundesbank and the ECB whose main monetary instrument is repurchase rate. The ECB asks the national central banks to conduct open-market operations to keep interest rates within its desired range, with:

- the ceiling being the rate which banks can borrow overnight from the central bank; and
- the floor being the rate at which banks with surplus cash deposit overnight funds.

In addition to this, the ECB will impose a minimum reserve requirement: banks must deposit at the central bank the equivalent of 2 per cent of their outstanding loans, as reserve requirements, giving a central bank tighter control over bank lending and helping to smooth out money market interest rates. Unlike other central banks, the ECB will pay a rate of interest on these bank deposits.

Over the years repos have developed into flexible instruments. Central banks use repurchase agreements to help commercial banks in terms of liquidity. This is the issue which will primarily occupy us in the present chapter, with emphasis on the fact that a repurchase agreement is committing one party to sell a security to another and buy it back at a later date.

In principle, banks and other companies enter into asset sale and repurchase agreements both for trading and for treasury management purposes. But outside the realm of central banks this tends to be a speculative transaction because such deals are often done for leveraging reasons. From a macroeconomic viewpoint, dematerialisation sees to it that the same security might be pledged in a repo several times: by its owner, its custodian and the exchange. Repos have become more common as lending has been increasingly securitised. *If* the asset in a repo is certain to come back to the selling institution at some predetermined date, *then* the credit risk on the asset sold remains in full risk with the seller.

However, an additional credit risk arises from the possibility of default of the counterparty to the repo deal. The potential size of this counterparty exposure depends on the type of security involved, the arrangements made, the margin and interest payments, the maturity of the repo movements in market prices, and other reasons. The exposure is the net cost of replacing the particular asset should the counterparty fail.

2 Basic features of sales and repurchase agreements

Sales and repurchase agreements are deals under which assets are sold by one party to another on terms that provide for the seller to repurchase the asset under certain conditions. Many institutions consider securities borrowing and lending and generally repo operations as being strategically important. This is particularly true of those able to capitalise on AAA or AA credentials, and those who have access to substantial custodial holdings of customers' securities (see section 6).

A variation of a repurchase agreement is an arrangement under which one party holds an asset on behalf of another. Another form of repo is outright forward purchases. They are less common than the more classical repurchase agreements, but the full credit risk remains; therefore it is not considered prudent to offset forward sales against forward purchases in assessing credit risk unless the transactions are with the same party. Even then there may be legal issues to be considered before netting.

Combined with the globality of their operations, the activity in securities borrowing and lending enables financial institutions to deliver more diversified services to customers in different financial markets. This policy capitalises on the fact that a bank or investor holding an inventory of assets (for instance, bonds) can fund his position in the repo market, doing so either on term or overnight.

Since repurchase will take place on a specified day in the future, this effectively means that the seller is borrowing money. The repo operation connects the underlying cash market and the futures market. The sale price may be market value, but it could also be another mutually agreed price. The difference between the buy-back price and the selling price is, for any practical purpose, the interest.

Basically, repurchase agreements are a form of collateralised lending by which one party sells securities and agrees to buy them back in the future at a higher price. For instance, to enhance its liquidity, a bank may be borrowings against US Treasury bonds or bills, mortgage-backed securities, or collateralised mortgage obligations (CMOs) which it holds. These securities are temporarily given by the bank as collateral to the lender, but the bank then retains the right to buy back the securities at a fixed price.

The repurchase is usually within a day or two of the 'sale', though it may extend over a number of months. Because typically the resale price is in excess of the purchase price, reflecting an agreed rate of return effective for the period of time the purchaser's money is at play, it introduces two key variables to the repurchase agreement: the mutually agreed *time* and *price* (see also section 4). The *repurchase price* may:

- be fixed at the outset;
- vary with the period for which the asset is held by the buyer; or
- be equal to the market price at time of repurchase.

The repurchase price can also be calculated to permit the buyer to recover incidental holding costs (such as insurance). Another crucial variable is the *nature of repurchase provision*. Whether this is an unconditional commitment for both parties, an option for the seller to repurchase (call option), an option for the buyer to resell to the seller (put option), or a combination of put and call, repurchased provisions are integral part of the repo.

The repo market is growing steadily although, as Figure 12.1 shows, not exponentially. Market expansion impacts on risk. Therefore, prudent policy must see to it that repurchase agreements are at all times fully collateralised in an amount at least equal to the purchase price, including accrued interest earned on the underlying securities. Instruments held as collateral should be valued daily, and *if* the value of repo instrument(s) declines, *then* the bank should ask for additional collateral.

Securities lending has its risks. One of the main stumbling blocks in the merger of the Mellon Bank with the Dreyfus Fund has been the divided management attention because of troubles at Mellon's Boston Company. This was an investment management firm that Mellon bought from American Express for $1.4 billion in May 1993.

In November 1994, Mellon said it would write off $130 million as a result of losses on derivatives holdings by Boston Company's securities lending business, rather than pass the losses on to clients. Dreyfus sources thought these pressures prompted deeper cuts in spending for business development, compensation and technological improvements than either company originally contemplated. (*Business Week*, 16 January 1995.)

Repurchase agreements with correspondent banks and with hedge funds carry credit risk, since the counterparty can default. They may also be counterproductive in terms of diversification (see Chapter 11) because sometimes

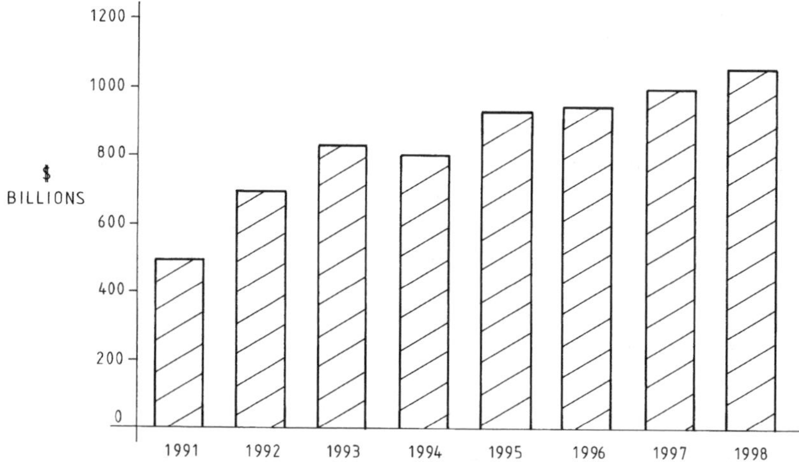

Figure 12.1 Outstanding repurchase agreements in the USA during eight consecutive years

they lead to a greater level of exposure to a single name, industry sector and, of course, type of instrument. Credit risk models have not evolved to a point where this type of concentration is taken care of.

3 Using repurchase agreements for going short and for other trades

Originally, the practice of borrowing and lending securities was more widespread in the USA, where it has been used for going short in a particular security and for arbitrage between short-term and long-term issues, or for engaging in reverse repurchase agreements with a variety of conditions attached to them.

A short seller typically expects prices to fall and hopes to buy the securities back at cheaper levels. By acquiring securities through a repo transaction, the short seller can deliver them to the buyer while maintaining his bet that the market will fall. Speculation aside, the ability to go short is essential for market-makers because they have to make two-way markets: they must be willing to buy securities they might not own, and to sell securities they do not have at the time of the transaction.

Investors may enter into repos for a variety of reasons. Say, for example, that an investor wants a certain government bond but is short of money with which to buy it; rather than take out a bank loan, it would be cheaper to buy the bond while simultaneously posting it as collateral for a loan. This process is often compared to pawn-broking, but this is for investment and trade reasons; with government paper as security, the lender will charge a lower rate than a bank.

The mortgage roll arbitrage model is a variation of repurchase agreements. A writer sells mortgage-backed financing (MBF) instruments to a buyer and agrees to repurchase an equal amount of substantially the same securities at a specified future date and at a set price.

In this transaction, the writer/borrower receives cash equal to the spot market price on the opening settlement date in return for the securities. On the closing settlement date, the seller pays the buyer the forward price, and the securities are returned. The difference between the spot and forward prices (drop) provides the seller's incentive to enter the roll transaction. The buyer/lender receives the interim cash flows from the securities as compensation for lending the cash.

Mortgage rolls benefit sellers and buyers in a similar manner to repos. They allow sellers to convert MBFs into cash at short-term, lower cost funds rate; reinvest the funds for the term of the contract at a higher rate; and earn a spread on the transaction. For their part, the buyers often use rolls to cover their obligations to deliver mortgage securities.

Mortgage rolls differ from repos in that the ownership of the securities is actually transferred and therefore the buyers are entitled to receive the intermediate cash flows from these MBF securities. Over and above this, roll buyers need only return substantially similar securities but are under no obligation to give back the identical pools on the repurchase date.

One kind of repurchase agreement that grew in popularity is flex, or floating rate repo, with MBFs as collateral. However, the mortgage-backed securities market is less liquid than the US Treasuries market.

The two primary considerations in mortgage roll analysis are the *cost of carry* and the *drop*. A mortgage roll arbitrage model is needed to determine the profitability of possible roll transactions under different prepayment assumptions, particularly concerning:

- the detailing of mortgage security information; and
- the provision of arbitrage information of forward drops by a prepayment scenario.

Although each investor has his own information requirements, a sound practice is that results are presented in terms of both arbitrage dollar amount and implied cost of carry, preferably in graphics. A breakeven drop for given market repo rate should be computed for each prepayment assumption. Models permitting experimentation on different scenarios give an advantage to the trader who has access to them.

The position taken by the central bank in connection with repurchase agreements and the prevailing rules of the game has a significant impact on the market. The Bank of England was the first central bank to introduce repos, in 1830. But more recently it restricted the privilege of lending or borrowing government bonds to the institutions that were willing to act as gilt-edged market-makers (GEMMs). They can borrow gilts to cover short positions, and are obliged to make two-way prices.

Unlike other central banks the Bank of England also insisted that trades must be settled at home so that it could keep a close eye on the market. Neither did it accept the need to level disparities in the tax treatment of investors. But then, at the end of 1995, the Bank of England opened up the repo market. Why did it change its mind?

Analysts say that one of the reasons is monetary policy. In an open market, reserve banks can use repos to change the level of liquidity. Another reason is probably that a growing number of players, among them hedge funds, now prefer to finance their purchases through repos. A third reason lies in the market's size. As seen in Figure 12.1, in America outstanding repos approached the $1 trillion level as 1995 came to a close. Cognisant people in the City suggest this influenced the Bank of England in changing the rules.

Part of the bet which every central bank of the G-10 is making is that the opening-up of the repo market will attract more investors, especially foreigners, and therefore increase liquidity. In turn this will reduce the government's borrowing costs. Even today, however, the British gilt repo market is small compared with its foreign counterparts.

The French repo market has grown faster than the British, probably because both the French government and the Bank of France have actively encouraged this market's development. Among other things, they helped to draw up a new contract that made repo transactions easier and more secure.

In Germany, the repo market was established in the late 1980s and today about two-thirds of turnover in its government bonds is repos. But most deals are booked in London because, unlike other central banks, the Bundesbank slaps reserve requirements on domestic trades in order to diminish counterparty risk.

4 The valuation of securities owned and securities sold

Borrowing and lending securities is risky. It takes place in an unregulated market without minimum capital requirements, position limits, margins and other constraints or restraints; therefore it can lead to uncontrolled speculation with potentially disruptive effects on the functioning of financial markets and, by extension, to systemic risk.

Though securities lending is done through clearing agents, there is a dispute about their role and legal responsibility in connection with these transactions. As we saw in section 2, the question of what constitutes adequate assessment of creditworthiness, or lack of it, is also open, and the same is true of repos' impact on diversification.

Since a broker enters into collateralised agreements to resell and to repurchase, securities lending arrangements and certain other secured transactions may result in significant credit exposure in the event that the counterparty to the transaction is unable to fulfil its contractual obligations. Therefore agreements to repurchase and securities borrowing arrangements are generally collateralised by cash or securities with a market value in excess of the company's obligation under the contract.

A broker attempts to minimise credit risk associated with these activities by monitoring them and requiring additional collateral to be deposited with or returned to the company when deemed necessary. Interactive computational finance, and its models, will probably help to refine this practice, inevitably affecting the method of valuation of securities owned and securities sold.

Past problems with failed firms clearly show the hurdle that can be created once the practice of borrowing and lending securities spreads beyond an inner circle of operators. Yet credit risk is not always taken into account in the valuation of securities which are handled through repos. This is not dissimilar to failures in options pricing.

In principle, as we will also see in section 5, securities owned and securities sold but not yet purchased must be recorded on trade date and carried at fair value. The valuation of government securities considers yield and time to maturity, as well as the closing exchange prices of related futures contracts. For state, municipal and corporate debt obligations, valuation is based on closing exchange quotations, dealer quotes, or OTC market prices.

Certificates of deposit (CDs) and bankers' acceptances represent short-term debt obligations of major financial institutions and are valued based on dealer quoted prices. Equity securities are generally valued using quoted market prices. The fair value for mortgage and other asset-backed securities and collateralised mortgage obligations issued by quasi-government agencies and corporate issuers is based on dealer quotes and the bank's pricing modelling techniques, which consider:

- coupon;
- yield;
- credit quality;
- prepayment estimates;
- average lives.

Other factors, too, are incorporated in estimating fair value when market value is not readily available. In addition, for control purposes it is wise to take into consideration the prices of transactions in related or similar securities if and when such prices are available.

The risk connected with derivatives should be part of the pricing equation. Securities sold but not yet purchased represent obligations to deliver specified issues at contracted prices, creating a liability to repurchase securities at prevailing market prices. Accordingly, these transactions result in off-balance-sheet risk as the bank's ultimate obligation to satisfy the sale of these securities may exceed the amount recognised in the consolidated statement of financial condition.

A sound risk management practice advises that derivative positions are valued in real-time by marking to market or marking to model. Inventory values are affected by changes in interest rates and credit spreads, market volatility and liquidity. Most changes can be monitored through the use of analytical techniques.

Subordinated liabilities consist of items related to secured demand note collateral agreements, subordinated revolving credit facilities, subordinated deferred compensation and other items. Loans payable include bank loans and borrowings bearing interest at contracted or prevailing money market rates at the time of the borrowings.

In the USA, these liabilities are subordinated to the claims of general creditors. They are available in computing net capital pursuant to the uniform net capital rule under the Securities Exchange Act of 1934. In terms of net capital requirements, securities houses are subject to the uniform net capital rule under the alternative method, net capital of not less than 2 per cent of aggregate debit balances arising from client transactions.

Restrictions may be imposed to prohibit a firm from expanding its business and declaring dividends if its net capital is less than 5 per cent of aggregate debit balances. Brokers are also subject to minimum financial requirements under the Commodities Exchange Act, which requires them to maintain net capital equal to 4 per cent of client funds.

5 Regulatory and accounting practices connected with securities lending

As the market for repurchase agreements has been growing, today repos can make up as much as 50 per cent of a major investment bank's balance sheet. It therefore comes as no surprise that the FASB is concerned about their regulation and associated financial reporting practices.

Since the securities lending system is overleveraged, it is easy to understand why regulators are worrying about the risks that they may have ignored in the past regarding settlements and clearing operations. Custodian banks and exchanges must be pressured by regulators to acknowledge and guard against the risks that they run by setting aside capital, but without increasing custody fees, and hence passing the buck to the users.

FASB originally intended that two-party repurchase agreements, which constitute a substantial portion of the repos market, would be considered sales. What lay behind this opinion was the fact that in two-party repurchase agreements, the institution which sells the securities is, in effect, transferring control since the second institution is free to sell the securities. Therefore, two-party repos are sales and should be marked to market.

By contrast, FASB held the position that three-party repos, in which a third institution holds the collateral, would still be considered financings. In 1995, however, FASB had to modify its position on financial reporting regarding repos following a Supreme Court ruling. The US Supreme Court decision, which involved the Nebraska Department of Revenue, found that most repos create liabilities, and therefore they are not sales requiring marking to market accounting.

As a result, many parties adopted the position that only a relatively small portion of the repo market should be considered sales requiring current-value accounting. This change of concept was particularly promoted by bankers who feared marking repos to market would curtail their ability to lend money, and hurt bank profits.

Community bankers also warned that considering repos transactions as sales would reduce their members' liquidity and have an adverse impact on the availability of credit within the communities these bankers served. Also, they pointed out that accountants have historically viewed repos as financings, which remain on the balance sheet.

FASB's Statement No. 125, *Accounting for Transfers and Servicing of Financial Assets and Extinguishments of Liabilities* did not wholeheartedly agree. Under certain conditions it obliges banks to value most repos at current market prices, but it also characterises sales of borrowed securities as *short sales*. This definition includes: (1) selling a security, (2) borrowing a security, (3) delivering the borrowed security, (4) purchasing a security, and (5) delivering the purchased security.

While a contract that involves activities (2) and (5) has two of the three characteristics of a derivative instrument, it is not taken as a derivative. Neither are contracts for activities (1), (3) and (4) taken as derivative financial instruments. However, if a forward purchase or sale is involved, and the contract does not qualify for a specified exception, it is subject to marking to market.

Particularly regarding repurchase agreements and *wash sales*, FASB has made a distinction between the initial exchange of financial assets for cash, which is not a sales-purchase transaction involving a derivative, and the accompanying forward contract which gives the right and obligation to purchase the transferred asset. If the forward contract requires delivery of a security readily convertible to cash it is subject to fair value requirements.

Furthermore, FASB Statement No. 133 draws a fine line by saying that financial guarantee contracts are not subject to marking to market, fair value accounting, and its other rules, *if* they provide for payments to be made only to reimburse the guaranteed party for a loss incurred because the debtor fails to pay when payment is due, which is an identifiable insurable event. By contrast, they are subject to marking to market if they provide for payments to be made in response to changes in an underlying factor, such as a decrease in the debtor's creditworthiness.

The bottom line of these dichotomies in the nature of financial reporting involving repos is that *if* indeed securities lending is primarily a financing and investment business, *then* investors should exercise due diligence. Reporting should be done in a way that permits them to:

- ask rigorous assets/liabilities questions; and
- seek out a strategy that suits their objectives and appetite for risk.

Post-mortem one can say that because hedging is a motor in the repo market and hedging involves risk, the FASB's original position was not that far wrong. There is also the fact that institutional investors are increasingly interested in repos given that strategies have been developed using Treasuries to hedge derivatives whose underlying price is a US Treasury price. Examples include structured notes, and interest rate swaps.

Emerging-market repos, most of which are dollar-denominated *Brady bonds*, expanded rapidly in 1994 only to be knocked down by Mexico's near-bankruptcy in December of that same year. After the Mexico crisis, the volume of business went back to what it had been a couple of years earlier, but nobody can say that this or similar crises will not recur, as proved in Brazil in January 1999.

Brady bonds are debt securities that resulted from debt-restructuring deals between banks and sovereign governments after several emerging countries' governments, particularly in Latin America, could not repay their loans. Such bonds are usually denominated in dollars, but can also be in other currencies depending on the organisation which arranged the restructuring. Before the 1994 bond débâcle, the most liquid markets were in Mexican, Argentinian, Brazilian and Venezuelan Brady bonds, which were all denominated in dollars but bore (along with the emerging markets' debt):

- price risk;
- liquidity risk; and
- counterparty risk.

Their advantage has been that they did not feature the currency risk of an emerging market. In most cases, repayment of at least half the principal was guaranteed because the Federal Reserve holds a supply of zero coupon Treasuries for this purpose. Investment banks dealing in Brady bonds are typically based in the USA and use them to finance their positions. Other Brady dealers are financial institutions in the debt's country of origin that repo their Brady bonds as a cheap source of financing.

These country of origin institutions often use as counterparty an American repo dealer. That dealer does a reverse repo with a US cash investor to balance his books, employing the International Securities Lending Association (ISLA) master agreement for Brady bond repos, as for other kinds. Brady bond repos are typically sold on the quality of the counterparty, not the quality of the collateral. This is the opposite of the way repos are usually marketed to willing parties in other transactions.

However, the dynamics of the market can rapidly change. After the 1994/95 Mexican crisis, the market demanded 10 per cent larger margins depending on the creditworthiness of the counterparty and the underlying collateral. There have also been rumours of substantial losses with repos. Some new players in the market offered lower margins (haircuts) to gain market share. In a market that is still counterparty-sensitive, small haircuts can be a very costly and unwise strategy.

In conclusion, repo agreements can become shaky once the underlying market, like that of Brady bonds, starts to sputter, showing signs of fatigue or even some repayment uncertainty. In the case of Brady bonds, the source of the paper's market strength was the Latin American governments who are the counterparties. By moving currency risk out of the equation, Brady bonds have put all emphasis on exposure associated with the state of counterparties, although some of these are shaky.

6 Is there a dividing line between custodian duties and repurchase agreements?

As every financial expert knows, admitting publicly that a business is for sale lowers its price; hence the unwillingness of the Morgan Bank to confess that its global-custody arm was up for sale, but the market said that it was for sale and that Morgan had put a $1 billion price on its securities lending business.

Opting out of securities lending has come as a surprise since, in addition to its own activity, Morgan is also the operator of Euroclear, the securities depository and settlement firm in Brussels and Luxembourg. On the other hand, J.P. Morgan is not the only institution to move out of custody. Bank of America sold its custodian business to a rival, Bank of New York. NatWest took a similar view and sold its custody operations to Lloyds. One explanation for these decisions to sell has been that banks fear tougher regulation, which is in reality long overdue. Until recently, custody operators attracted little interest from banking supervisors, but the rules may be changing.

Unbundling securities lending from custody and cash management from securities lending is intuitively appealing because of the loopholes which currently exist. One of the loopholes in the system is that custodians do not tie up capital for exposure and do not invest too much money in risk management. This allows them to make profits from thin margins. But if risk management reserves are applied, as should be the case, securities lending and custody would suddenly become a less attractive business.

This can be stated despite the growth in this market. Demand for custody services has increased as international investment has grown. Since 1990, the major pension funds in the First World have allocated more money for cross-border securities holdings, at the average rate of 10 per cent a year.

As demand for monitoring these cross-border holdings has grown, custodian banks with global networks have benefited, while new events such as *outsourcing* have further promoted the custodians' business. For instance, in November 1994 Prudential Insurance, Britain's biggest life insurer, turned over its £40 billion ($66 billion) of assets to an outside custodian. Other financial institutions followed suit.

Custodians with international networks are best positioned to gain share; State Street and Chase Manhattan are examples. Also, since the mid-1990s, Germany's Deutsche Bank and Holland's ABN-Amro have been trying to increase their share of the market by undercutting rivals. This has led to price wars. In Chase's European custody operations, banks' minimum charges have dropped by 75 per cent since 1990, in spite of rising costs. The evident effect is that of shrinking profit margins which help in explaining the sales wave, as noted in the earlier paragraphs in this section.

There are other challenges as well. Clients often own securities in many different markets which increases the administrative work, particularly when they make new demands for daily, rather than weekly, valuations of their holdings. To meet their clients' requirements banks must constantly upgrade their computer systems.

Quite clearly, only the strongest and biggest custodians can afford large sums and still make money. As margins are wafer-thin, projected revenues do not justify spending a fortune to keep up with the competition, if it were not for securities lending. However, this greater emphasis on repos by custodians is guaranteed to give fresh impetus to the whole debate as to whether *custody* and *securities lending* should be separated. Custody banks are under competitive pressure to get revenue forgone from falling custody fees. If securities lending were unbundled, they would be more careful with fees, and situations such as that at Harris Bank might not arise.

Technology also plays a key role in cutting costs and, even more so in exercising a rigorous risk control. An example is provided by the Tokyo-Mitsubishi Bank which, in the mid-1990s, invested in a new system, ReadQ, to process repo transactions more rapidly. Once a trade is made, it updates the position, computes the bank's exposures, sends an order to the clearing bank for delivery, and updates the general ledger, all at the same time.

As cannot be repeated too often, banks are in the risk-taking business and whoever takes risks must use first-class technology. Otherwise, the dual effect of costs and exposure would see that it does not survive. While high technology alone is not enough to keep exposure under control, the use of low technology is sure to open Pandora's box of risks, while simultaneously raising the unit cost of transactions to unacceptable levels.

13

Redefining Reporting Requirements and Opening New Frontiers

1 Introduction

The focal point of this chapter is leading trends in regulation of the financial industry, in particular, the new rules which have become necessary or are currently under development in connection with reporting practices because of the huge transformation taking place in banking and in the financial industry at large. A second objective is to compare how authorities in different countries deal with the supervision of derivatives exposure, and a third is to identify the new frontiers in financial reporting and explain what more could be offered through high-technology solutions.

First we will briefly compare similarities and differences between what is implied by the Financial Accounting Standards Statement 133 in the USA and the regulation which brought to life the Statement of Total Recognised Gains and Losses (STRGL) in the UK. Then we will take a look at possible re-regulation on a global scale, and some new frontier issues in prudential financial reporting.

This is followed by an overview of the way the Swiss have solved derivatives reporting by the banking industry which is different from the British-American model. The next issue concerns the German regulations for reliable financial reporting, including the cash flow approach to the control of exposure. Intrinsic value will be examined as a function of cash flow, a concept underpinning the valuation of securities as well as risk control.

Having covered the foremost financial reporting trends today, we will examine the use of simulation and experimentation for marking to model the trading book. This analytical approach to the representation of exposure will help to clarify the problems and opportunities present in the valuation of derivative financial instruments in the bank's portfolio.

Finally, this chapter addresses some new frontier issues in financial reporting. These inevitably arise when the instruments used by the banks leapfrog current regulations. The careful reader will also notice that, at the same time, there exists a bifurcation in reporting practices followed by some institutions; reports for internal management accounting purposes, and reports to the supervisory authorities for regulatory reasons do not necessarily need to be identical. Sometimes the regulators themselves are divided as to what they would like to see in financial reporting. For instance, some regulators point out that a bank's risk management problems do not end with the trading book; they also concern market risk exposure in the banking book making it necessary to account for this in a dynamic computation of prudential capital. As Chapter 11 has underlined, models have a great deal to do with the redefinition of capital requirements as well as with the efficient use of early warning signals, but this practice, too, has its limits.

2 Are there critical differences between the British, American and Swiss Regulatory Requirements?

While the UK's STRGL was still a discussion paper and the publication of Statement of Financial Accounting Standards (SFAS) No. 133 by FASB was delayed in the USA, on several occasions I heard a certain doubt expressed by cognisant bank executives and accounting experts I was talking to in London: 'Will the Americans come on board?' 'Will they adopt the solution of the Accounting Standards Board?' The implication was that, short of this, 'It would not be easy to unify the financial reporting practices on an international level.'

There are reasons for thinking this way. At the time – that is, in mid- to late 1997 – FASB had proposed the use of current value for derivatives only. By contrast, the British ASB advanced the principle that current value should be used in connection with all financial instruments, whether derivatives or on-balance-sheet. Because it provides a more global view, the British approach:

- tends to present fewer hedge accounting problems, and
- does not require a distinction between on-balance-sheet and off-balance-sheet financial instruments.

Financial Reporting Standard 13 (FRS) 'Derivatives and Other Financial Instruments Disclosures', by the Accounting Standards Board (ASB) was released in 1998 – and is effective for accounting and financial reporting with years ending after 23 March 1999. FRS 13 rules apply to March 1999 year-ends to companies that have any quoted securities, and to all banks.

At present, the ASB has issued this standard on disclosures but is working towards another standard on the recognition and measurement of financial instruments, including derivatives. The overall objective of FRS 13 is to create improved transparency by having companies provide information about the impact of financial instruments on their risk profile. Specifically:

- how the risks might affect their performance and financial condition; and
- how senior management exercises effective control over these exposures.

Narrative disclosures are required to deal with the role that financial instruments have in creating or changing the risks a company faces; as well as the company's objectives and policies in using financial instruments to manage its risks, including a description of its hedging activities.

Numerical disclosures need to be given to interest rates; currency rates; liquidity; maturity; market value of instruments, compared with book value; and issues relating to the effects of hedge accounting. The role of numerical disclosures is to show how the entity's objectives and policies were implemented in the reporting period.

An example of market risks which exist on-balance-sheet is the loans portfolio (a part of the banking book). The banking book is not addressed (at least for the time being) by the Basle Committee's 1996 Market Risk Amendment; yet, as every bank should appreciate, the loans book does not cover credit risk only. It also features:

- interest rate risk; and
- liquidity risk.

Some banks weed out of the loans portfolio the mismatch risk in interest rates by means of internal interest rate swaps (IRS) making interest rate risk taken with loans part of the trading book. In a regulatory sense this is not necessarily an acceptable practice, but it constitutes a method for risk appraisal within the bank's own IAMIS.

Neither are loans the only example of market exposure embedded into the banking book: another case is equity risk in proprietary positions. The economic temptation to add stocks to one's portfolio is understandable, since equities in the long run yield higher average returns than bonds. But this is because returns on equities are much riskier.

In its way, equity risk explains why private pension funds investing mainly in stocks, such as TIAA-CREF, do not guarantee a fixed retirement income. Prices in the stock market fluctuate much more than bond prices. How should the bank's proprietary positions be marked?

The new American financial reporting rule defined by SFAS 133 answers this query through the notion of *management intent*. If the intent of the board and senior management is to hold these positions long term, then the accruals method should be used; otherwise, they must be marked to market.

A difference between British and American viewpoints concerns loans and related hedges. FASB views floating rate loans as cash flow exposures (see section 3). In this sense, a swap that converts a loan from fixed to floating rate may be considered as a hedge whose price impacts on the cash flow. In regard to *comprehensive income*, FASB uses this notion as a temporary parking place for gains and losses on hedges regarding uncontracted future transactions. In a later period, these gains and losses will be transferred to earnings. This is not so different from what ASB implies with STRGL.

The careful reader of both SFAS 133 and of the STRGL rules will appreciate that on many issues, and most particularly in terms of accounting culture, the British and American viewpoints are not that far apart. This opinion is based on the fact that FASB has clearly stated its belief that *current value* is the most relevant measure for financial instruments at large, and is the only relevant measure for derivatives.

The regulatory authorities are fully justified in their insistence that any financial instruments other than long-term investment should be measured at *current value*, even if this runs contrary to the traditional accruals method. Where an instrument is traded in an active market, the market price should be used. Where there is no such market, and therefore market prices are not available, quoted prices for similar instruments may be used, with appropriate adjustments to reflect any differences; or, alternatively, valuation techniques may be used, including option pricing models such as binomial distribution and Black–Scholes (see D.N. Chorafas, *Advanced Financial Analysis*, Euromoney Books, London, 1994).

Current value is the term British regulators are using. FASB speaks of *present value* (PV). The definition of the two terms is not exactly the same, and *fair value* is used too (also by the FASB). Fair value is the price a willing buyer will pay a willing seller for an asset or liability, under non-fire-sale conditions.

Whether we talk of current value, present value or fair value, one of the practical problems is that measuring all financial instruments at current value could represent a major task. Therefore, FASB has somewhat constrained the scope of marking to market by not demanding that all financial instruments undergo this process, while requiring that all derivatives are recognised and measured at current value in the balance sheet. In its own way, Swiss National Bank made this solution mandatory as of 1996 (see section 3).

Let me now integrate the foregoing concepts. The dividing line between those instruments to be marked to market and those that can stay in the books on original value is *management intent*. However, the implementation of management intent in regulatory reporting is anathema to continental European bankers, with Britain being somewhere between the American and continental positions.

Whether management intent is or is not clearly stated in financial statements, a basic preoccupation of practically all regulators is that while derivatives were originally designed to mitigate risk, now they have themselves become the origin of large exposure. A number of recent meltdowns (as in East Asia and Russia), corporate mismanagement scandals, and crises in local government finances because of derivatives have brought many problems to light at devastating cost to investors and taxpayers.

In my humble opinion, regulators should be distinguishing between small amounts, large sums and very large sums in play with all sorts of financial instruments. This is partly done through the definition of large exposures with CAD (see Chapter 11). Regulators should also focus on the frequency of an event happening, which may range from very low to high. As shown in Figure 13.1, these two variables have an inverse correlation, therefore combining them permits one to distinguish between normal (or expected), unexpected and extreme events.

1. Expected losses, for instance with loans, can be taken care of through the annual profit and loss statement.
2. Unexpected losses call for special reserves. Credit risk eigenmodels, used by commercial banks, focus on this type of exposure.
3. Extreme events are a sort of super-catastrophe which cannot be matched through reserves, but which might be approached by means of a reinsurance underwritten by the capital markets.

In conclusion, the answer to the title of this section is that indeed there are differences in prudential regulatory requirements, not so much between the British and the American position but between current rules and those

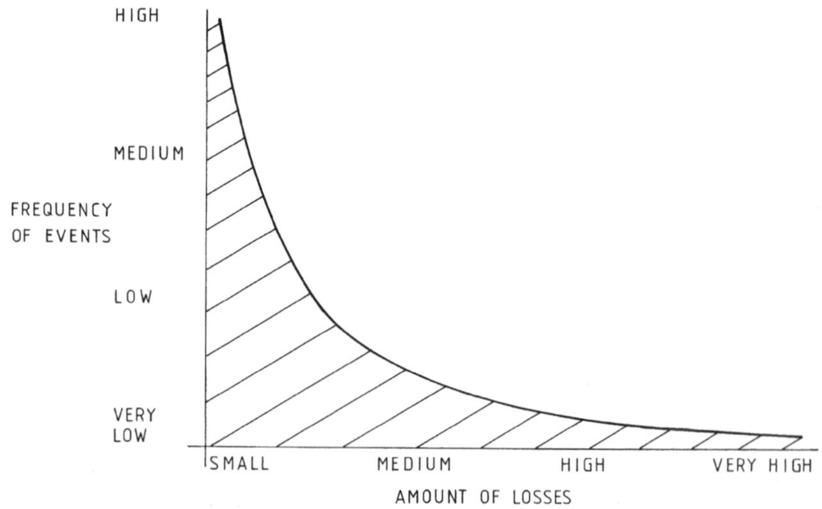

Figure 13.1 Frequent events have a small price tag, while extreme events may represent catastrophic losses

which will crystallise during the next five years following the conclusion of the Basle Committee, known as 2000+.

3 Working Parties and the Gordian Knot cut by the Swiss National Bank

The fact that Europe has so many sovereign states, each with its own jurisdiction, has led to a shower of working parties in search of a common solution. In accounting, for example, the Fédération des Experts Comptables Européens (FEE), the International Accounting Standards Committee (IASC) and the British Bankers' Association, among others, are looking for a new accounting standard. The Basle Committee also has a subcommittee addressing itself to the same job.

The usual procedure is to assemble a task force and invite guest members to assist in the discussions. Examples are nominees of FEE member bodies; the FEE Insurance Working Party; the Fédération Bancaire; and the European Commission. Typically, the agenda of the task force is to:

- review documents containing precedents;
- determine which are relevant; and
- try to agree on an outline format for its report.

Working parties perform this mission by allocating specific tasks to their members. They consider relevant parts of national legislation and standards for banks and financial institutions; suggest extensions or changes to what already exists, as warranted by new developments in the market; and put forward some basic concepts for decision.

The members of the working parties contribute their time individually. They compare standards under discussion with the Bank Accounts Directive (BAD) of the EU, as well as other directives where relevant. They classify the results as 'Not covered by directives', 'In agreement with directives' or 'In conflict with directives', and submit them to FEE for collation and circulation.

Typically, a position paper is discussed by the full working party and its members try to agree on outline provisions to be considered for addition, deletion or amendment. The position paper also brings up additional matters that should or could be covered in a future BAD or other relevant document. Also, the members of the working parties prepare recommendations outside the meetings, and elaborate sections of a draft report.

Of course, all this takes time, and there is considerable duplication of effort since the missions of the different task forces, commissions and working parties tend to overlap. No doubt a single organisation endowed with the appropriate authority could come up with a much more coherent and universal set of rules. As Henry Ford once commented: 'A committee cannot drive a company, like a committee cannot drive a car.'

One of the best examples of a financial reporting document produced by one authority rather than a multinational working party is that on the disclosure of gains and losses derivatives by the Swiss National Bank. In compliance with the regulation prevailing in Switzerland since 1996, Figures 13.2 and 13.3 map the on-balance-sheet and off-balance-sheet assets and liabilities of one of the big Swiss banks, as reported in its annual statement. According to the new regulation:

- off-balance-sheet gains are shown in the balance sheet as *other assets* (Figure 13.2).
- off-balance-sheet losses are also shown in the balance sheet, but as *other liabilities* (Figure 13.3).

The careful reader will appreciate that in this specific case, both other assets and other liabilities increased rapidly in the five-year timeframe mapped on the two figures. Other liabilities have grown faster and by Year 5 exceeded other assets. This means that at year-end the institution had losses rather than gains in derivatives contracts.

Through this financial reporting framework, the Swiss authorities are integrating market risk into the assets and liabilities the bank reports to supervisors. Gains and losses are also made transparent to correspondent bankers, investors and the general public. By making exposure visible both to the authorities and to business partners, this solution helps the bank gain public

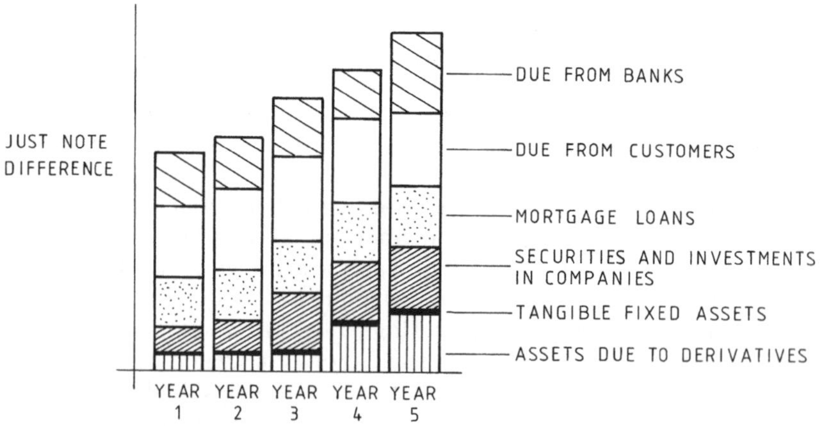

Figure 13.2 Assets in the balance sheet and off-balance-sheet of a major financial institution (up to $300 billion)

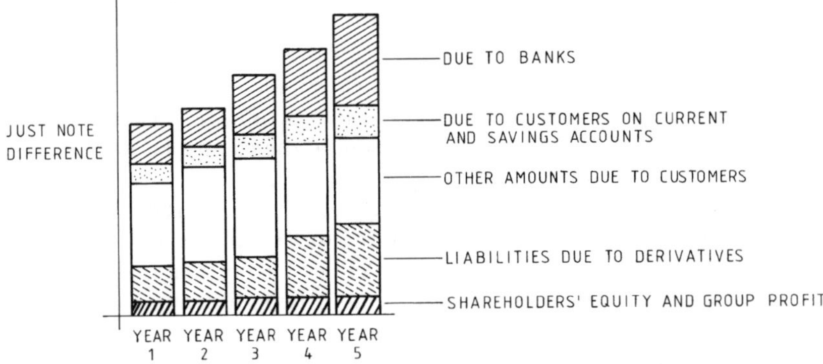

Figure 13.3 Liabilities in the balance sheet and off-balance-sheet of a major financial institution (up to $300 billion)

confidence. This is, of course, a major departure from past practices. Classically, the balance sheet talks of *positions*, not of risk, and the items shown in it do not switch from one column to the other because of market price changes.

Conceptually, however, the fact is that all reported positions – whether in assets or in liabilities – have embedded into them an element of exposure which is positive. The cutting of the Gordian knot by the Swiss authorities dramatises the fact that in a dynamic market the concept of an asset and of a liability is relative rather than absolute, and it could change with time. This is the sense of position risk. Therefore the 1996 Swiss rule of reporting market value in derivatives is a refinement, not a contradiction. As every banker, trader or investor should appreciate, it is inescapable that every position shown in assets and liabilities has an exposure associated with it.

In this way, the balance sheet becomes a statement which maps all financial instruments that form the trading and non-trading portfolios, and makes it possible to focus the analyses according to the heading under which they are included. This is important at a time when interest-bearing banking products are no longer the dominant components of income of major banks. They are increasingly being replaced by:

- transaction-based earnings from trading activities; and
- fee income from portfolio management.

On the other hand, the growing level of trading activities brings with it an increase in leveraging. Many bankers assert that the absolute size of these positions does not necessarily reflect a higher level of risk. I personally think the opposite. Either way, the nature of the principal financial instruments or classes of financial instruments being used, the basis for their inclusion in the accounts, the valuation methods and the accounting treatment of gains and losses have been clearly specified by the Swiss authorities, and they have become transparent.

Another supervisory initiative to bring to the reader's attention is the 1997 regulation by Swiss authorities which stipulates the way reporting entities should be disclosing some types of transaction. For instance, security dealers must adjust the level of disclosure to the client's knowledge and understanding of financial instruments.

Particularly where the level of risk exceeds what is considered to be a 'normal level', the client must state in writing that he understands this transaction is high risk. Also, in terms of guidelines for portfolio management the client must be informed about what he is being offered. Means must be available to confirm this understanding.

4 Concepts underpinning the Bundesbank's *Mindest Anforderungen für Handelsgesellschaften* and the cash flow method

The best way of looking at the CAD (see Chapter 11) is as being half-way between a guideline and a framework. More concrete than a guideline are the national regulations which are elaborated and published by the reserve bank. As the Swiss example has demonstrated, every regulatory authority applies its own reporting rules which are much more precise.

Another interesting example is provided by the rules established by the Bundesbank in connection with minimum requirements and reporting procedures. In a nutshell the framework is shown in Table 13.1. The first column indicates those financial activities to which minimum capital requirements apply, while the second column lists the exclusions.

On 1 January 1997, the *Mindest Anforderungen für Handelsgesellschaft–* (MAH) became law. Theoretically, MAH is the German version of the EU's CAD (see Chapter 11), but practically it follows its own patterns of rules which are concrete and thoroughly studied: MAH looks at the risk involved in banking on a product basis, and specifies that every trading activity must satisfy capital requirements.

The basic statement establishing capital requirements is that all instruments being traded, including securities, money market, swaps, options and futures must be marked to market every day. The definition MAH gives to *trading* is that an instrument is exchanged between two willing parties. This opens up some challenging possibilities from a mathematical modelling viewpoint. For instance, a bank which issued a fixed rate bond gets essentially involved in three trading operations:

- the issuing of the fixed income security;
- a swap to hedge interest rate risk; and
- the funding of the trade.

Table 13.1 Deutsche Bundesbank: range of applications subject to minimum requirements

Included	*Excluded*
All trading activities, whether for the bank's own account or for the account of third parties, including those based on: – Money market activities – Securities – Borrower's notes – Stock lending – Foreign exchange transactions – Trading in precious metals – Trading in derivatives regardless of whether relating to: – The trading book – Investments held as fixed assets – The liquidity reserve	Funds invested by customers for a fixed period Trading in coins Travellers' cheque business Genuine commissions in securities and derivatives Specified commissions in foreign exchange, precious metals and fixed-price trading in securities Securities issue business

According to MAH, these three operations must be marked to market. This is not as simple as it sounds; for instance, to mark to market a loan to Siemens which is made in Germany but in dollars, it is necessary to split this loan into the parts identified by the following four points:

- the fixed-rate loan itself;
- the swap to hedge the fixed rate with variable rate;
- the currency exchange operation, hedged over the term of the loan; and
- the funding of the loan position.

Credit risk enters into the fixed rate loan as the loan is carried in the banking book. The other three points have more to do with market risk. The second and third items are part of the trading book, and hence subject to the 1996 Market Risk Amendment by the Basle Committee. The fourth point belongs to the banking book (like the first).

MAH's directives also contrast with SFAS No.119 (which preceded SFAS 133) whose rule is to write derivatives gains and losses in a supplementary statement to be attached to the income statement (profit and loss). Neither is MAH similar to the STRGL by the British ASB.

In its way, MAH builds upon the Bundesbank's adoption of cash flow as the control element of exposures taken by a credit institution. The German central bank chose cash flow as a measure of financial health in the autumn of 1993. To refresh the reader's memory, the simplest way to think of *cash flow* is money received minus money paid out. This is as true of the whole bank as of any of its departments, projects, channels, or financial instruments it trades. In very simple terms:

Cash flow = Inflow – Outflow

The term *cash flow*, however, does not have just one definition and method of computation, as some textbooks suggest. Cash assumes many forms and into the cash flow equation enter net income, depreciation, amortisation, interest expenses, income taxes and dividends (see D.N. Chorafas, *Financial Models and Simulation*, Macmillan, London, 1995).

The Bundesbank is not alone among central banks placing emphasis on cash flow as a means of measuring exposure: other jurisdictions in G-10 countries follow a similar strategy. Cash flow contributes to an entity's financial staying power. Also, regulatory guidelines necessarily account for the fact that investors greatly value the ability of a company (or of a portfolio) to generate net cash flows. They look at *assets* as a source of prospective cash inflows, and at *liabilities* as obligations that probably will generate cash outflows.

The role played by the *present value of expected cash flows* should not be underestimated. It takes into account both inflows and outflows resulting from transactions that can be expected to happen in the ordinary course of business. Well-managed companies steadily use discounted cash flow to evaluate the present value of their portfolio, their investments and their holdings. As a matter of principle, both cash flow and liquidity should be constantly analysed in a detailed and global sense. This can be done effectively through models, real-time computation and visualisation of results.

Largely developed as a result of the Third World debt crisis of the 1980s, the concept underpinning the cash flow approach is, in my judgement, an excellent way of looking at exposure, because it represents an important aspect of the counterparty's dependability. For instance, loans, positive cash flows enhance the debtor's ability to:

- pay the interest; and
- repay the loan.

Measurements and reporting procedures based on cash flow have also been adopted by the Bundesbank in connection with derivatives. In this case, the German reserve bank sees cash flow as the best method of controlling exposure embedded into the derivatives portfolio of commercial banks. Because a cash flow stream is longer term, it is not biased by passing problems of governance.

Let me add this in conclusion. Discounted cash flows and other algorithms provide analytical information on which factual judgement can be based. Cash flow is one of the better measures, and it follows orthodox accounting standards. There is also a body of professional knowledge available because the actuarial method used in insurance is based on discounted cash flows. As of the late 1980s many Wall Street analysts have made cash flow, rather than profits, the primary measure of a company's health.

5 Using simulation, experimentation and public pricing information for compliance with the rules

The bottom line is that the control of exposure is, first and foremost, of greatest importance to the commercial and investment banks themselves. Therefore, they should appreciate the regulators' initiative which says that they have to disclose details about derivatives and other off-balance-sheet financial instruments, showing them in their accounts at current value. Let us always keep in mind that until very recently most commitments made in derivative products were not entered into a balance sheet at all or, at best, they were shown in a footnote which failed to reflect their true significance in terms of risk taken by the institution.

The ASB has been right to insist that all financial instruments, not just those linked to a hedged position, should be marked to current value. The problem is doing so in such a way that reported results are credible. A dependable procedure has now been established, though it is expected to evolve as experience is gained in its usage.

Critics say that marking to market the loans book and using the cash flow method are one-sided, and that they fit better the case of impaired loans than those which have no problems. Bad debt provisions are currently made on an undiscounted basis. Usually the same critics also add that marking to market the loans portfolio factors in bad news that may occur in the future, but forgets about future good news. The charge against marking to market the loans portfolio is connected to the fact that, under current accounting, the process of putting a loan into the banking book creates a *de facto* loss because of administrative and other costs. Such loss is generated as operational costs have to be charged.

The answer to this argument is that this seeming imbalance will not necessarily affect the way the market perceives the value of the loan because the evaluation made by the market is matter-of-fact rather than strictly procedural; but it will have an impact in terms of marking to model, when established accounting methods are followed. It is therefore necessary to clarify how operational cost charges can or should be counterbalanced, say, by a value-added factor to be associated with an ongoing loan (if there is one). Indeed, this issue is an example of the fact that it is not enough to publish new regulations, it is also necessary to:

- establish rigorous solutions;
- study all possible consequences; and
- simulate worst-case scenarios.

What I mean by worst-case scenarios when evaluating procedural steps is the tricks which can be played with balance sheets and with off-balance-sheet reporting. For instance, when reading a company's balance sheet statement, beware of one-time write-offs. Also, look twice at extraordinary items and what may be hidden behind them.

Say, for a moment, that all listed companies and public interest bodies had to use current values for loans and borrowings, as well as instruments such as swaps, forwards, futures and options. The only exception would be the company's own equity shares. This would not only revolutionise accounting procedures which date back to Luca Paciolo and his seminal work published in 1494, but also lead to a new industry of published prices.

As soon as marking to market the contents of trading book and banking book becomes a pan-European requirement, and is also adopted by the G-10 countries outside Europe (America, Canada and Japan), the market for quoted prices for securities and other instruments will suddenly become so large that information providers will rush to fill the need:

1. Pricing schemes will capitalise on the globalisation of markets, and the fact that the Internet can ensure a cost-effective access to databases of even the smallest institutions.
2. Effective solutions will use interactive computational finance for timely and accurate reporting 24 hours per day, 7 days per week, any-to-any using the Internet.
3. Algorithmic solutions will provide in real-time a pricing mechanism dependent on the bank's investment horizon, as well as prevailing volatility and liquidity.

Simulation in finance can be assisted by experience gained in other fields, such as physics and engineering. Which is the most basic rule concerning the modelling of physical systems? The answer is abstraction and idealisation, a process which suppresses all finer points to reach a simplified but (one hopes) valid solution.

For starters, let me give a vivid example about the simplification which we seek from the natural real world in which we live our daily lives. With very few exceptions, the body of all animals can be idealised as a living cylinder pierced doubly by two tubes or passages, one for the breath of life, the other for food and water. The reason for this bifurcation lies deep in the secret of life which biologists are actively searching to unlock. The cells of any animal require an uninterrupted double uptake. All animals routinely breathe through one compound passage, while they gain sources of energy, by eating and drinking, through another. The breathing cylinder works in real-time. Practically every second we draw a new breath. Although no less essential, foods and liquids enter in timed batches.

With this metaphor in the background, which are the financial market's two cylinders if we abstract, as in the case of animals, the limbs, wings, fur, fins and bones? The cognisant reader will answer:

- *volatility* which works in real-time; and
- *liquidity* which acts in timed batches.

Whether we consider interest rate risk, currency exchange risk or any other market risk, the exposure which we take will be underpinned by liquidity and volatility. Add cash flow as the third part in the algorithm and you get the simplified model.

Once this has been appreciated, we can idealise the financial risks embedded in the banking book and the trading book, splitting them according to counterparty, financial instrument and other criteria. We can also develop a procedure capable of transiting from one three-dimensional representation to another:

- *cash flow* has to be carefully calculated on each bank's books' content;
- *liquidity* and *volatility* are those prevailing in the market;
- *interest rate risk* is easily tractable in marking to market terms, and the same is true of *currency exchange risk*.

Cash flow from assets and operations defines a company's liquidity as well as its ability to service its debt. Properly done, cash flow analysis succeeds in exposing a firm's mechanisms to sustain liquidity and therefore it constitutes one of the best tools available in modern finance (see also section 4).

Another important element publicly quoted prices will have to provide is counterparty exposure. This is greatly helped because of the work done by independent rating agencies such as Standard & Poor's, Moody's and Fitch IBCA. *Credit risk* estimates can be based on these opinions for borrowers big enough to be tracked by rating agencies; or, alternatively, on internal but audited credit grading models for smaller borrowers. Expert systems can be instrumental in developing and sustaining grading models.

A rigorous solution will also require an input from regulators, as well as *backtesting*, as the 1996 Market Risk Amendment has specified. Furthermore, a valid approach will also demand building a *modular* implementation which is adaptable, flexible, verifiable and easily updated.

Past experience can serve as a guide. We know how to develop securitisation models with house mortgages which reflect real-life policies and practices because some valuable algorithms are already on hand. But we would need to embed a stronger credit risk factor for corporates and other types of loan, which means that more focused research still needs to be done.

Valid approaches in regard to loans will invariably involve taking a look at securitised products, and working by analogy. For example: can we manage the loans book *as if* it were a bonds book? For marking to model purposes, a rigorous simulation procedure would account for the fact that many profitable investments require long-term commitment of capital unless they are converted into publicly traded securities.

At the same time, any model which focuses on wealth risk should take due account of cash on hand and of cash flow. There is no universal practice on how to treat cash holdings, but a growing body of opinion suggests that it is wrong to integrate the *cash book* into the *banking book*, a practice followed because of cash management experience. Many cognisant treasurers believe that a better position for the cash book is to be part of the *trading book*.

Factual and documented solutions will evidently require rules and regulations which make tampering with fair value estimates a criminal offence and curtail the different creative accounting practices. A sound initiative is ASB's position on *hedge accounting*, especially for companies which commonly take out hedges against future transactions. The Board correctly suspects there is some abuse in this area and that it is necessary to close the loopholes. ASB also states that the advent of sophisticated approaches to trading and risk management blurs the dividing line between:

- *hedging*, for which gains and losses are deferred; and
- *trading* proper, for which gains and losses are recognised as they occur.

In addition, the accounts are more difficult to analyse if hedge accounting is used because it creates debits and credits in the balance sheet that are not assets or liabilities but paper gains and paper losses. The answer to the above two points is *management intent*, of which we spoke in section 2. The board and senior management of a credit institution should be able to state in unambiguous terms why a commitment was made.

6 Policy risk, choice of hedging and extreme events in wealth management

A banker, a treasurer or an investor can create hedged positions through balance sheet and off-balance-sheet instruments. His hedging plans, however, will remain valid only as long as the market is steady. By contrast, they may well turn upside down when the market changes in a significant way, or the monetary authorities alter their policy. The disintegration of hedging plans has happened time and again during the 1990s, so it is not an issue open to argument.

Take the stock market as an example. Bull markets rarely die a normal death. Most often they are killed by inflation, some unexpected regulatory measures such as higher reserve requirements, or a sharp rise in interest rates, whether by the market or by the regulators. Hence, besides other risks there is also a *policy risk*: a change in the policy of the regulators can alter or even turn on its head the basis of a given hedge. This happened in 1994 when the Federal Reserve increased the short-term interest rate six times, the first two shocks being enough to unravel the highly geared bond market.

A change in policy can create significant losses in hedges as well as gains in unhedged positions. The irony of this is that, given a relatively high rate of volatility, it is not inconceivable an unhedged position will behave better than a hedged one. Besides, not hedging at least some of the positions is for any practical purpose unavoidable, let alone that it is practically impossible to create a perfect hedge for assets and liabilities, no matter what the theorists and the salesmen say.

What many bankers, investors and treasurers fail to realise is that *hedging* and *not-hedging* are asymmetric aspects of the management of wealth. Just as the trading book has a *trading risk*, portfolio management always involves a *wealth risk*. In today's global economy, fine-tuned wealth management depends on:

- the money supply;
- the velocity of circulation of money;
- the money's purchasing power;
- inflation and deflation;
- exchange rates;
- interest rates; and
- factors reflected in liquidity.

We know more or less how to estimate liquidity in a given market: what is more difficult is to estimate global liquidity. There are several measures of transnational market liquidity such as *turnover ratios* which measure the total value of all trades divided by a country's market capitalisation; most approaches, however, rest on hypotheses.

Not only is hedging for wealth management purposes not as simple as many books on 'modern portfolio theory' suggest, but in addition the bank's own protection system for loans may unravel when a super-catastrophe hits. A similar statement is valid in connection to another gimmick: 'portfolio insurance', a dynamic asset allocation scheme supposed to protect against falling markets.

The US security firms who suffered the worst losses in the 1987 equity market crash had relied on portfolio insurance rather than market know-how. Other mis-hedging examples are more recent. Even large loans taken for trading (read, speculative) reasons can turn around and bite the hand that feeds them. A *gate-keeper* is therefore needed to screen and contain extreme events, as well as irrational trade-offs of risk and return.

Such a function is not covered by popular theories and neither are currently available rules and regulations tackling the aftermath of extreme events: for instance, permitting banks to tap the capital markets with a reinsurance programme in a way similar to that followed by the more classic reinsurance industry. Solutions protecting the interest of banks and investors, while avoiding systemic risk, will not come easily. They will require a great deal of regulatory attention, as well as rigorous schemes for financial super-catastrophes, and financial products priced according to their risk as possible outliers.

Figure 13.4 restructures the concave relationship between frequency of events and amount of losses which was presented in Figure 13.1. It does so by distinguishing between those losses which can be seen as part of the profit and loss statement, those requiring special reserves as insurance and the case of super-catastrophes. Super-catastrophes could be supported in either of two ways: taxpayers' money, when the reserve bank steps in and salvages the defunct institution, or event-triggered catastrophe derivatives sold to the capital market.

The reference to the gate-keeper serves well in the case of extreme events because, contrary to what their name might imply, they are not purely stochastic, but also exhibit a momentum effect. This momentum may build up for different reasons, such as superleveraging, which brought down sovereigns (Indonesia, South Korea, Russia and Brazil), and also financial companies from Continental Illinois and Credit Lyonnais to LTCM.

Practically all financial institutions have in them a bit of the leveraging that these last three companies had. As an article in *Business Week* put in

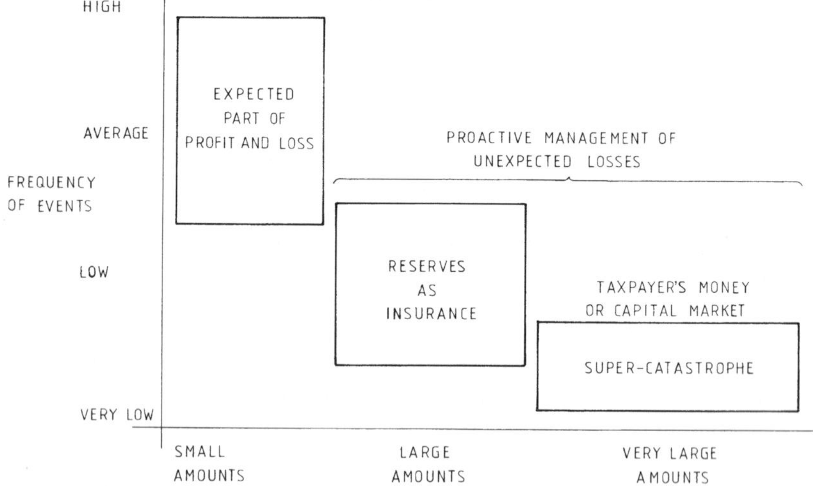

Figure 13.4 Expected events, unexpected events and super-catastrophes with corresponding size of financial loss

(25 January 1999): 'A huge slice of Goldman's earnings come from proprietary trading... Embedded in Goldman Sachs is a hedge fund.' This applies to practically all big banks and many of the smaller ones.

A thorough analysis of transnational economic conditions, to unearth extreme events-in-the-making, has as much to do with prudential supervision as it has with wealth risk. A rigorous gate-keeper will look at stock market volatility and the openness of a country's capital market, doing so country-by-country without forgetting the correlations between risk factors. It is also wise to examine how closely different indicators are correlated with very rapid economic growth and its opposite: stagflation (stagnation with inflation). A strong market links with liquidity: countries with the most liquid stock markets tend to grow faster. Investors are wary of illiquid markets and of illiquid instruments, and hence they avoid them.

People who think they are experts in hedging should appreciate that because of the global market's complexity and the fact that it takes time to understand the behaviour of new instruments, there will always be a residual wealth risk which extreme events may hide. Ironically, wealth risk – and, by extension, systemic risk – is sometimes courted by monetary authorities when they suddenly change their policies and their rules.

Sharp changes in policies, practices and rules are no recent phenomenon, but one which has been going on for centuries. Therefore institutions which want to do a perfect job have to analyse long time series to flush out trends as well as inconsistencies in public policy. Similarly, databased market data can be mined to increase our sensitivity to market behaviour, since market sensitivity and the ability to hedge disasters correlate. Sensitivity is put on the backburner when investors, treasurers and bankers follow the herd.

Beware, too, of extravagant claims. Some companies say they have developed a 'no-risk portfolio', but 'no-risk' can often mean 'high risk'. Let me close this chapter with one more thought: Brandon Davies, of Barclays Bank says, 'As we get more sophisticated we find we consume time trying to develop solutions other banks do already.' Brandon is right. Sophistication is a self-feeding cycle. Its appetite for pushing forward the frontiers of knowledge and of technology never ends, but only those who prove to be up to the task can benefit from it.

14
Regulators and the Wave of Mergers in Banking

1 Introduction

There is no evidence that regulators have interfered in banking mergers, other than to push a weak, nearly insolvent bank into the arms of a strong bank to save it from bankruptcy. But in early 1998 regulators did take action to stop the merger of two giant certified public accountancy firms because this would have reduced competition in the outsourcing of financial services.

It is still too early to say whether this could be seen as the forerunner of a more activist position by regulators in mega-mergers concerning the banking industry, or if it has been a one-off event. What is sure is that in finance, as in any other industry, globalisation has been a major drive behind many, if not all, new initiatives including mergers and acquisitions.

Next to globalisation and technology the biggest factor which characterised financial institutions in the late 1990s has been consolidation through mergers. This has created a seamless, borderless environment shifting attention away from traditional policy in lending and trading activities which looked for diversification in counterparty risk.

Because of mergers, counterparty risk is on the increase as mergers and acquisitions lead into dealing with a handful of big banks. If the experience of the late 1990s is used to gain a factual opinion on where concentration of credit risk leads, this opinion is negative. Banks failed to assess the risks associated with hedge funds even though they used this form of lending in a big way.

The merger drive has produced alliances between banks who may at one time have been seen only as competitors. The now evolving financial landscape requires companies able to communicate across language barriers, a diversity of product lines, cultural differences and technological incompatibilities. Along with advanced networks, which make improved co-ordination possible, come practical business requirements: tier-1 banks use enablers that address customer needs in a more customised and personalised way than has ever been possible; they employ technology to develop revolutionary new financial products and processes that provide for faster and more sophisticated financial solutions.

Both in banking and in manufacturing, many mergers are a way of spreading research and development costs and of capitalising on technological virtuosity. But the merger drive is not without challenges. One of the problems is that the grand vision of company leaders is not always shared by their subordinates. Another problem is that many financial entities do not have the ability to capitalise on the human resources and the opportunities opened up through advanced technology even after the merger.

Many financial analysts have start to wonder whether a merger is worth the disruption that its prospect, let alone the reality, brings to a bank's daily business. Apart from the cost of capital, the average economic value-added of institutions that have merged in the past ten years fell after the merger. Why, then, do they do it? And why have mergers in the banking industry taken on such a large dimension?

These are by no means idle queries. They are issues challenging commercial bankers, investment bankers and regulators. Central banks and governments also face the prospect of mega bank failures which are much more difficult to contain, or salvage, than if the banks were smaller. The case study in section 6 also demonstrates that a whole financial sector might fall apart.

2 A bird's-eye view of mega bank mergers

While the regulators are concerned about the increasing amount of exposure taken by credit institutions, the stock market has been the first to react. In America and in Europe the equity of some banks dropped by almost 50 per cent in September and October 1998, and this decline dramatised a shift in sentiment since the spring of 1998 when a series of huge deals were agreed. In the first six months of 1998:

- Travelers merged with Citicorp, in a deal which at the time valued Citicorp at $82.5 billion;
- NationsBank merged with BankAmerica for a tab standing at $66.6 billion;
- Banc One agreed to buy First Chicago for $29.5 billion;
- Norwest of Minneapolis announced it was buying Wells Fargo of San Francisco for $31.17 billion.

But, as the size of the banks' exposure in East Asia and in Russia hit the news, shares in all the money centre banks plummeted. The market's judgement on Citicorp, Travelers, BankAmerica and Banc One has been particularly savage. Analysts suggested that they had alienated investors by not keeping them fully informed.

In a snowball effect, market reverses led to nervousness over non-interest fee income, from activities such as capital markets, fund management and investment banking, and most particularly from trading exposure. Whether acquired or acquiring, each and every one of these banks is regulated. When market crises hit, the whole regulatory mechanism is on alert (see also Chapter 3 on systemic risk).

Figure 14.1 gives a bird's eye view of the top mergers in the 1998 wave in the USA alone, plus the Chemical Bank's take-over of Chase Manhattan which preceded this fever activity. The figure in the top box indicates the assets of the resulting institution, but it does not tell us much about the exposure embedded in these mergers, once the risks the individual banks carry in non-performing loans, derivatives and other instruments are brought together in the combined books.

In the Citicorp–Travelers merger (see section 4), Citicorp's $3.1 trillion in notional principal amount in derivatives has been combined with Travelers' extensive holdings and its exposure through its Salomon Smith Barney subsidiary. Some analysts estimated the new group would have nearly $6 trillion in notional principal amount connected to derivative instruments, in its portfolio.

Other US institutions, too, are at the $6 trillion level with derivatives over and above the undisclosed amounts concerning troubled loans. In fact, in notional principal the three big US banks (Citigroup, Chase and Morgan) have an exposure of more than twice the GDP of the USA.

The fact that Citigroup has $700 billion in assets is not just a statistic. Apart from the financial strength, this number also means that a single mega-failure could bankrupt the US deposit insurance fund. At just $30 billion, the fund of the FDIC suddenly looks inadequate. Citigroup holds roughly $50 billion in US deposits, and in a worst-case scenario, speculation by aggressive bond traders, or faulty underwriting, or large derivatives losses would cut deeply into the group's capital structure. Regulation, too, becomes more problematic as the very wide range of the institution's activities brings it under different jurisdictions, while consolidation is doubling the number of too-big-to-fail banks which in the past reserve banks and governments kept alive at a high cost to taxpayers. According to the Federal Reserve Bank of Minneapolis, there were 11 too-big-to-fail banks in 1984 with assets of $38.2 billion or more. By 1997, the number had reached 21 and was growing. At the same time banking industry assets were barely up in real terms but, in virtual money (that is, in leveraging the assets) there was a huge growth.

Even the smaller (in assets) mega banks resulting from mergers look vulnerable. The NationsBank–BankAmerica merger combined the fifth- and sixth-largest derivatives holding banks in the USA, yielding an institution with huge principal amounts, and therefore with a significant amount of exposure to the derivatives.

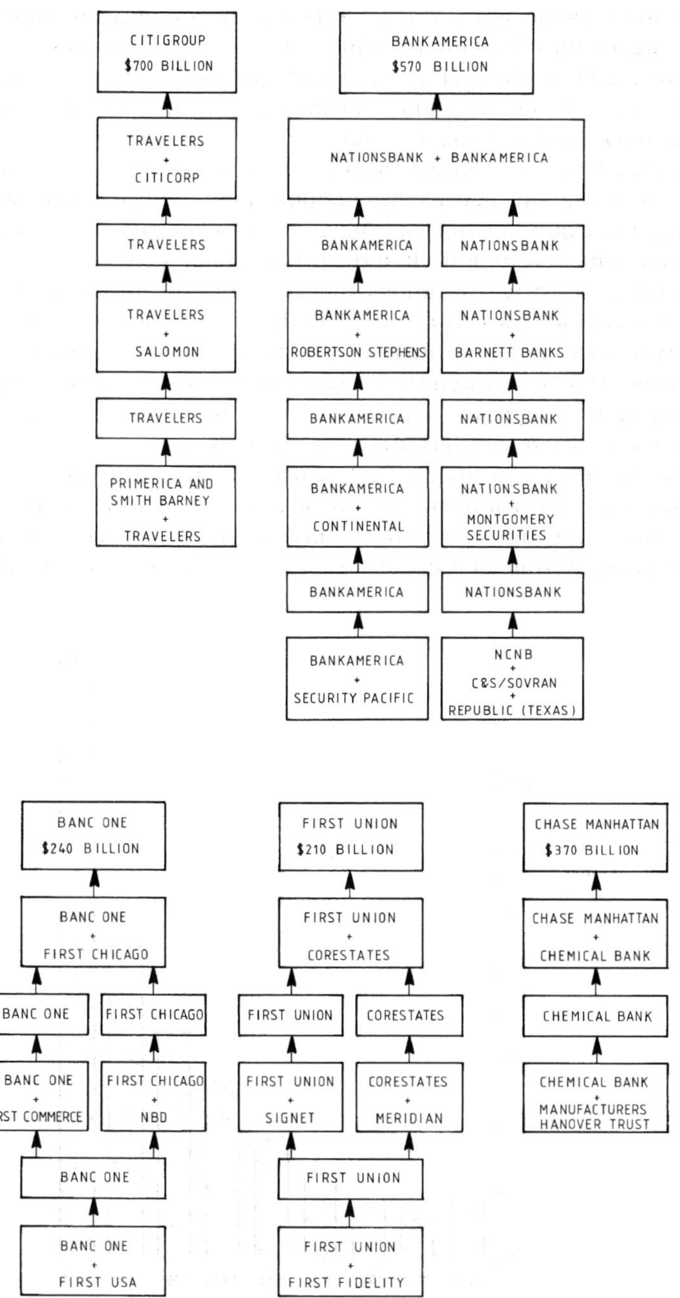

Figure 14.1 Mergers of major institutions in the USA

The main reason given when the merger of NationsBank and the old BankAmerica into the new BankAmerica was announced was to create a coast-to-coast institution and boost competitiveness. The new BankAmerica said it could trim its $19 billion in combined expenses by 10 per cent and cut up to 8000 positions nation-wide.

The Banc One–First Chicago NBD merger looks better in terms of exposure because Banc One had avoided jumping on the derivatives disaster train, but with the acquisition of First Chicago NBD and its $1.4 trillion in derivatives, Banc One now finds itself in the trillion-dollar derivatives club.

Of course, all these institutions are exposed in other product lines, too, such as good old loans with their counterparty risk and interest rate risk. The reason why I pay more attention to some instruments rather than others is that the skyrocketing derivatives exposure is today the prime danger of a meltdown. This exposure undermines the value of announced US bank mergers in 1990–98, which is shown in Figure 14.2.

The regulators are justified in feeling overwhelmed. Examiners trained to monitor banks for loans may not be able to get their arms around new mammoths like Citigroup and BankAmerica. 'The marketplace is moving so fast that the government is unable to keep up with it', said William M. Isaac,

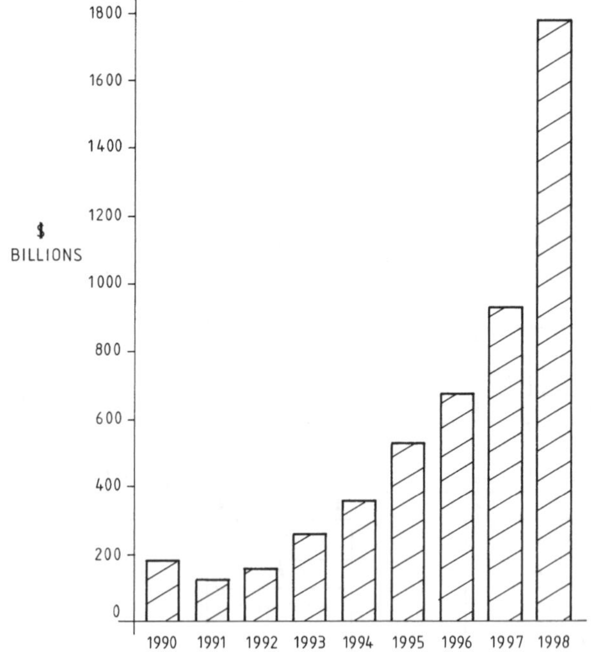

Figure 14.2 Value of announced US bank mergers, 1990–98

former chairman of the FDIC. 'Federal regulatory systems are 10 years out of touch' (*Business Week*, 27 April 1998).

In other terms, the legislators, the Administration and the supervisors must rethink how banks are regulated and what sort of rules should apply. This subject is at the heart of the new global financial architecture, which we discussed in Chapter 2. Two of the concepts which are currently under discussion are:

- encouraging the banking industry to police itself in a factual and documented manner; and
- shifting more of the risk of failure of any single institution on to private investors.

The message conveyed by this second point has been explored in Chapter 13, section 6. My suggestion has been to address the financial markets through structured instruments designed to cover super-catastrophes, in a way similar to the one under study by insurance companies to cover the loss from extreme events such as earthquakes and hurricanes.

Regarding the issue of self-policing, this is not new, but so far self-policing has not proved terribly effective. Only ten months have passed since Swiss Bank and Union Bank of Switzerland joined forces to form the new UBS, as the world's biggest financial institution with end-1997 assets of $700 billion until the LTCM catastrophe emerged. Self-policing was one of the announced goals of that merger, but at the time several analysts argued that the complexity of big banks can make it harder to manage risks. Indeed, in September/October 1998 the new UBS reported losses totalling SF 1.6 billion ($1.2 billion) from misjudging the risks of derivatives trading and hedge-fund lending over the past year. This came over and above losses of $600 million, also incurred in derivatives in October 1997, just prior to the merger, which *The Economist* characterised as 'being as high as the Alps'.

Neither have America's big banks been much more prudent. As we have also seen, in September 1998 they became prominent losers in loans to a big hedge fund, LTCM, which subsequently they had to rescue under pressure from the New York Fed.

If the board is the organ which looks after self-policing, then one has to admit that this is bad news because self-policing is not always at the top of the priorities list. In the wake of these huge losses, the UBS chairman was forced out, along with three of his closest associates. The president of the new BankAmerica also had to quit, after the revelation of a $529 million trading loss and a $374 million write-off for silly loans to D.E. Shaw. Then in mid-January 1999, a palace coup at Goldman Sachs forced out Jon Corzine. Corzine is a trader; those who replaced him are investment bankers.

Whether the origin is stockholder activism, interference by regulators or an internal palace revolution, initiatives bringing new blood to the top are needed to break the cosy relationship among board members. Goldman Sachs' vaunted ability to manage risk suffered a blow in the summer of 1998 when it lost an estimated $500 million to $1 billion as the market caved in following Russia's default and the ensuing turbulence.

Many banks lost very large amounts. While none of these losses has so far proved life-threatening, the loss-making trend does reflect the difficulty of running big banks which are extraordinarily diverse and so much more difficult to manage than the old-style commercial bank under the Glass–Steagall Act. Because practically nobody has experience of how to deal with such complex situations, governments coming to the rescue also stumble.

The French taxpayer having to fork out billions of dollars in successive instalments to pull Credit Lyonnais from an abyss of its own making is by now a classical case in both bank mismanagement and rescue incompetence. Less well known is that after the American taxpayer poured between $160 and $180 billion into the rescue of the savings and loan sector in the early 1990s, it now faces a libel which will cost many more billions of dollars in public money (see section 6).

3 Some merged institutions tend to create second-class clients

With the recovery in the New York stock market in mid-October 1998, merger activity has been stepped up. There were mergers worth $50 billion in October and an estimated $140 billion in November 1998. The Exxon–Mobil merger, if approved, will be the largest single merger in history in total dollar value. Let us not forget that the consolidated treasury of the two oil companies is bigger than a big bank.

Mega consolidation appears to be an outgrowth of global competitive conditions that put a squeeze on profits in many industries. Analysts think that large-sized mergers are related to deflation and the loss of pricing power which hits the bottom line. A near consensus in the market is that the major combinations in the financial industry reflect globalisation and product line expansion, while deflation in raw materials and pricing power are prominent merger reasons in the natural resource industries.

Many analysts now look at mergers as another form of restructuring to bring costs down and under control. Since the bulk of purchases are for stock, mergers may also be an indication that corporations are trying to take advantage of inflation in stock prices while the market is still friendly. In the general case, the management of merging banks and other companies finds plenty of reasons why the merger is a good idea but, despite these assurances, in many cases the evidence points the other way (see also section 4 on Citigroup).

The majority of deals fail to earn back their cost of capital and some have been real disasters for their shareholders. Because of the gamble taken on a number of issues, many mergers and acquisitions are performing well below expectations. Therefore, the board and senior management must clearly understand the financial, strategic and implementation issues of deals *before* approaching the negotiating table. There is plenty of up-front planning that should drive shareholder value consideration, and there are also several requirements concerning risk control. These should be considered before, rather than after, the merger.

Not only is global risk management proving to be extraordinarily difficult, because of size and clash in cultures, but also the banks resulting from mega mergers seem unable to hold on to their clientele. In less than a year, the new UBS lost 150 000 customers from its retail base in Switzerland.

Economics is one of the reasons why big banks feel happier when small customers move to another institution. It costs money to administer a client account. Costs accumulate from several sources, including the teller's time, supervision and information technology, but the 'merger dividends' do not materialise as expected, or perhaps whatever is gained is swamped by big losses in other channels.

In the case of the new UBS, the economies of scale it hoped to achieve by shedding 8000 personnel were far outstripped by the huge derivatives losses. As far as the profit and loss statement is concerned, the merger dividend has been singularly negative. There is also the banking public's viewpoint to be considered and this has two different aspects: the generally negative public reaction because of massive downsizing, and the reduction in the quality of banking service. Survey after survey indicates what many customers feel are the results of mergers:

- less personal service;
- higher banking fees; and
- less credit, in the case of small business.

In fact, one survey that came to my attention had focused on small-business owners and it showed that in the past five years mergers had prompted 25 per cent of these firms to switch banks. This survey also found that 32 per cent of people interviewed said they would look for a new bank if their current bank were taken over. Another survey, a Gallup poll, was hardly more encouraging for banks contemplating a merger. It suggested that 23 per cent of a credit institution's customers typically left for another bank in the wake of a merger, citing as reasons:

- poor or impersonal service;
- fees that were too high; and
- better rates elsewhere.

Regulators might not be unduly upset by the haemorrhage suffered in the bank's client base, but they are evidently concerned because it diminishes the bank's income, assets and financial staying power. All this enters into the algorithm of management control which must consider not only exposure in derivatives and in loans but social and other issues as well.

In the drive to become bigger and bigger, few board and chief executives pay enough attention to the fact that a major problem with mega mergers in the banking industry is that organisation is wanting, and this has a very significant impact on efficiency, all the way from management results to client handling and risk control. Executives of banks who went through mega merger turmoil complain that over a protracted period of time:

- the musical chairs effect continued at unprecedented levels;
- the lines of authority and responsibility were completely unclear;
- nobody seemed to know 'who was who' in the organisation; and
- sometimes there were two or three bosses for the same department.

This state of disorganisation is not the unique experience of one institution but of many who underwent merger pains, and it is the rule rather than the exception, particularly with a merger of equals. Almost a year after the merger of the Union Bank of Switzerland with Swiss Bank Corporation (SBC), many departments had two heads (one from each organisation) and sometimes the right hand did not know what the left was doing.

When in September 1998 the LTCM disaster hit the market and the new UBS lost big money, the executive vice president of finance made a statement that 'he did not know' of this particular commitment which the old UBS had made. While it is a little difficult to swallow this kind of statement, I have no doubt that many other similar cases exist among the bigger financial institutions.

The careful reader will appreciate that a huge exposure in derivatives is not the only worry. As shown in Figure 14.3, there has been a little over \$22 trillion in credit market debt in the USA as of the end of 1998, part of it underwritten with lower standing counterparties. For instance, in 1997, some \$119 billion in junk bonds were issued, more than three times the \$32 billion issued in 1986 at the peak of the Drexel Burnham Lambert era. One of the key worries is that credit and debt pricing depends only partly on risk-and-return trade-offs, the real movers are marketing strategies. Consequently, in a significant number of cases, the pricing of the debt leaves something to be desired.

Sometimes debt pricing strategies disregard asset quality, or pay only lip service to the appraisal of collateral. Haircuts are too small, and favours are too big, while the borrower's equity is not evaluated in a rigorous manner, and pledges and covenants cannot be legally enforced. In other cases, the triggering events are ill-defined.

These approaches have to change because with credit derivatives *credit risk volatility* and *debt* are today globally traded commodities. During 1997,

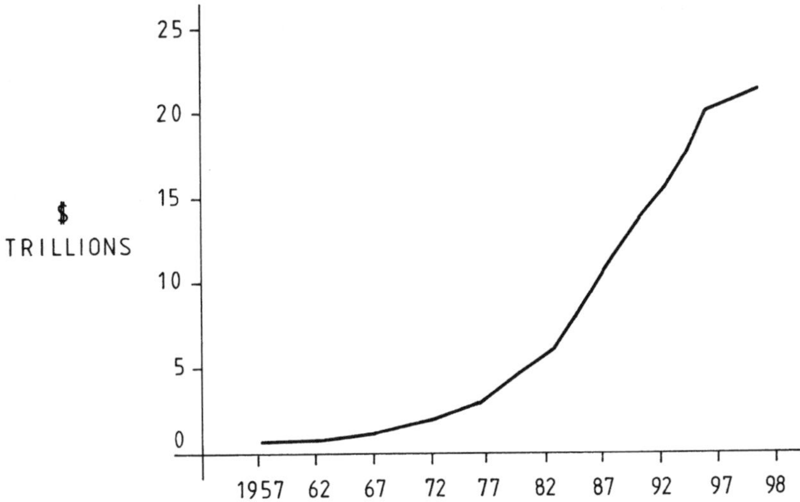

Figure 14.3 Credit market debt in the USA, 1957–98

companies issued some $150 billion in investment grade debt and $195 billion in mortgage-backed securities. Each of these two amounts is in excess of the record $118 billion raised from 1335 stock issues, including $19 billion from real estate investment trusts. Another $43 billion was raised from initial public offerings.

Investment grade corporate debt has an average cumulative default rate of 6.4 per cent over 20 years, which is far from negligible. Junk bonds defaults average 43 per cent, while the worst grade of junk shows an average cumulative default rate of 66 per cent. These default rates mean significant exposure, but such risk figures are not necessarily considered, let alone revealed, in the case of bank mergers. In fact, the resulting mega banks may not be banks at all, if by that is meant an institution that takes deposits in and then lends the money out in the form of home mortgages, credit-card debt and business loans.

Apart from the fact that they buy money rather than depend on deposits, big banks invest depositors' money almost immediately in the stock market, in their own brand of mutual fund, or a retirement annuity issued by their insurance subsidiary. Just the same, as the LTCM case has shown, most of the loans they give out are going into options and swaps, bundled with other loans and sold off to institutional investors such as money-market funds and pension funds.

Some financial analysts believe that a new generation of superbanks may be built around the Fidelity and Vanguard mutual funds, General Electric Capital or giant brokerage houses, rather than the more classical former commercial banks. Some experts also think that eventually only five to ten of these trillion-dollar giants will dominate the global financial services industry, and at the other end of the spectrum there will be lots of small players. This bifurcation will pose a number of major challenges for regulators.

4 The aftermath of Citigroup and other mergers

Let me start with a disclaimer: this is not a critique *per se* of the Citigroup merger; it is only a case study about events happening time and again in bank mergers. Let me also add to this statement some more flavour: a 1998 study by A.T. Kearney, which examined 115 multi-billion-dollar mergers from 1993 to 1996, found that:

- 58 per cent failed to produce any benefit to shareholders; and
- 62 per cent failed to outperform their peers in terms of profit growth after the merger.

The Kearney study also concluded that mergers of equals were less successful than acquisitions of smaller companies, and that 80 per cent of successful mergers were between companies in related businesses. There are a number of reasons why mergers of equals fail to deliver. The three most potent are:

- clashes of personalities at the top and senior management levels;
- the magnitude of the job of putting together two diverse organisations and structures; and
- the difficulty of focusing on goals and strategic issues, as senior management's attention is distracted by the above two issues.

Having made this reference, I would start with the good news. According to many financial analysts, Citicorp has been the only successful *global brand* in consumer banking. After nearly going bust in 1991 because of bad loans, Citibank had established impressive lending controls. For marketing reasons, the institution features branches in 100 countries, mostly serving better-off individuals; it has been one of the world's leading credit-card operators, and has had a technological edge over its rivals which makes it hard to overtake.

Travelers, its counterpart in the 1998 merger, was built up through a series of astute acquisitions to become an insurer and investment banker with a range of interests, from property insurance and mutual funds to shares and bonds. On paper, the merger made sense. Travelers had different distribution networks from Citi, ranging from its Salomon Smith Barney investment bank to insurance products for everybody, both upmarket and downmarket.

Citigroup was formed from the merger of Citicorp and Travelers in a deal announced on 6 April 1998; it has about $700 billion in assets and has set itself a challenge to reinvent banking. The goal is that of creating a full-service company that can market a range of financial products to corporations and consumers, leapfrogging the competition.

Now for the bad news. The concept of a global financial-services supermarket has been tried before but it has yet to be a winner. Neither customers nor investors are convinced, though investors grasp the benefits of a good old-fashioned industry consolidation which, over and above other benefits, is able to cut costs with a sharp knife.

The full financial services concept seems rather linear: two big institutions merge, combine operations, eliminate jobs and produce a tidy and predictable jump in earnings and in share price. But there is always a significant difference between theory and practice. Real life does not necessarily work in a linear way.

Few merger-oriented bank presidents take account of the fact that there are *diseconomies of scale* and a loss of clients (see section 3). There is also a shift in financial industry appeal. The Federal Reserve has calculated that banks' share of household financial assets has fallen from 90 per cent in 1980 to just over 55 per cent in 1998, while mutual funds have grown from around 10 per cent to more than 22 per cent. Commercial banks now hold only a 28 per cent share of *consumer credit*, as opposed to 72 per cent for non-banks. Banks' share of *business credit* has fallen from nearly 50 per cent in 1980 to around 35 per cent, while electronic commerce looms as a new threat.

Major risk areas in post-acquisition management aside, mergers in the banking industry have not bucked this trend. In many cases, the expected gains and synergies, or cost-cutting, never worked out as expected, while some deals have been troubled from the start. Wells Fargo's 1996 acquisition of First Interstate Bancorp had still not been completely ironed out before it was acquired in turn by the Norwest Bank. Yet Wells Fargo had spent at least $150 million in unexpected integration-related write-offs, while it had lost more than $5 billion in deposits.

Some analysts see the current race for size as a dangerous excess, driven simply by egos and inflated share prices. Others advise great caution because size creates its own problems. The BankAmerica deal, for example, combines two brokerage firms with a long history of professional incompatibility: NationBank's Montgomery Securities and BankAmerica's Robertson, Stevens & Co.

While many performance challenges built into pre-acquisition or pre-merger prices do not materialise, first reactions tend to be off the mark. Articles published shortly after the announcement of the Citicorp–Travelers merger had nothing but praise: 'There is the central justification of the deal: cross-selling each other's products, mainly to retail customers.' Then came the projections:

- over the next two years, Citigroup ought to be able to generate $600 million more in earnings because of cross-selling;

- 'Citigroup hopes to double its $7.5 billion in revenue in five years.'(*Business Week*, 20 April 1998.) But what is the basis for such hopes?

One of the news items suggested that the arrangement could solve the two organisations' biggest problems. John Reed, Citicorp's Chief Executive Officer, gets a stronger direct-sales force to market Citi checking accounts, mutual funds and credit cards. This competitive condition was projected on the premise that Travelers had 10300 Salomon Smith Barney brokers, 80000 part-time Primerica Financial Services insurance agents, and so on; in short, *une Grande Armée*.

Citi's contribution to the merger is expected to add to this army of agents and bankers. At Travelers, Sandy Weill will have control of Citicorp's 750 branch offices outside the USA; some 464 in Europe, 166 in Latin America, and 93 in Asia. This, the media suggested, will transform Travelers into an international player.

However, eight months down the line it was no longer the same story that the media had originally reported. In late October 1998, after Citigroup's stock had collapsed because of the global financial crisis, long-simmering tensions came to the surface. Insiders were saying that friction between various factions have been wracking Citigroup for months. Eventually the bickering exploded into public view.

Acting together, John Reed and Sandy Weill, the two Chief Executive Officers of Citigroup, asked for James Dimon's head. At Travelers Dimon had been Weill's heir-apparent. At the end of the day this was no longer true due to losses at Salomon and other reasons. Beyond the executive shuffle, other events help to show that 'the deal of the century' was in trouble, plagued by:

- turf battles;
- cultural clashes;
- a general malaise; and
- unsettled decisions on strategies.

Said one insider: 'This is an organisation of dukes and earls. If your liege goes, unless you can quickly find a line of authority and loyalty to someone else, you're gone too' (*Business Week*, 16 November 1998). The careful reader will not fail to notice the huge difference between the 20 April and 16 November 1998 reports.

As 1998 came to a close, the buck did not stop anywhere in particular at the biggest financial company known to man. It was not at all clear who was running the show. 'The real issue is the rate of speed at which this stuff was put together', suggested Carole S. Berger, a partner at Berger Jackson Capital Management. 'For Travelers to buy Salomon and then do the merger with Citicorp within the same year is a very tough thing.'

Senior management had also to cope with a sharp drop in capitalisation which unsettled shareholders. Back in April 1998, when Citicorp and Travelers announced their intention to merge, the deal was valued at $70 billion. But by the time it was closed on 8 October, the price had fallen to $37 billion, reflecting the sharp declines in both institutions' stock prices (partly because of the general stock market malaise).

The other mega mergers of 1998 did not fare any better, but for different reasons. The new $570 billion BankAmerica, formed by the 30 September takeover by NationsBank of the old BankAmerica was quick to announce that the combined bank had less than $300 million in exposure to hedge funds. However, when the third quarter results were released on 14 October, it reported a $372 million write-off, on a $1.4 billion loan to D.E. Shaw and a $529 million trading loss (some $400 million of which came from the old BankAmerica and the rest from NationsBank). There have been musical chairs as well.

5 Bank mergers in Canada and in Europe

The message section 4 has given is that in real life mergers rarely work out as smoothly as they are supposed to, and this is particularly true of mega mergers. For many years to come, financial historians will be asking questions to which there are no easy answers: why do mergers that looked good on paper fail in reality? What does it take to make synergy between big institutions come to life? How can we increase the likelihood that a merger will be a long-term success?

In order to respond to such queries, one has to analyse the role of mergers from a strategic perspective, and study the best practices of organisations known for their ability to digest what they buy. Another subject for analysis is why original plans fall victim to turf wars among far-flung parts of a big organisation. There are few examples of banks which have built their businesses resulting from a merger into a textbook case of customer appeal and product efficiency.

In April 1998, the Canadian Imperial Bank of Commerce (CIBC) bought Toronto Dominion Bank for 22.7 billion Canadian dollars ($15.8 billion). The deal brought together Canada's second and fifth largest banks and made the new CIBC slightly smaller than the $23 billion combination of Royal Bank of Canada and the Bank of Montreal which was announced in January 1998.

The Royal Bank of Canada and Bank of Montreal had combined assets of 481.4 billion Canadian dollars (US$335 billion) when they merged. The new CIBC has combined assets of 460 billion Canadian dollars (US$320 billion). CIBC shareholders will own 51.5 per cent of the bank, and Toronto Dominion stockholders will hold 48.5 per cent. The merged institution featured 2350 branches and 69 000 employees at the time of the merger.

These two mega mergers in Canada's history were preceded by other bank mergers involving some of the same institutions which, analysts say, were not quite settled when the new wave began. In 1997 CIBC had acquired Oppenheimer, a New York investment house. Toronto Dominion owned Waterhouse Investor Services, the world's third-largest discount brokerage, and just prior to the CIBC merger it had bought Jack White of San Diego (also a discount brokerage).

The same years, late 1997 and 1998, had seen a spate of bank mergers in Europe, including the take-over by the Dutch banking group ING of Belgium's Banque Bruxelles Lambert; a Bavarian marriage of Bayerische Vereinsbank with Bayerische Hypo-Bank, and the often mentioned merger of SBC with Union Bank of Switzerland, to name but a few.

Not all these combinations of assets, liabilities, products, management and clients had worked as planned or were free of friction. An example is HypoVereinsbank, which became Germany's second-largest institution. Both Vereinsbank and Hypo-Bank were primary lenders. Trouble erupted after an early November 1997 admission by the bank that it would have to take a DM3.5 billion ($2.1 billion) charge to cover losses, mainly on property loans made by Hypo-Bank in the early 1990s.

Albrecht Schmid, the merged banks' chairman and formerly boss of Vereinsbank, suggested that both managers of the former Hypo-Bank and the auditors had shown negligence. This rattled Eberhard Martini, Hypo's former chairman, who sits on the new bank's supervisory board. It also posed a number of queries, at least from the financial analysts' viewpoint:

1. How was Vereinsbank's *wish-list* determined?
2. What was the economic vision of the deal that justified the merger?
3. Was another big Bavarian bank the right target?
4. What does it take, other than the will to merge, to make the deal work?

Due to its relatively slight exposure to emerging markets and hedge funds, HypoVereinsbank had hoped to outshine rivals such as Deutsche Bank and Dresdner Bank, which had been badly hit by market turmoil, particularly in loans to emerging countries. But the synergy does not seem to have worked as originally thought. Some of the friction has come from the fact that the Vereinsbank and HypoBank cultures are very different: Vereinsbank's bankers tend to be rather conservative, whereas the risk-takers all seem to come from Hypo-Bank's side.

Neither are German banks who ventured into acquisitions abroad free of digestion problems. An example is provided by the Deutsche Bank which began life in 1870 with a licence from Kaiser Wilhelm I to conduct banking business of all kinds. In the late 1980s, more than a century later, as capital markets became global, Deutsche struggled to keep up, largely due to acquisitions which left much to be desired as regards efficiency, synergy and the bottom line.

As with mergers, acquisitions have a nasty habit of defying the hopes of those who spend money on them. Theorists say that successful acquisitions are the result of far-sighted strategies. The practical issues are more mundane. Acquirers need to:

- understand why and how an acquisition is going to help achieve established goals;
- make the deal work in an efficient manner through a rapid timetable; and
- convince the market that the resulting institution is superior to the one which preceded it.

Consequently, practitioners answer the theorists' strategic-type arguments by saying that to determine whether an acquisition opportunity is attractive requires a rigorous analytical framework which not only reflects criteria for value but which also thoroughly examines internal and external factors that help to establish the wisdom of a merger, including its cost-effectiveness. Deutsche is believed to have spent upwards of $3 billion since 1989 on vain efforts to join the top league. The haemorrhaging of money started in 1989 when Deutsche bought Morgan Grenfell, a British merchant bank. First, it left Morgan Grenfell largely to its own devices, without much of an integration effort. Then, after five years of disappointments, it decided to integrate its acquisition more fully. With this came numerous problems and defections. A fund-management fraud itself did not help, raising questions about the institution's internal controls and leaving Deutsche hundreds of millions of dollars worse off than it had planned to be as a result of acquiring a City bank.

Neither were the strategic moves that successful. During 1997 and 1998 Deutsche Bank's strategy has been to pirate teams of investment bankers from top-name rivals, paying extravagant sums. This did not work out, as management control seems to have got out of hand. Then Deutsche Morgan Grenfell, the parent company's investment-banking arm, was incorporated into a new group: Deutsche Bank Securities.

Rumour, however, had it that Deutsche Bank was actively looking for another acquisition in America. Sometimes the Morgan Bank was mentioned as the target, and in other cases Bankers Trust; both were wounded from losses in East Asia, in Russia and in derivatives, while neither seemed to be a good match which would fit well in a merger and fill the blanks left in Deutsche.

The search for an acquisition ended with a $9.2 billion purchase. This is hardly cheap, at over twice Bankers Trust's book value. On Wall Street, many analysts doubted the wisdom of this acquisition which will simply promote Deutsche Bank from the third division of global investment banks to the second. That is a small jump which is hardly worth spending more than $9 billion on, and over and above that the big money needed to solve indigestion problems.

6 After the shock: the cost of the savings and loans failure

This section presents a case study on high costs which may follow as an aftermath years after the original commitment. This is not an inevitable result of mergers and take-overs, though both were present in the US thrifts industry. It has, however, much to do with the salvage of institutions which went astray largely because of mismanagement. This is also a message-bearer for defunct sovereigns (the subject of Chapter 15).

Here is, in a nutshell, the background of this case. In the 1980s, after watered-down lending rules and a real estate collapse left many thrifts with plenty of bad loans, regulators decided that the cheapest way to handle the lenders was to encourage them to merge with healthier institutions or get an infusion of new capital. As a result, regulators struck deals with the Bass family, Ronald O. Perelman, Jay A. Pritzker, Lewis Ranieri and William E. Smith to act as white knights for the thrifts. It is precisely these investors who stand to gain from the damage claims because of a particular twist of fortune.

In the early 1990s, the failure of the savings and loan industry had cost taxpayers $160–$180 billion (see Chapter 3). With that money lost, everybody thought the worst was over. But in 1998 the savings and loan salvage operation came back to life, threatening to become more expensive. The reason for the revival was a 1996 ruling by the US Supreme Court, which stated that the government had betrayed investors by changing the rules of the bailout; this change of rules happened at the height of the savings and loan crisis.

The sense of betrayal to which the US Supreme Court made reference came from the fact that many of these white knight deals were criticised in Congress as being overly generous. To this, the regulators responded that they had no choice, because Congress itself refused to provide money to back the insured deposits of the bleeding savings and loan sector. Therefore, to attract investors they gave the savings and loans permission to use an unusual accounting rule.

This exceptional and irrational rule had the effect of letting many thrifts satisfy their capital requirements by booking huge liabilities as assets. Such a curious accounting principle allowed the buyers of weakened savings and loans to take the difference between their purchase price and the market value of the institution and count that as an asset. It was called *supervisory goodwill.*

As the price often consisted of the assumption of the insolvent institution's liabilities, the move by the regulators essentially converted liabilities into capital that could satisfy regulatory requirements. A Federal appeals judge ultimately referred to this curious definition of supervisory goodwill as 'a euphemism for spinning straw into gold'.

The freedom to use such a twisted accounting procedure led new investors and other savings and loans to bring capital to the weaker thrifts. But even creative accounting has its limits. As the savings and loan crisis reached a pitch in 1989, these twisted accounting arrangements were phased out by tough legislation endorsed by President Bush and approved by Congress. But the new law's provision ending 'supervisory goodwill' turned what had appeared to be healthy balance sheets into shaky ones; stripped of supervisory goodwill, the balance sheets of several savings and loans could no longer meet minimum capital requirements.

In the aftermath, many savings and loans collapsed, while others came to the brink of failure. Some were bought by healthier companies, resulting in further consolidation, while the savings and loan industry unleashed a barrage of lawsuits, accusing Congress and the Administration of having perpetrated an enormous bait-and-switch.

It took the thrifts industry some time to understand that the Supreme Court ruling had opened the gates to a goldmine-in-waiting. More than two years after the 1996 Supreme Court decision, in November 1998, a Federal court in Washington, DC, got ready to begin assessing the costs. That sum, experts say, could add up to anywhere from $4 billion to $50 billion, and even the high end is only a guestimate.

The Supreme Court dismissed the Clinton Administration's arguments that the contracts did not provide insurance against a legislative change. 'It would, indeed, have been madness', Justice Souter wrote, for the industry to have entered into the contracts without some guarantee that they were enforceable, 'for the very existence of their institutions would then have been in jeopardy'.

It will be up to the Chief Judge of the US Court of Federal Claims to decide the size of the award to Glendale Federal Bank, a California savings and loan that nearly collapsed after Federal accounting rules were changed in 1989. The judge, Loren A. Smith, has already indicated that he will order a sizeable settlement for the savings and loan, which is seeking $1.9 billion.

That may set a standard for more than 120 cases brought by savings and loans, and their shareholders. While the exact size of the awards is likely to be determined by appeals courts, and this will take years, the bottom line is that taxpayers will have to pay whatever the courts decide. Government officials calculate that every $1 billion awarded to the thrifts industry will cost each American household $10.

More than anything else, this promises to be another lawyers' paradise. Anxious not to miss out, many savings and loans have engaged legions of lawyers and some Nobel Prize winners. The Justice Department, which acts for the defence, is devoting more resources to this issue than to any other matter, including the famed Microsoft case. Ironically, two different Federal agencies are on opposing sides of the legal battle which is now starting, and two Nobel Prize-winning economists have been pitted against each other on the meaning of their own past collaborative work.

Dr Merton H. Miller is a $1000-an-hour expert for the Government, while Dr Franco Modigliani is paid, at the same rate, by the savings and loans industry. Dr Miller's position is that the Government's changes to the financial assumptions regarding the savings and loan sector did not take away anything except accounting smoke and mirrors. Dr Modigliani's response is that the elements of his and Dr Miller's own theory are completely irrelevant to the thrifts litigation, and have been dragged in as a red herring.

While the Justice Department is a defendant, the FDIC has aligned itself, in many cases, with the plaintiffs. It is a fundamental axiom that the USA cannot sue itself, the Justice Department has stated. FDIC has replied that it must pursue the cases because of its legal obligations as a receiver representing the institutions that collapsed. Some lawyers suggest that the government cannot emulate the mega companies and think it is above the law. This is not, however, everybody's opinion, and the courts will decide. Such major cost added to that already paid with taxpayers' money in connection with the failure of savings and loans (US building societies) is a good example on how, like old soldiers, old financial sins never die.

15

Debt Management Strategies and the Restructuring of Assets and Liabilities by Sovereigns

1 Introduction

A most basic equation in economics and finance involves investments and their risks. These are a function of the type, importance and number of trade decisions which we make, whether the underlying reference is that of a private investor, financial institution, sovereign or even a curious merger of private companies and sovereigns because the latter own the former through nationalisation or crony capitalism.

While institutions which are not careful about their exposure accumulate a huge amount of credit risk and market risk, governments have their own leveraging ways. They tend to collect deficits as far as the eye can see. They pile mountains of debt upon each other, burdening future generations, and at the same time they lack regulators who could set the rules and supervise the execution of a prudential policy.

Prudence would dictate that governments, like company management, should err on the side of caution. But this never really happens. More frequently than not, governments project that the economy will pick up and do away with the deficits. Such forecasts are inherently uncertain. This is not too dissimilar from the behaviour of boards that are not capable of bringing the exposure of their institution under control.

Traditionally prognostication by economists working for the government tends to project that there will be low unemployment and high capacity utilisation, while the authorities will keep inflation tamed. Others advance the opposite forecast, though they admit the effects of intensification of global competition and greater cost reduction with the help of information technology.

Chapter 1 made the point that globalisation has been a tremendous force. For the top 100 companies, approximately 43 per cent of revenue in 1999 will come from overseas, compared with 37 per cent in 1995. This increase is a direct result of greater business opportunities for many of the large corporations on a world-wide basis, and this brings government policies and practices into the picture.

Some governments also tend to control their budget deficits much better than they did in the past, with the result that inflation statistics have been very positive. Other governments have liberalised foreign exchange regulations, and still others offer foreign companies coming into the country significant tax breaks. But no government has been able to conquer volatility, which remains a function of the behaviour and nervousness of the capital markets.

Since it is unavoidable that debt management strategies, inflation, deflation, privatisation, and the restructuring of national economies have an impact on the banking industry, this chapter addresses itself to these subjects. Regulatory policies and rules are not made in the abstract. Other things being equal, they would be crisper and more rational in a sound economy than in one which is full of troubles.

2 The global impact of debt management policies

Walter Wriston, the former Chief Executive Officer of Citibank, once said that countries do not go bankrupt because they always own more money than they owe. While in the general case there is truth in this statement, due to political reasons countries may be unwilling to deliver in accordance with their obligations, may be unable to service foreign debts due to lack of hard currency, or may choose to service their debt through excessive inflation, effectively eroding their debt's value.

Lenders usually bet on creditworthiness of sovereigns because a government has the legal power to tax its residents, apply currency exchange controls and monopolise foreign earnings of all entities in its territory. But there is no assurance, other than historical precedence and political stability, that the loans contracted with foreign banks or other institutions will be honoured in full.

Most governments are reluctant to renege on their debt, not for religious reasons but because they understand that the cost of default is not only high but has also increased during the last 10 years. Penalties have become greater as globalisation tends to provide for greater transparency and the capital markets significantly increase the risk premium for loans immediately after a default.

At the same time, to attract foreign investors governments know they have to pursue a liberal economic strategy. While, however, these are important factors in shaping national policy, they are by no means an assurance that sovereigns will not default.

This is the perspective from which debt management policies and practices by sovereigns should be examined. It must also be kept in mind that governments, supranational organisations, banks and industrial corporations are currently handling billions of dollars, their volume strongly influencing the global financial system and the way in which it works.

Since the banking industry has been a lender to sovereigns, a discussion about public debt – particularly in foreign exchange – necessarily involves credit institutions. And because sovereigns compete with private companies for funds, a fairly accurate frame of reference will consider other debtors rather than just the needs of government treasuries. In principle, both borrowers and lenders must have a clear understanding of whether they want to bet on:

- equity or debt;
- subordinated or non-subordinated debt;
- fixed or floating interest rates; and
- the denomination of their assets and liabilities in one or more base currencies.

A financial institution has different ways of measuring the costs and risks associated with a borrowing strategy as well as with lending. Discounted cash flows are very useful, as we have already seen in Chapter 13, and the same is true of marking to market the value of debt. Analytical approaches are important because they provide insight and foresight in a world where indebtedness increases at rapid pace. In just 22 years, from 1975 to 1997, in nominal terms the issue of international bonds grew from $20 billion to $500 billion per year while, during the same time, medium- to long-term syndicated loans increased 20-fold.

A major reason for this trend has been the sharp rise in government indebtedness. Finland provides a good example of how fast the national debt can grow. In 1990, the public debt/GDP ratio was relatively low, at 14.5 per cent. But in the early 1990s, after the break-up of the Soviet Union, the Finnish economy experienced a severe economic recession. With this, a decrease in GDP and a massive deficit saw to it that at the end of 1995 the debt/GDP ratio had jumped to 60 per cent: a four-fold increase in five short years, although thereafter it more or less stabilised (see also the plight of neighbouring Sweden in section 5).

Is there a correlation between deficits and interest rates? Based on American statistics, Figure 15.1 suggests that despite all the hype about the importance of a shrinking budget deficit to the sustenance of a healthy bond market, there has been little connection between the steady decline in the deficit in 1992–96 and the direction of interest rates, even if interest rates have become a political issue.

The fact that the Fed and other central banks now focus more on the cost of money than on money supply gives further weight to the need for forecasting interest rate risk. For the borrower, interest rate risk exposure is the degree to which debt costs are exposed to changes in the level of interest

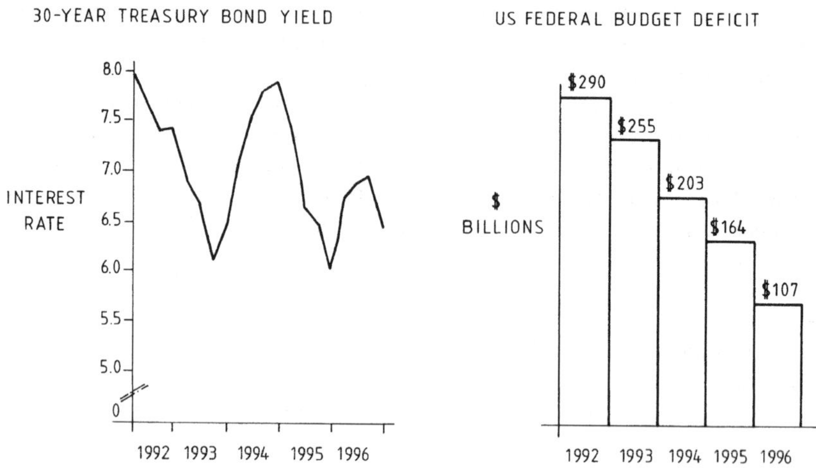

Figure 15.1 The lack of correlation between US budget deficits and interest rates

rates. Basically, this exposure can be divided between market risk and cash flow risk. The latter calls for the prognostication of debt servicing costs, taking into account fixed rate and floating rate loans as well as derivative financial instruments contracted to hedge market risk. For sovereigns, the issue of interest rates is complex and polyvalent because it involves both internal and external factors.

For example, prior to the crash of East Asian economies, domestic interest rates were high and this made it attractive for domestic borrowers, including banks, to go for foreign financing. Foreign banks, for their part, were happy to lend at rates they could not obtain in G-10 countries. Many analysts today think foreign banks were so eager to lend to emerging cronies that they did not perform with due diligence. These foreign banks were not prudent enough to examine whether the exchange rates of such countries were sustainable, or whether the central bank had enough foreign reserves to permit payment of interest and repayment of loans.

Apart from interest rate risk, to which not enough attention has been paid, both borrowers and lenders in the international money market and capital market were faced with volatility in exchange rates. For lenders, the classical foreign currency funding (using local deposit to serve local loans) did not work in Third World countries, while the solution of cross-currency swaps provided only partial protection.

In the short run, currency risks constitute the single largest exposure for sovereigns. Unlike multinationals, governments lack major external monetary assets, and hence they are not in a position to match liabilities and to protect themselves against major changes in foreign exchange markets.

Investment banks have for some time presented themselves as rescuers advising the use of derivatives, but when the real meltdown came in Thailand, Indonesia, South Korea, Russia and Brazil, their advice did not help much.

Technically speaking, but also theoretically, swaptions are the answer to sensitivity to changes in rates causing options exercise. This is important with investments in, or issuance of, bonds with put/call features. The answer to sensitivity issues concerning rates between a transaction and its completion is often hedges arranged at time of commitment.

Due to such considerations, the mid- to late 1990s have seen a swap-intensive debt management of many sovereigns. In practice, however, this introduced swap counterparty risk which forced issuers to confront the fact that in addition to interest rate and currency exchange exposure they were also running a large credit book full of counterparty risk.

A better job than the sovereigns was done by supranationals which maintain substantial liquidity reserves, partly in order to avoid being forced to borrow from the market when large disbursements are forthcoming. In recent years, for example, the World Bank maintained its reserves at 40–45 per cent of its next three years' estimated cash requirements. While the pork barrel of the World Bank is always under siege, it is not in the same position as the pork barrel of the sovereigns.

In conclusion, whether we talk of sovereigns, supranationals, money centre banks or other institutions, comfortable resources enable their holders to decouple their own funding from their lending operations. This avoids tight back-to-back financing and makes feasible an optimisation of lending operations taking advantage of the most opportune movements in the market.

3 Who are the watchdogs for government deficits?

The statement was made in the Introduction that governments do not have regulators who set the policies and the rules regarding the amount of their red ink, and supervisors who control the execution. This is not 100 per cent true, however. Sometimes the Constitution and in other cases Parliament (when it keeps itself out of the pork barrel) will play the role of regulator, while the national auditing office acts as the supervisor of the administrative services of the government.

For instance, this is the role of La Cour des Comptes (the Accounts Tribunal) in France, a super-auditor of all branches of the French government, from ministries and other public services to state-owned enterprises. La Cour des Comptes publishes its findings and by so doing it has often exposed irregularities. But, although it fights waste, it does not enter into budgetary red ink and high deficits in any way other than to point out money thrown down the drain.

In America the watchdog of all administrative services of the government and of the executive itself is the GAO. GAO reports directly to the US

Congress, and it is a demanding auditor which also makes its accounts public. The Administration has often been put in an embarrassing position by GAO, because the latter brings to general view waste, spoilage and other irregularities.

In a way, the best regulator of government red ink is the national Constitution. Under Article 115 of the German Constitution, annual government borrowing cannot exceed annual spending on investment. If it does, the government must declare as the reason a grave disruption of economic balance. This emergency declaration is *not* a state bankruptcy, and it has only been invoked a handful of times in the years after the Second World War.

Sometimes, the classes embedded in the Constitution make life tough for the government. For instance, in 1997 the German deficit, which had to be financed by new borrowing, was DM70 billion (about $40 billion). This is way beyond the DM53.5 billion projected in January of that same year. With investment spending standing at DM59 billion, the gap was some DM11 billion. While the main source of the budget gap was soaring, government spending on unemployment wages, too, had an impact.

In 1997 alone, Bonn had to spend over DM180 billion on unemployment benefits for the 4.3 million jobless. This was a record not seen since the depression peak of 1932–33, and the situation has only slightly improved since then. The Constitution should act as regulator, but governments will always try to find a way round. What the German government did was an attempt at repricing the gold stock, which would have given a paper profit (see also section 6). In this case the watchdog became the Bundesbank, reminding the government that this move, too, was against the Constitution.

The other side of the deficit equation is inefficiency: the biggest part of unemployment benefits filters through to the bureaucracy rather than going to those for whom the money is intended. The German government must pay DM41 000 for every jobless worker, though the worker sees only DM12 095 of that money. The rest, a hefty 70.5 per cent, disappears in social security 'overheads'. In short, money is going to the pockets of bureaucrats employed as intermediaries.

Policies, too, played a role in the booming federal deficits. The Lower House and the Senate have been lenient with wage control, and when the wages run high the overheads skyrocket. Trying to make some sense in a world of runaway wages, Dr Hans Tietmeyer, head of the Bundesbank, said on repeated occasions that Germany needed a moderate round of wage increases and lower budget deficits. He also pointed out that although the Bundesbank laid the monetary groundwork for balanced and non-inflationary economic growth, there were four areas that needed to be addressed to ensure such growth:

- the budget deficit;
- wage costs;

- social and labour policies; and
- innovation.

Not only in Germany do social and labour policies have to be liberalised in order to reduce costs and help promote competitiveness. Tietmeyer also suggested that monetary policy can only lay the groundwork to make stable growth possible. These words also apply to the economies of other nations which overspend on social benefits and overheads, then overtax to make ends meet.

The French crisis of that same year, 1997, provides an example of why overspending by government is counterproductive. Keeping up with electoral promises, in September 1997 the Socialist government announced 'the creation of 350 000 jobs' for unemployed people under 26 years of age. The aim sounds plausible, but these are five-year jobs, to be financed by the state up to 80 per cent (hence, through deficit spending). The other 20 per cent is to be paid by future employers, business associations and regional authorities.

The first piece of bad news is that while such measures are temporary they tend to increase in a permanent manner the social charges rather than reducing them. They also avoid the difficult issue of *job market deregulation*, because this runs contrary to embedded interests and governments do not have the stomach to confront these interests. Yet this would have been the only fundamental measure able to get the employment machine moving again.

The second piece of bad news is that the jobs the government wanted to create are not renewable at the end of their term, which leaves the problem of unemployment entirely unsolved. Even worse is the fact that there was not one single productive job being offered through the aforementioned plan. As a result, the expenses added to the overhead rather than reducing them.

It is indeed surprising that in their drive to avoid change governments manage to produce a totally bureaucratic jobs policy. Most of the 'new plans' they bring forward are characterised by a massive need for 'mediators' and therefore involve overheads which represent no added value. Yet the French Socialist government was persuaded that such jobs represented real careers for youth. Here are some examples of what the 'new professionals' are supposed to be doing:

- help children at school;
- help youth in social revolt in the cities' suburbs;
- help the aged in old folks' homes;
- help reintegrate sick people just out of hospital; and
- help reintegrate former criminals.

All these people will be employed in the context of projects being carried out by the ministries of education, the environment, social affairs, justice, culture and the interior. Interestingly enough, this policy has been condemned by several trade unions, who denounced the fact that it will lead to the creation of second-tier civil service jobs which give no professional qualification and which are not for life. In other words, as if the fact that they lack added value – while costing lots of money – was not enough, they do not offer any sort of career prospects.

At the end of the day, when governments overspend on overheads the probability of bankruptcy cannot be ruled out. Default scenarios which increase the likelihood of a sovereign going belly up include:

- a severe world recession;
- very high real interest rates;
- a commodity price collapse;
- a meltdown of the national financial system;
- a shrinking base of taxable income or business profits because of tax evasion or stress; and
- overleveraging in foreign loans by the sovereign in collusion with local business and industry.

The final default scenario is the case when, because of crony capitalism or other reasons, private companies get government guarantees for their loans with foreign lenders. Contributing to a sovereign default scenario are: labour market inflexibility; the drying-up of private capital inflows as past loans become due; too many short-term loans which require frequent servicing in a nervous market; and the inability of national political leaders to mobilise public support for belt-tightening.

4 Positioning the national economy against the globalisation forces

Restructuring the national economy in such a way that it can face the globalised market forces is a tough task, not only because imagination is in short supply but also because the measures to be taken are of necessity unpopular since they are bound to hit some of the embedded interests as well as some of the people. As a result, new far-reaching measures are not being pushed through, or even discussed in a convincing manner, and there are even cases where certain timid steps in the right direction are being reversed after a change in government.

Right-wing governments are just as incapable of turning the situation around as the socialists, or even more so. The three-week long strike of the French rail workers in November/December 1995 forced the Juppé administration to dump a key measure in its plan to slash welfare deficits: rail employees will continue to retire very young, at the age of 50.

Just for the record, this perk dates back to the early twentieth century when coal dust in the lungs of rail workers led to severe illnesses. Today, no trains run on coal in Western Europe, but over the years the perk has produced more railway retirees than active employees, brought huge deficits to the nationalised railsystem, and led to crippling strikes as workers resist the curbs on the benefits derived from old-fashioned regulations.

The Juppé government also killed a plan to close uneconomic train routes, despite a rising rail deficit that will hit $6 billion annually. These give-backs and cave-ins have practically killed a big chunk of the reforms which were planned by the right-wing government, proving once more the dictum that it is better to amputate a leg in one single operation, if it is unavoidable to do so, than to lengthen the process by chopping it off two centimetres at a time.

The most disturbing roll-back executed by the Juppé administration under pressure from strikers, was its 10 December 1995 promise of a constitutional amendment to perpetuate state control of public services: power production, telecommunications, trains and other sectors are to remain under state control, feeding their inefficiency from the pork barrel. This has doomed French taxpayers to subsidising inefficiency as far as the eye can see, and has also kept the government's head in the sand, while free markets have been transforming the world economy.

At the time of these events Jacques Chirac, the French president, said the government would tough it out: 'We were not elected to organise the decline of France.' But, as the influential newspaper *Le Monde* commented, the strikes had so discredited Juppé that he was no longer the best person to lead the survival exercise. The bottom line is that those who will pay the final bill are the young because the labour market is becoming tighter, and they will find it more and more difficult to find a job.

Just as maddening is the task of trying to reform the deficit-plagued welfare state. The Juppé government did not bother to tell French citizens why that mattered. It did not explain that in the final analysis it is the taxpayer who pays, since the money must come from somewhere. Neither did the government convince the populace that restructuring is synonymous with job creation yet, at the time, unemployment in France was 11.5 per cent and rising; unwise 'social' programmes kept the cost of labour and taxes high; and the disinvestment climate prompted French businesses to export jobs.

As with German and other Western European companies, French companies have been on an investment drive abroad for some time. While their global reach because of this strategy is good, the job market at home suffers. Right-wing, centre, or centre-left, the governments of continental Europe have been singularly unable to position their national economies against the forces unleashed by globalisation.

By forcing the hand of the government through prolonged strikes (even the unemployed strike in France), what the social unrest essentially managed to do was to maintain practically every country's outmoded motto: tax, spend, protect. Most labour bosses refused to see that a sluggish economy and ageing population cannot support the old social programme. New departures call for sacrifices, but the only thing everyone is in agreement about sacrificing is the next generation.

The careful reader will appreciate that I have avoided talking about the euro and its possible effects. The euro is not the subject of this book. Also, and this is very important, what I have just highlighted is so crucial that it can make or break the euro. Governments should understand that they cannot depend on a fragile new currency to pull them out of the mess.

However, there is also a silver lining in this long story with no proactive measures. While the cost of keeping immobile is a heavy toll in terms of unemployment and a stagnant labour market, the steady export of jobs by businesses and slow growth in GNP will one day waken the dormant public conscience. For bureaucrats, doing nothing at least means making no wrong decision, therefore not putting one's career in jeopardy; but for everybody else in the population, doing nothing translates into continuing stress and pain. The only other option to positioning the national economy against the forces of globalisation, through rigorous restructuring measures, is covert acts of protectionism. Protectionism, of course, will lead to an international trade collapse. Let me remind you of a historical precedent.

With the global economy in a tailspin in the early 1930s, countries tried to relieve domestic suffering through stiff import barriers. Some of the actions by 'emerging countries' in the late 1990s, after the meltdown in East Asia, resembled the protectionist frenzy that was followed by the world-wide financial crisis of the late 1920s and early 1930s. As shown in Figure 15.2, in less than four years it cut world trade by 66 per cent, and it sent every country in the globe into a great depression.

The root of the problem is that most nations in the so-called emerging markets have not passed the basic tests of a capitalist society, and this has untold consequences for the global banking industry. Nations which are

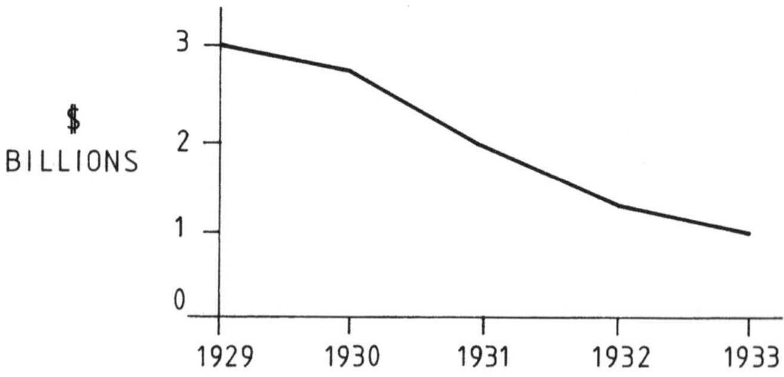

Figure 15.2 Trade collapse because of protectionism: a lesson from the 1930s

economically mismanaged and resisting open markets do not improve their bottom line through capitalism because cronyism carries the day.

These reminders are timely as Malaysia and Russia have been reversing course, dropping out of the global economy. There have also been other calls (this time from the German socialists), to curtail the world-wide system of floating exchange rates and free flows of capital, with the inevitable result of erecting stiff barriers to global economic progress.

On 29 January 1999, during the World Economic Forum at Davos in Switzerland (28 January–2 February 1999), Al Gore called for a curb on corruption and greater transparency, essentially saying that a new financial architecture (see Chapter 2) would not work without these two measures. Theoretically, Gore is right; in practical terms the problem is that to weed out corruption one has to regulate human nature, and this is not feasible.

There should be, however, a new financial architecture which could slowly but surely steer in the direction Al Gore suggested. Many cognisant analysts now think that it is time for an early warning system for financial and economic weaknesses of individual nations. Also long overdue is information which will assist in the understanding of:

- how collapses of a certain magnitude, such as the ones in 1997 in East Asia, in 1998 in Russia and in 1999 in Brazil, can happen; and
- how their spread can be stopped (already the Brazilian example suggests that this might be possible).

Answering these two issues is tantamount to calling for global regulators with authority over sovereigns. Anticipating trends may be a journalistic stock in trade but here we are talking about something much more fundamental. What is needed is a system of checks and balances which permits us to make out just where the tracks of the global economy are going; this would be a sound approach to starting to regulate globalised markets.

5 The effort to privatise the public debt

Structured financial transactions are usually derivative financial instruments which pool assets and transfer all or part of the originator's credit risk to new investors. The term structured instruments comes from the fact that they are designed in such a way as to answer the customisation requirements of buyers. These sometimes call for unbundling credit risk and market risk; in other cases, what investors want is to recombine credit risk and market risk in novel ways.

The concept of structured financing started in the 1920s with second mortgages on office buildings and it developed some momentum in the residential mortgage market. To find that vector, one can go back more than 60 years to 1938, when the US government established the Federal National

Mortgage Association (FNMA), also known as Fannie Mae. The goal was to provide mortgage capital to home owners.

Fannie Mae bought qualified mortgages and issued securities. In 1968, another effort at securitisation centring on mortgages saw the light when the Government National Mortgage Association (GNMA) was split from FNMA and was authorised to guarantee the principal and interest on mortgage securities from other issuers. GNMA invented the 'Ginnie Mae pass-through'. However, it is only during the 1980s that MBF has become a huge market.

Other types of personal debt, too, were securitised in the 1980s; for instance, credit card receivables and car loans. This happened after investment banks realised the potential for underwriting pools of small loans that could not be sold off separately. By contrast, the securitisation of corporate loans took off only in the late 1990s with credit derivatives. (D.N. Chorafas, *Credit Derivatives and the Management of Risk*, New York Institute of Finance, New York, 1999).

Now there is talk of public sector debt securitisation using private-sector techniques for the management of assets and liabilities. Governments have begun to realise that to improve their borrowing performance they have to adopt methods originally devised to help investors choose and allocate assets. To make their new look more attractive, governments have started seeing to it that their finances are given a new perspective by being drawn up in the form of a corporate balance sheet available to public scrutiny, while the prospect of earnings fees from state borrowings, larger in some cases than the GDP, is exciting the imagination of investment bankers.

No one has yet gone so far as to privatise the national debt, but some novel activities are worth watching. In 1990, the Irish Government set up the National Treasury Management Agency (NTMA), free from civil service conventions and based on industry-competitive pay and promotion. NTMA features primary and secondary trading desks, and has a telesales team for short-term Irish paper.

The NTMA sees itself as akin to a corporate treasury removed from the classical culture of government bureaucracy. Actually, it is similar to the trading floor of an investment bank reporting directly to top management. NTMA has a direct line to the Irish finance minister rather than being a part of the finance ministry infrastructure. Since other initiatives similar to NTMA may follow, it is legitimate to ask how big may be the sovereign debt involved if the privatisation of national debt becomes a way of life?

Generalisations are not possible. The answer varies from country to country and from year to year. Table 15.1 presents the high end of national debt as a percentage of GDP with four highly indebted countries in 1994–96. Notice that two of these countries (Italy and Sweden) are members of G-10. In each of these countries, debt is greater than 100 per cent of GDP. Notice also how fast the Swedish public debt has risen year-on-year.

Table 15.1 The high end of government debt as a percentage of GDP

	1994	*1995*	*1996*
Belgium	142.0	140.0	137.3
Italy	123.2	125.7	126.1
Greece	120.8	121.3	121.4
Sweden	93.8	102.7	110.5

There are no rules to us tell what the low end should be. Statistics, however, indicate that today it is rare to find a country with national debt lower than 50 per cent of GDP, so I have used this 50 per cent milestone as the threshold below which we can talk of a low end. Only two countries, among those examined, qualified under this criterion, as shown in Table 15.2, and I hope for their sakes that they will continue to qualify.

Table 15.2 The low end of government debt as a percentage of GDP

	1994	*1995*	*1996*
Australia	34.9	36.7	37.3
Norway	46.7	47.8	48.5

Neither are there any rules to say how fast or how slowly the national debt ceiling could or should be raised. The answer is largely political and to a significant measure it depends on *who* twists the other party's hand: is government or parliament holding the high ground? Furthermore, which one is more greedy or prone to use other people's money?

To appreciate the possible size of securitisation of public debt, it is instructive to look at the policies of the G-7 and see where they stand in terms of government debt. This is also an indication of how well they manage their current budgetary deficits. Statistics for the same three years are shown in Table 15.3.

Table 15.3 G-7 government debt as a percentage of GDP

	1994	*1995*	*1996*
Canada	95.6	96.4	96.2
France	56.0	58.8	60.2
Germany	53.2	61.2	60.4
Italy	123.2	125.7	126.1
Japan	78.7	83.4	88.2
UK	51.8	54.0	54.1
USA	64.6	64.7	65.0

As the careful reader will see, leaving out Italy which is stuck at the high end of government deficits (see also Table 15.1), the worst-off in terms of red ink among the G-7 are Canada and Japan. If the estimated $2.0 trillion necessary to stop the huge banking crisis has to be spent by the Japanese government, then the Japanese public debt would surpass that of Belgium as a percentage of GDP, given that $2.0 trillion represents about half the country's gross financial product, and there are also other gaping holes in the Japanese economy demanding attention.

The bottom line is that year after year, well into the new millennium, Japan will need to refinance tremendous amounts of debt. The government is finally responding to the eight-year downturn of the Japanese economy with a major fiscal stimulus, but all of it will be debt financing. Astute analysts will notice that Japan is not alone in this plight; over the next few years, vast amounts of debt must be financed and refinanced in many parts of the world.

Looking once again at Table 15.3, in absolute figures, as of the mid-1990s the best placed country in public debt terms was the UK. Its government debt stood at 54.1 per cent of GDP. France, Germany and the USA tended to cluster together, but from 1994–96 the German situation deteriorated faster than the others, followed by the French.

What about the privatisation of state-owned enterprises which some of these countries, (for instance, the French and the Italians) had planned in order to improve the government's cash flow? Would not this help in paying back some of the public debt? Can such policies help to lighten the debt load of future generations? Are privatisations the opposite of the theme of section 6, which is not nationalisation but investment in equities by governments made through stock exchanges?

Since state-owned enterprises are notoriously inefficient, disposing of them through privatisation will surely save the taxpayers from being forced to dip into their pockets to pay for other people's pleasures. How far this is going to relieve the tax load of future generations is open to discussion. Much depends on how much of the money is used to diminish the national debt and how much is spent on short-term political fancy. As for the comparison between privatisation and the retirement of national debt, these two processes go in opposite directions: privatisation essentially means giving to private ownership companies thoroughly rotten after decades of state ownership, whereas investments in private firms through government agencies, such as Social Security, risk bringing no-growth bureaucratic habits into prospering enterprises.

There is also the question of the appeal of those companies to be privatised at anything other than bargain-basement prices. Governments do not own high-tech firms; what they control is mainly smoke-stack, brown-industry types and banks with weak balance sheets. Yet it is the technology sector whose capitalisation virtually doubled between October 1998 and

February 1999 in the US stock market. Keep that in mind when discussing privatisation.

6 Are investments in equities by governments a good solution?

The statistics which were given in section 5 speak volumes about the challenges facing countries struggling with heavy government debt burdens, but also of the challenges facing financial markets if public debt is privatised. Since there is unrelenting pressure to ensure loans are raised and serviced, the question becomes: 'How long will it be before a finance minister is persuaded that a privatised public debt has many merits?'

The roots of an answer to this lie in the fact that up to a point comparisons can be drawn between treasury management in a corporation and a country's debt burden. Such comparisons make sense when governments understand that they need to achieve certain gains in asset and liability management at the national level, though the motivation for such action is primarily political. On the technical side there is the transition from looking at individual government loans to treating public debt as a portfolio. A major part of the solution which might be adopted is to allow for risk reduction through combining different exposures.

A crucial element in assets and liabilities management at the national level, as well as in regard to the privatisation of national debt, is that of matching liabilities to cash flows. Because of globalisation, this job involves many currencies and it has similarities to that of the treasurer of a transnational corporation and the way he has been running his job in the 1990s. Like corporate treasurers, ministers of finance will have to look at a bifurcation of debt into:

- internal, which can be serviced through taxation; and
- External, requiring hard-won foreign currency.

One of the ways being discussed in connection with external debt is to use the country's foreign trade structure as a guide for deciding on current account balances. In the last analysis, it is a question of bringing a number of factors into equilibrium, such as central bank reserves, current account balance, trends in trade in hard currencies, and the government's ability to raise capital in the domestic and international markets.

To whom should the securitised government debt be sold? The answer is to institutional investors and the retail market. There are precedents for this, like Italy's drive in 1994 to push its yen bonds into the hands of Japanese households, or Ontario's moves abroad in 1992/93 with US$2 billion in bonds. Both were prompted by the need to raise more funding than the government thought the domestic or state market could bear.

There is also the channel of derivatives which sovereigns have so far not exploited in any big way, though some local governments – such as Orange County and the London Borough of Hammersmith and Fulham – thought that leverage through derivatives was a great idea, but paid dearly for it. With derivatives a whole new way of looking at liability management is possible, and with that comes a range of huge risks.

Hammersmith and Fulham provide a useful lesson which should be taught at business schools and law schools. Because of budgetary constraints imposed by the central government throughout the late 1980s, the Borough entered into floating rate obligations so that it could benefit from a fall in interest rates. It also took outright positions in swaps, unmatched by any underlying borrowings, to the tune of about £3 billion ($3.9 billion).

However, because the UK economy was overheating and inflationary pressures were building up, the government was forced to raise interest rates. As a result of its leveraging through derivatives, the Borough – which had an annual budget of £44.6 million ($71.2 million) – faced a loss on its swaps portfolio of some $300 million ($490 million). Bankruptcy was averted only because of a judgment by the House of Lords in 1991 that the local authority had indeed acted outside its powers.

After the securitisation of public debt starts rolling, it would be interesting to see how much of the paper to be issued would be illegal tender. The courts will tell when some of these cases are tested through legal action.

Nevertheless, if disposing of domestic and foreign debt through securitisation is one of the options governments are currently examining with the help of international investment banks, amassing equity in private companies (provided budget surpluses permit) is another puzzle. In fact, some people think that this is an option even if there are no budgetary surpluses. Take Social Security as an example: there are three ways of pulling it back from the brink of the abyss: raising taxes, cutting benefits, or investing payroll (tax dollars) to get a better return. The third option practically means investing in the stock market. A host of measures will have to be brought together to make money available for this solution: making people retire later, forcing the few professions which currently do not contribute to the system to join, and so on. Those favourable to the partial privatisation of Social Security and its equity investments think this is feasible. What then?

Should sovereign governments invest in equities? Should they do so only in case of surpluses? Only for Social Security reasons? Or to put some of the money they make through the securitisation of public debt on a capital gains track? There are, of course, precedents. In August 1997 it was announced that the Norwegian government was going to build an equity portfolio to invest and hold its surplus funds from its petroleum sales. The Norwegian government's fund is expected to reach in excess of $150 billion within the next ten years. All of this money will probably be invested in various stock market indexes in the major exchanges of the world.

Similarly, worried about the long-term solvency of Social Security, the US government has on the table a proposal to buy stocks with $800 billion of budgetary surplus. This has been the pension funds' strategy. If such sovereign equity investments happen in a big way, and in a proactive sense, that will mean the end of the stock markets as we know them. The regulators will also become the gamblers, and vested interests and inside trading will combine to run the show.

Even if only part of the government's hoard is thrown to the stock market (for instance, investments by Social Security currently under discussion in the USA and other countries), this will radically change the way stock markets tick. The sovereign's heavy hand will be a constant reminder that every time investors become worried about near-term fundamentals, all they need to do is to demonstrate (à la French farmers) to keep rolling the torrent of funds pouring into the market from the government's coffers.

Which regulators will have the authority to tell sovereign governments how to value the equities in their books? Will it be accruals or marking to market? Since governments will manipulate the books to have a surplus they can spend, what if the market caves in? Will they write down the losses? Will these capital losses increase the public debt? What then? Will the gaping holes be privatised?

Let me briefly repeat an example I have given. In 1997 the German government wanted to reprice the gold in its vault to make the deficit that year look smaller. This did not happen because the mighty Bundesbank discouraged it through a public statement. But on this occasion it was revealed that the French and Italian governments had *revalued* their gold reserves, for the same reason, when the gold price was over $400 per ounce. In 1997, however, the gold price was under $300 per ounce, yet the two governments had not devalued their gold reserves by marking them to market.

Creative accounting by governments converted to a 'market economy' risks being far worse than the illegal manipulations of the same name by private commercial and industrial firms. After all, governments push the laws through parliaments, and lawmakers understand the pork barrel well. Also, when the central banks are compliant as usually happens (the Fed, Bundesbank and, more recently, the Bank of England and the ECB being exceptions), governments can print money to supply the stock market practically at will.

Unless there is a very significant negative event, equities will be not just the asset of choice but also the asset supported by somebody with big shoulders. This somebody would tend to contain stock market corrections and not allow them to turn into substantial prolonged downturns, until a huge crash happens such as the one in 1929 in America or in 1991 in Japan. At the same time, this high-handed approach will not only take potential losses out of the picture; it will also put a lid on profits.

Pessimists say that though there is considerable speculation over when the nationalisation of stock markets will happen, there is little doubt that one day it will take place. Optimists think it would never happen, because there is no mechanism for accomplishing such a colossal task. This argument does not forget the wit of politicians and their egos, but the intersection of greed and politics has led to rampant fiascos rather than long-lasting reform.

Index